NEXT GENERATION
GRAMMAR
2

David Bohlke

Arlen Gargagliano

Series Editor
David Bohlke

Next Generation Grammar 2

Pearson Education, 10 Bank Street, White Plains, NY 10606

Staff credits: The people who made up the *Next Generation Grammar 2* team—representing editorial, production, design, and manufacturing—are Andrea Bryant, Aerin Csigay, Dave Dickey, Nancy Flaggman, Gosia Jaros-White, Mike Kemper, Maria Pia Marrella, Amy McCormick, Liza Pleva, Massimo Rubini, Ruth Voetmann, and Adina Zoltan.

Development: Goathaus Studio
Cover art: Diane Fenster
Text composition: ElectraGraphics, Inc.
Text font: Minion Pro

Library of Congress Cataloging-in-Publication Data
Cavage, Christina.
  Next generation grammar 1 / Christina Cavage, Stephen T. Jones.
    p. cm.
  ISBN 978-0-13-256063-4 — ISBN 978-0-13-276054-6 — ISBN 978-0-13-276055-3 — ISBN 978-0-13-276057-7
  1. English language—Grammar—Study and teaching. 2. English language—Study and teaching—Foreign speakers.
I. Jones, Stephen T. II. Title. III. Title: Next generation grammar one.
  PE1065.C528 2013
  428.2'4—dc23
                                                                                                    2012024734

For text, photo, and illustration credits, please turn to the page following the index at the back of the book.

PEARSON ELT ON THE WEB

PearsonELT.com offers a wide range of classroom resources and professional development materials. Access our course-specific websites, product information, and Pearson offices around the world.

Visit us at **pearsonELT.com**

Printed in the United States of America

ISBN 10: 0-13-276054-1 (with MyEnglishLab)
ISBN 13: 978-0-13-276054-6 (with MyEnglishLab)

2 3 4 5 6 7 8 9 10—V082—18 17 16 15

Welcome to *Next Generation Grammar*

When do we use one of the present forms for future, as opposed to using *will* or *be going to*? Which modal verbs do we tend to use to make requests, from least formal to most formal? In what types of writing might we find more instances of passive forms than active forms? And how and why do we reduce certain adverbial clauses? These and many other questions are all answered in *Next Generation Grammar,* a groundbreaking new series designed to truly meet the needs of today's students. In addition to learning through the textbook, learners engage with innovative digital content, including interactive learning software, video, and continuous online assessment.

At its heart, *Next Generation Grammar* is a comprehensive grammar course that prepares students to communicate accurately in both writing and speaking. The grammar points are presented naturally, through a variety of high-interest reading texts followed by extensive practice and application. Each new grammar point is practiced using all four skills, with extra emphasis on grammar for writing. This task-centered approach allows immediate feedback on learning outcomes so students can track their own progress.

The series is truly for a new generation—one that is busy, mobile, and demanding. It respects that learners are comfortable with technology and use it as part of their daily lives. The series provides a traditional textbook (in either print or eText format) along with dynamic online material that is an integral, not a supplementary, part of the series. This seamless integration of text and digital offers a streamlined, 21st century learning experience that will engage and captivate learners.

Next Generation Grammar boasts a highly impressive author team. I would like to thank Sigrun Biesenbach-Lucas, Donette Brantner-Artenie, Christina Cavage, Arlen Gargagliano, Steve Jones, Jennifer Recio Lebedev, and Pamela Vittorio for their tireless dedication to this project. I would also like to thank Pietro Alongi, Andrea Bryant, Gosia Jaros-White, Amy McCormick, Massimo Rubini, and the entire Pearson editorial, production, and marketing team for their vision and guidance through the development of this series.

David Bohlke
Series Editior

About the Series Editor. David Bohlke has 25 years of experience as a teacher, trainer, program director, editor, and materials developer. He has taught in Japan, Korea, Saudi Arabia, and Morocco, and has conducted multiple teacher-training workshops around the world. David is the former publishing manager for adult courses for Cambridge University Press and the former editorial manager for Global ELT for Cengage Learning. He is the coauthor of *Listening Power 2* (Pearson Education), *Four Corners* (Cambridge University Press), and *Speak Now* (Oxford University Press), and is the series editor for *Interchange,* Fourth Edition (Cambridge University Press).

What's next in grammar?

Imagine a grammar course that gives you the freedom to devote class time to what you think is most important; a grammar course that keeps students engaged and on-track; a grammar course that extends learning beyond the classroom through compelling digital content.

Introducing *Next Generation Grammar*

Print or eText?
You make the choice. The course book content is presented in two formats, print or eText, offering maximum flexibility for different learning styles and needs.

Blended instruction
Optimize instruction through a blend of course book (in either print or eText format) and online content. This seamless integration will allow for spending more class time on meaningful, communicative work. Learners will practice and apply new language online and can also access our engaging video reviews if they have missed a lesson, or simply need additional help with a grammar point.

Rich online content
Explore the online component. It offers a wealth of interactive activities, grammar reference material, audio files, test material, and video reviews with our Grammar Coach, Jennifer Lebedev, YouTube's *JenniferESL.* The dynamic multimedia content will keep learners focused and engaged. You can also track class progress through an intuitive and comprehensive learner management system.

Ongoing assessment
Use the extensive assessment suite for targeted instruction. The interactive nature of the assessments (including timely feedback, goal tracking, and progress reports) allows you to track progress, and also allows learners to see for themselves which areas have been mastered and which require more effort. In the course book, assessment occurs at the end of each unit. The online component offers pre- and post-unit tests, as well as end-of-chapter tests.

The **next generation of grammar** courses is here. **Anytime, anywhere, anyplace.**

Teacher-directed

Student-centered

Print or eText

Practical tasks

Seamless integration of course book and digital

Grammar coach

Ongoing assessment

Anytime, anywhere, anyplace

CONTENTS

Tour of a Unit

Each unit in **Next Generation Grammar** begins with an engaging opener that provides a quick overview of the unit. A list of learning outcomes establishes each chapter's focus and helps students preview the grammar content. The outcomes can also be used as a way to review and assess progress as students master chapter content.

Before they begin the unit, students go online and complete the **What do you know?** section to assess what they already know about the grammar featured in the unit. This directs students' focus to the grammar and also helps teachers target instruction to their learners' specific needs.

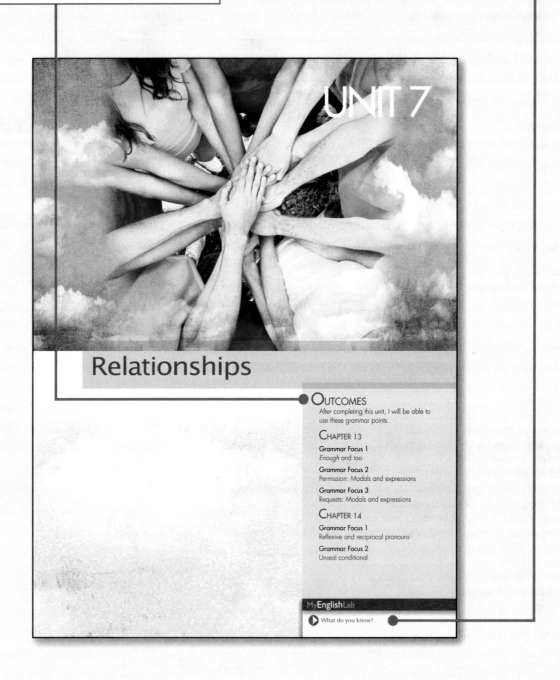

UNIT 7

Relationships

OUTCOMES

After completing this unit, I will be able to use these grammar points.

CHAPTER 13

Grammar Focus 1
Enough and too

Grammar Focus 2
Permission: Modals and expressions

Grammar Focus 3
Requests: Modals and expressions

CHAPTER 14

Grammar Focus 1
Reflexive and reciprocal pronouns

Grammar Focus 2
Unreal conditional

MyEnglishLab

▶ What do you know?

The **Getting Started** section begins with the introduction of the chapter's themes. Students engage in lighthearted, motivating, and personal tasks that introduce and preview the chapter's grammar points.

In the **Reading** section students are further exposed to the chapter's grammar through high-interest, real-world texts that reflect the unit's theme. Beginning with a pre-reading warm-up, tasks progress from schema building to a detailed comprehension check.

The **Vocabulary Check** activities on *MyEnglishLab* allow students to review and practice the vocabulary necessary for reading comprehension. Students are encouraged to complete these activities before they begin the **Reading** section.

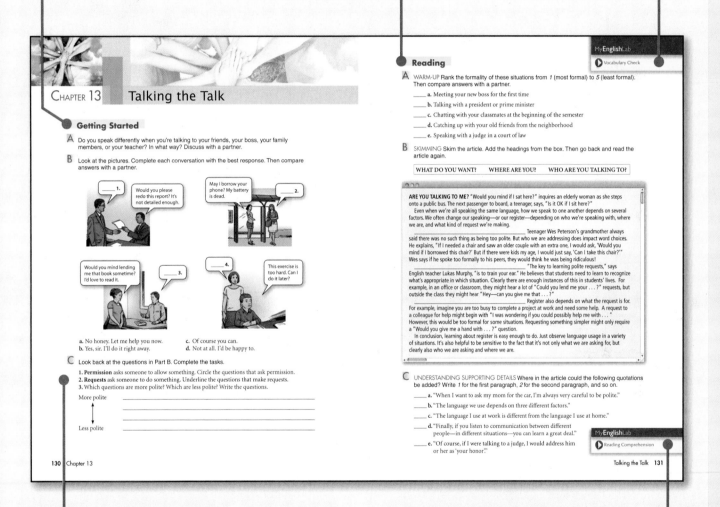

This section culminates with an important inductive step that asks students to look back at the previous tasks and focus on form or function. By circling, underlining, charting, or answering questions, students focus on differences in meaning.

Upon completion of the **Reading** section, students can further engage with the chapter's reading selection on *MyEnglishLab*. The **Reading Comprehension** activities provide students with an additional check of understanding.

The **Grammar Focus** sections present the chapter's target structures in clear, easy-to-read charts. Each chart presents example sentences taken from the chapter reading that illustrate the structure in context.
The language notes give short and clear explanations of the form, meaning, and use of the target structure.

Grammar Focus 1 *Enough* and *too*

Examples	Language notes
(1) She was **smart enough**, but she didn't try. Did he finish **quickly enough**? I **didn't study enough**. I failed the test.	As we saw in Chapter 11, the word **enough** means "sufficient" or "the right amount." It has a positive meaning. In addition to modifying nouns, **enough** can also modify **adjectives**, **adverbs**, and **verbs**. Use: **adjective / adverb / verb + enough**
(2) This report is **not detailed enough**. He didn't work **fast enough**. You aren't **eating enough**.	**Not enough** means that something is insufficient or less than the right amount. Use: **not + adjective + enough** **not + verb + adverb + enough** helping verb + **not** + verb + **enough**
(3) He didn't move fast **enough to get** a seat. Do you think she has **enough to do**?	We often add an **infinitive**: **enough + infinitive**
(4) Don't be **too friendly** with strangers. Does he speak **too formally** to his peers?	As we saw in Chapter 11, the word **too** means "more than is needed." The meaning is usually negative. In addition to modifying quantifiers, **too** can also modify **adjectives** and **adverbs**.
(5) My kids aren't **too interested** in history. Don't work **too hard**!	We use **not too** to say that something is **lacking**. Use: **not + too + adjective / adverb**
(6) You are **too busy to complete** a project. Did he arrive **too late to get** into the movie?	We often add an **infinitive**: **too + adjective / adverb + infinitive**
(7) There are **too many people** on the bus. There are **too few seats** on the bus. **Q:** Did the teacher present **too much information**? **A:** No, she presented **too little**. / She **didn't present enough**.	As we saw in Chapter 11, we can also use **(not) enough** and **too** with **count and noncount nouns**. • The opposite of **too many** is **too few** (for count nouns). • The opposite of **too much** is **too little** (for noncount nouns). We more commonly say "not enough."

Grammar Practice

MyEnglishLab
Grammar Plus 1
Activities 1 and 2

A Complete the sentences. Use *enough* or *too*.

1. I don't have _____ money to pay my taxi fare.
   Could you lend me some?
2. You are speaking _____ quickly. Would you mind slowing down?
3. Kevin hates to wait. He has _____ little patience.
4. I had no trouble finding your house. Your directions were easy _____.
5. Your instructions aren't clear _____. Can you say it in a different way?
6. Hal is _____ short to get the book off the shelf. He needs a ladder.
7. Nancy doesn't have a driver's license. She's not old _____.

8. The movie is sold out. We arrived _____ late.
9. My grandma says I'm too thin. She always says, "You don't eat _____."

B Rewrite these sentences to say the opposite. Use *enough* or *too*. More than one correct answer may be possible.

1. She is walking too quickly. *She is not walking fast enough.*
2. He is old enough to enter the contest. _____
3. We were too slow to get seats on the subway. _____
4. There are too many people in our discussion group. _____
5. She was strong enough to lift the box. _____
6. There are too few grammar exercises in this book. _____

C Look at the picture. Write sentences with *enough* or *too*.

1. _____
2. _____
3. _____
4. _____
5. _____
6. _____

In the **Grammar Practice** sections, students are given the opportunity to apply the grammar structures in a variety of contextualized, controlled exercises that allow them to practice both the forms and the uses of the new structures.

MyEnglishLab

Grammar practice continues online in the **Grammar Plus** activities. Each **Grammar Plus** includes two additional practice activities to further reinforce new structures. Instant scoring and meaningful feedback show students their progress and highlight areas that may require more effort. Students also have the opportunity to see a video review featuring our expert grammar coach. The videos provide a quick, engaging review—perfect for allowing students to check their understanding before proceeding to further assessment.

In the **Listening** sections students have the opportunity to hear the target grammar in context and to practice their listening skills. Activities are developed to practice both top-down and bottom-up listening skills.

MyEnglishLab

Listening activities continue online with **Listen for it**. These activities assess both grammar in context and listening comprehension, and include instant scoring and feedback.

MyEnglishLab

Before students do the **Writing**, they go online to complete **Linking Grammar to Writing**. Several guided writing tasks link the grammar to the skill of writing, enabling students to then move back to the textbook and complete the **Writing** section with full confidence.

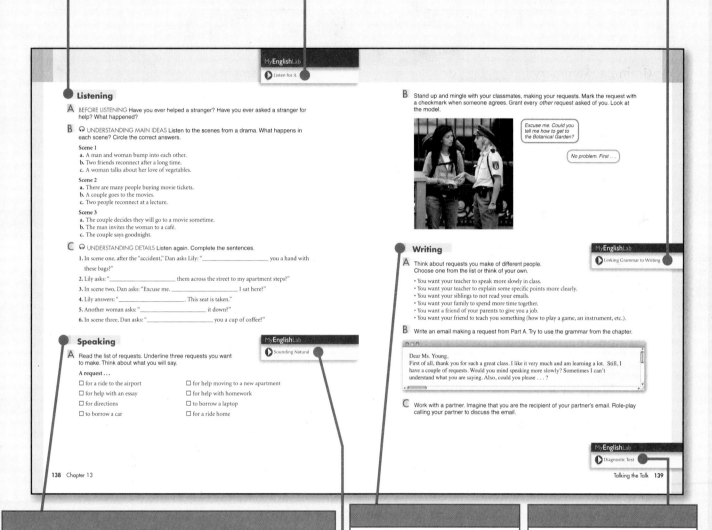

MyEnglishLab
▶ Listen for it.

Listening

A BEFORE LISTENING Have you ever helped a stranger? Have you ever asked a stranger for help? What happened?

B 🎧 UNDERSTANDING MAIN IDEAS Listen to the scenes from a drama. What happens in each scene? Circle the correct answers.

Scene 1
a. A man and woman bump into each other.
b. Two friends reconnect after a long time.
c. A woman talks about her love of vegetables.

Scene 2
a. There are many people buying movie tickets.
b. A couple goes to the movies.
c. Two people reconnect at a lecture.

Scene 3
a. The couple decides they will go to a movie sometime.
b. The man invites the woman to a café.
c. The couple says goodnight.

C 🎧 UNDERSTANDING DETAILS Listen again. Complete the sentences.

1. In scene one, after the "accident," Dan asks Lily: "_____ you a hand with these bags?"
2. Lily asks: "_____ them across the street to my apartment steps?"
3. In scene two, Dan asks: "Excuse me. _____ I sat here?"
4. Lily answers: "_____. This seat is taken."
5. Another woman asks: "_____ it down?"
6. In scene three, Dan asks: "_____ you a cup of coffee?"

Speaking

A Read the list of requests. Underline three requests you want to make. Think about what you will say.

A request . . .
☐ for a ride to the airport   ☐ for help moving to a new apartment
☐ for help with an essay   ☐ for help with homework
☐ for directions   ☐ to borrow a laptop
☐ to borrow a car   ☐ for a ride home

MyEnglishLab
▶ Sounding Natural

B Stand up and mingle with your classmates, making your requests. Mark the request with a checkmark when someone agrees. Grant every *other* request asked of you. Look at the model.

Excuse me. Could you tell me how to get to the Botanical Garden?

No problem. First . . .

Writing

A Think about requests you make of different people. Choose one from the list or think of your own.

• You want your teacher to speak more slowly in class.
• You want your teacher to explain some specific points more clearly.
• You want your siblings to not read your emails.
• You want your family to spend more time together.
• You want a friend of your parents to give you a job.
• You want your friend to teach you something (how to play a game, an instrument, etc.).

B Write an email making a request from Part A. Try to use the grammar from the chapter.

Dear Ms. Young,
First of all, thank you for such a great class. I like it very much and am learning a lot. Still, I have a couple of requests. Would you mind speaking more slowly? Sometimes I can't understand what you are saying. Also, could you please . . . ?

C Work with a partner. Imagine that you are the recipient of your partner's email. Role-play calling your partner to discuss the email.

MyEnglishLab
▶ Linking Grammar to Writing

MyEnglishLab
▶ Diagnostic Test

The **Speaking** section provides students with the opportunity to use the chapter's grammar naturally and appropriately in a variety of engaging interactive speaking activities.

MyEnglishLab

The **Sounding Natural** activities are pronunciation activities relating to the chapter's grammar and alternating between productive and receptive tasks. In the receptive tasks, students listen to prompts and select correct answers. In the productive tasks, students listen to prompts, record themselves, and compare their submissions with a model.

The **Writing** section provides students with the opportunity to use the chapter's grammar naturally and appropriately in a variety of activities. Students are provided with a whole or partial model and a more open-ended writing task.

Each chapter culminates with an online **Diagnostic Test** that assesses students' comprehension and mastery of the chapter's grammar structures. The test tracks students' progress and allows teachers to focus on the specific student needs.

The **Grammar Summary** chart provides a concise, easy-to-read overview of all the grammar structures presented in the unit. It also serves as an excellent reference for review and study.

A quick 20- or 25-point **Self-Assessment** gives students an additional opportunity to check their understanding of the unit's target structures. This gives students one more chance to assess what they may still need to master before taking the online **Unit Test**.

Grammar Summary

MyEnglishLab
▶ Grammar Summary

Enough means "sufficient" or "the right amount." Place it after adjectives, adverbs, and verbs. To say something is insufficient, use *not + adjective / adverb / verb + enough*. The meaning is usually negative. We can add an infinitive after *enough*.

Enough	Not enough
He's **tall enough** to reach the shelf.	He's **not tall enough** to reach the shelf.
She ran **fast enough** to catch the bus.	She didn't run **fast enough** to catch the bus.
I **studied enough**.	I **didn't study enough**.

The word *too* means "more than needed." Place it before adjectives and adverbs. The meaning is usually negative. We can add an infinitive after the phrase.

Too	
I'm **too tired**.	I'm **too tired to stay** awake.
He walks **too slowly**.	He walks **too slowly to keep** up with me.

We use *can*, *could*, and *may*, and other expressions to **ask permission**. We use *can*, *could*, and *would* and other expressions to **make requests**. By using expressions such as *Would you mind . . . ?* we imply that the action may be annoying or imposing. We can grant and refuse permission with *can* and *may (not): Yes, you can. / No you may not*. We can grant and refuse requests with a variety of responses. (*Sure. / Not at all. / Sorry.*)

Asking permission	Making requests
Can / Could / May I see your homework?	**Can you** open the door?
Is it OK if I sit here?	**Would you** say your name again?
Do you mind if I sit here?	**Could you not** make that noise, please?
Would it be OK if I sat here?	**Would you mind** turning down the TV?
Would you mind if I sat here?	**Do you mind** waiting?
I was wondering if I could sit here.	**I was wondering if** you'd mind helping.

Reflexive pronouns are used when the subject and object of a sentence refer to the same person or thing. We also use them for emphasis. *By + a reflexive pronoun* means "alone."

Singular	Plural
I forced **myself** out of bed.	We are pushing **ourselves** today.
Admit the truth to **yourself**!	You and Mika express **yourselves** well.
The cat gave **itself** a bath.	The children fixed breakfast **by themselves**.
He wanted to go hiking **by himself**.	

Use the **reciprocal pronouns** *each other* (for two people) and *one another* (for more than two people) when the subject and object refer to the same people or things.

Reciprocal pronouns
Bill and Carrie are looking at **each other**.
The group of students were helping **one another** finish the project.

We use the **unreal conditional** to talk about unreal or imaginary conditions. Use an *if*-clause (simple past or past continuous) + a main clause (*would / might / could* + base verb). Although the *if*-clause is in the simple past, it refers to the present or future.

If-clause	Main clause
If I **had** the time,	I **would travel** more.
If I **were** a pilot,	I **could see** the world.
If I **were earning** more money,	I **might travel** for six months.

148 Unit 7 Grammar Summary

Self-Assessment

A (5 points) Rewrite the sentences. Add *too* or *enough*.
1. Lara didn't eat. (enough) _____
2. I have little time to finish my report. (too) _____
3. Damien gave up the race easily. (too) _____
4. The presentation was not detailed. (enough) _____
5. They didn't read the map closely. (enough) _____

B (8 points) Circle the correct words.
1. Can / May you please speak more slowly?
2. Would you mind close / closing that window?
3. May / Would I please see your I.D. card?
4. I was wondering if you'd mind help / helping me.
5. Do you mind if I borrow / borrowed your notes?
6. Is it OK if I move / moved your bag over there?
7. Do / Would you mind if I sat here?
8. I was wondering if I can / could use your laptop.

C (6 points) Complete the sentences. Use reflexive or reciprocal pronouns.
1. Look at _____! You are wearing two different shoes!
2. After Pedro scored the winning goal, he and his coach looked at _____ in disbelief.
3. My coworkers always try to solve their problems _____.
4. No one knows why Mr. Parker decided to give _____ a haircut.
5. For their birthdays, the three best friends bought _____ dinner.
6. Some people prefer to travel with a group, but I like traveling by _____.

D (6 points) Complete the sentences. Use the unreal conditional.
1. If my friends _____ (go) out without me, I _____ (be) upset.
2. If I _____ (not / live) so far away from campus, I _____ (walk) to school.
3. Tom _____ (not / be) in this advanced class if he _____ (not / study) so hard.
4. Kara _____ (quit) her job today if she _____ (have) any savings.
5. If I _____ (be) a veterinarian, I _____ (specialize) in cats.
6. If I _____ (see) a crime, I _____ (call) the police immediately.

Unit 7 Self-Assessment 149

MyEnglishLab

Students can go to *MyEnglishLab* for a **Grammar Summary** review, which includes activities and a video to help students prepare for the **Self-Assessment** and **Unit Test**.

xiv Tour of a Unit

Each unit ends with an interesting and engaging group **Unit Project** that encourages students to synthesize the new grammar structures and to integrate the unit's theme and skills. The project promotes collaboration, creativity, and fluency and exposes students to a variety of real-world situations.

Unit Project: Sphere of influence

A We all have people who influence us. These may be family members, friends, colleagues, bosses, teachers, or others. These people are part of our "sphere of influence." Work with a partner. Create your sphere of influence. Follow the steps.

1. Think of four people who have positively influenced you the most.
2. Tell your partner about them. Describe how they have enhanced your life.
3. Collect images, short written stories, or other things that represent these four people. Put them on a poster or create a webpage.

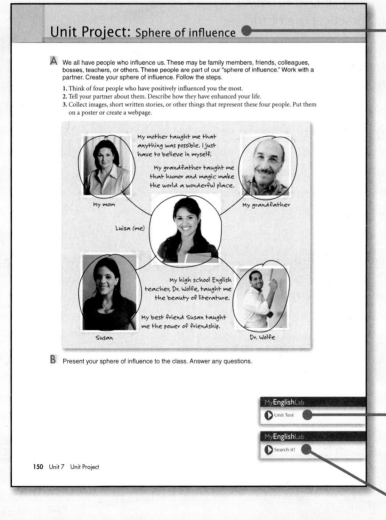

My mother taught me that anything was possible. I just have to believe in myself.

My mom

My grandfather taught me that humor and magic make the world a wonderful place.

My grandfather

Luisa (me)

My high school English teacher, Dr. Wolfe, taught me the beauty of literature.

My best friend Susan taught me the power of friendship.

Susan

Dr. Wolfe

B Present your sphere of influence to the class. Answer any questions.

My**English**Lab
▶ Unit Test

My**English**Lab
▶ Search it!

My**English**Lab

The unit's final, cumulative assessment is a comprehensive online **Unit Test**. This test allows students to check their mastery of the unit's grammar structures, see their progress, and identify areas that may need improvement. The test allows teachers to track students' progress and to focus on areas that might benefit from more attention.

My**English**Lab

The **Search it!** activity allows students to do a fun online search for content that relates to the chapter's theme. Teachers may choose to have students complete these real-world tasks individually, in pairs, or in small groups.

Next Generation Grammar Digital

MyEnglishLab

A dynamic, easy-to-use online learning and assessment program, integral to the *Next Generation Grammar* program

▶ **Original activities** focusing on grammar, vocabulary, and skills that extend the *Next Generation Grammar* program

▶ **Multiple** reading, writing, listening, and speaking activities that practice grammar in context, including *Linking Grammar to Writing*, which guides students in the practical use of the chapter's grammar

▶ **Video** instruction from a dynamic grammar coach that provides an engaging and comprehensive grammar review

▶ **Extensive** and ongoing assessment that provides evidence of student learning and progress on both the chapter and unit level

▶ **Individualized** instruction, instant feedback, and study plans that provide personalized learning

▶ A **flexible gradebook** that helps instructors monitor student progress

And remember, *Next Generation Grammar* is available both in print and as an eText.

ActiveTeach

A powerful digital resource that provides the perfect solution for seamless lesson planning and exciting whole-class teaching

- ◐ A **Digital Student Book** with interactive whiteboard (IWB) software
- ◐ **Useful notes** that present teaching suggestions, corpus-informed grammar tips, troublesome grammar points, and culture notes
- ◐ Instant one-stop **audio** and **video grammar coach**
- ◐ **Printable** audio scripts, video scripts, and answer keys
- ◐ **Capability** for teachers to:
  - Write, highlight, erase, and create notes
  - Add and save newly-created classroom work
  - Enlarge any section of a page

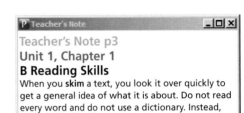

Teacher's Note

Teacher's Note p3
Unit 1, Chapter 1
B Reading Skills
When you **skim** a text, you look it over quickly to get a general idea of what it is about. Do not read every word and do not use a dictionary. Instead, look at the title, pictures, bold, or italicized words, and the first line of each paragraph to get a sense of the general idea.

About the Authors

David Bohlke has 25 years of experience as a teacher, trainer, program director, editor, and materials developer. He has taught in Japan, Korea, Saudi Arabia, and Morocco, and has conducted multiple teacher-training workshops around the world. David is the former publishing manager for adult courses for Cambridge University Press and the former editorial manager for Global ELT for Cengage Learning. He is the coauthor of *Listening Power 2* (Pearson Education), *Four Corners* (Cambridge University Press), and *Speak Now* (Oxford University Press), and is the series editor for *Interchange,* Fourth Edition (Cambridge University Press). He is also the series editor for *Next Generation Grammar.*

Arlen Gargagliano is an assistant director for Westchester Community College's English Language Institute in New York. Author of several textbooks and coauthor of the *Writing from Within* series (Cambridge University Press), Professor Gargagliano has taught for 25 years in the United States, Spain, and Peru. She is a well-known presenter throughout the States and the Americas, the author of several cookbooks, a regular contributor to several food-related blogs, and the creator of the blog *In the Kitchen with Arlen.*

Acknowledgments

I would like to extend a special thank you to Amy McCormick and Massimo Rubini for spearheading this project and providing leadership and support throughout its development, and to Andrea Bryant, Leigh Stolle, and Gosia Jaros-White for their tireless commitment and careful attention to detail. Finally, I'd like to express my gratitude to my friend and coauthor Arlen Gargagliano for her upbeat energy, keen judgment, and good humor. —DB

Thanks first and foremost to my coauthor and eagle-eye editor extraordinaire, David Bohlke. A thank you also to Leigh Stolle for her constructive comments, sharp editorial wisdom, and motivational support. Thanks also to my fellow NGG teammates: Donnette and Sigrun, Pamela and Jennifer, and Christina and Steve. Special thanks to those at the helm of this project: Andrea Bryant and Amy McCormick. Thanks also to Gosia Jaros-White for her digital savvy and guidance. Finally, a special thank you goes to my colleague and dear friend Massimo Rubini, whose foresight and vision brought us all together, and who continues to be an inspiring pillar of strength and support. —AG

Reviewers

We are grateful to the following reviewers for their many helpful comments:

Yukiko Arita, Ibaraki University, Mito, Japan; **Asmaa Awad,** University of Sharjah, Sharjah, United Arab Emirates; **Kim Bayer,** Hunter College CUNY, New York, NY; **Michelle Bell,** University of South Florida, Tampa, FL; **Jeff Bette,** Westchester Community College SUNY, Valhalla, NY; **Leslie Biaggi,** Miami Dade College, Miami, FL; **Celina Costa,** George Brown College, Toronto, Ontario, Canada; **Eric Dury,** University of Sharjah, Sharjah, United Arab Emirates; **Katie Entigar,** Kaplan's English Scool, Boston, MA; **Margaret Eomurian,** Houston Community College, Central College, Houston, TX; **Liz Flynn,** San Diego Community College, San Diego, CA: **Ruth French,** Hunter College CUNY, New York, NY; **Jas Gill,** University of British Columbia, Vancouver, British Columbia, Canada; **Joanne Glaski,** Suffolk County Community College, Selden, NY; **Sandra Hartmann,** University of Houston, Houston, TX; **Cora Higgins,** Boston Academy of English, Boston, MA; **Carolyn Ho,** Lone Star College-Cyfair, Cypress, TX; **Gretchen Irwin-Arada,** Hunter College CUNY, New York, NY; **Bob Jester,** Hunter College CUNY, New York, NY; **Patricia Juza,** Baruch College CUNY, New York, NY; **Liz Kara,** Alberta College, Alberta, Canada; **Jessica March,** American University of Sharjah, Sharjah, United Arab Emirates; **Alison McAdams,** Approach International Student Center, Boston, MA; **Kathy Mehdi,** University of Sharjah, Sharjah, United Arab Emirates; **April Muchmore-Vokoun,** Hillsborough Community College, Dale Mabry Campus, Tampa, FL; **Forest Nelson,** Tokai University, Toyko, Japan; **Dina Paglia,** Hunter College CUNY, New York, NY; **DyAnne Philips,** Houston Community College, Southwest College, Gulfton Center, Houston, TX; **Russell Pickett,** Sam Houston State University, Huntsville, TX; **Peggy Porter,** Houston Community College, Northwest College, Houston, TX; **Tahani Qadri,** American University of Sharjah, Sharjah, United Arab Emirates; **Alison Rice,** Hunter College CUNY, New York, NY; **Kevin Ryan,** Showa Women's University, Tokyo, Japan; **Yasser Salem,** University of Sharjah, Sharjah, United Arab Emirates; **Janet Selitto,** Seminole State College of Florida, Sanford, FL; **Laura Sheehan,** Houston Community College, Southwest College, Stafford Campus, Houston, TX; **Barbara Smith-Palinkas,** Hillsborough Cummunity College, Dale Mabry Campus, Tampa, FL; **Maria Spelleri,** State College of Florida Manatee-Sarasota, Venice, FL; **Marjorie Stamberg,** Hunter College CUNY, New York, NY; **Gregory Strong,** Aoyama Gakuin University, Tokyo, Japan; **Fausto G. Vergara,** Houston Community College, Southeast College, Houston, TX; **Khristie Wills,** American University of Sharjah, Sharjah, United Arab Emirates; **Nancy Ramirez Wright,** Santa Ana College, Santa Ana, CA.

Connections

OUTCOMES

After completing this unit, I will be able to use these grammar points.

CHAPTER 1

Grammar Focus 1
Simple present: *Be*

Grammar Focus 2
Present progressive

CHAPTER 2

Grammar Focus 1
Simple present

Grammar Focus 2
Simple present vs. present progressive

MyEnglishLab

 What do you know?

CHAPTER 1   Network of Friends

Getting Started

A Read the status updates. Answer the questions with names.

1. Who has a new job? _____
2. Who's watching TV? _____
3. Who's waiting for someone? _____
4. Who's taking a language class? _____

FAVORITES
NEW FEEDS
MESSAGES
EVENTS
MORE ▾

What's on your mind? ────────────────────────

Tina Lee   I'm taking Spanish this semester, but it's really hard. I need a good pronunciation dictionary. Any suggestions? Gracias!
Like • Comment • Share

Kevin Potter   Michael, where are you?? I'm standing under the big Coca-Cola sign outside the train station. It's raining—please hurry!
Like • Comment • Share

Teresa Sanchez   Mom, Dad, and I are watching an old movie on TV. Dad's crying, and Mom's laughing. I'm bored. Someone call or text me, please!
Like • Comment • Share

Young-ho Park   I have a new part-time job! I'm working at Omega Café. I'm learning how to make excellent espressos and lattes. Stop by everyone! :)
Like • Comment • Share

B   Comment on one of the status updates in Part A. Then compare with a partner.

C   Look back at the status updates in Part A. Complete the tasks.

1. The verb *be* in the **simple present** takes three forms: *am, is, are*. We use *be* to connect a subject to information such as location or state of being (*I am home. We are tired.*). The contracted forms are *'m, 's,* and *'re*. Circle the examples of *be* in the simple present form.
2. The **present progressive** is formed by the simple present form of *be* + base verb + *-ing* (*am taking*). Underline the examples.
3. Which examples of the present progressive are for actions happening right now, at the moment of speaking? Which are for longer actions in progress now, but not necessarily at this exact moment?

Reading

A WARM-UP Check (✓) the ways you communicate with friends and family. Then compare answers with a partner.

☐ phone   ☐ letter   ☐ blogging   ☐ social networking

☐ email   ☐ texting   ☐ instant messaging   ☐ other: _____

B SKIMMING Skim the messages on Lindsay's wall. What are three topics the friends are discussing? Then go back and read the messages again.

Lindsay Adams 9:47 P.M. I'm in the library. I'm studying for my chemistry final right now, but I'm also thinking about my ski trip to the mountains next week. Oh no . . . the guy at the next desk is sleeping . . . and snoring!

Jake Sanders 9:53 P.M. Hi, Lindsay! How are classes? How many are you taking? Are they going well?

Lindsay Adams 9:58 P.M. Nice to hear from you, Jake! I'm taking five classes this fall semester, so I'm studying all the time. And I'm working in a Japanese restaurant on weekends. I'm learning a lot about the restaurant business. Where are you right now? What are you doing these days?

Jake Sanders 10:01 P.M. I'm working at Mega Design now. It's exciting! I'm designing a lot of brochures and webpages on the computer. The hours are long—I get home after 7 P.M. some nights. But the pay is good.

Lindsay Adams 10:05 P.M. Are you still playing in your band? I'm just curious.

Jake Sanders 10:10 P.M. Yes! We're not playing very much during the week, but we're playing a lot on weekends at weddings. I'm not sleeping very much these days.

Rachel Carson 10:17 P.M. Your band is awesome! By the way, is your company hiring? I'm looking for a new job.

Jake Sanders 10:22 P.M. Sorry, Rachel, they aren't hiring at the moment, but I think Design Plus is. What kind of job are you looking for?

Rachel Carson 10:25 P.M. I'm looking at Design Plus's website right now. They're advertising for a new graphic designer. That's perfect! Thanks!

C UNDERSTANDING DETAILS Write *T* for the true statements and *F* for the false statements. Correct the false ones.

    studying for
__*F*__ 1. Lindsay is ~~taking~~ her chemistry final right now.

_____ 2. Lindsay is working at a restaurant on weekends.

_____ 3. Jake's band is playing a lot during the week.

_____ 4. Jake is getting enough sleep.

_____ 5. Jake is looking for a new job.

_____ 6. Mega Design is advertising for a graphic designer.

_____ 7. Rachel is sending in a job application right now.

Grammar Focus 1 Simple present: *Be*

Examples	Language notes
(1) **Present** Past ——— X ———→ Future **I am** in the library. **She is** bored. **You are** a good student.	We often use the verb **be** in the **simple present** to connect the subject to information such as current location, state of being, or category. The verb *be* has three forms in the simple present: (*I*) **am**, (*he, she, it*) **is**, and (*you, we, they*) **are**.
(2) **I'm** in the library. **She's** bored. **You're** a good student.	In statements, we often **contract** the simple present forms of *be* after pronouns.
(3) She**'s not** / She **isn't** in the classroom. We**'re not** / We **aren't** at work. I **am not** home.	We add **not** to make a statement negative. There are two ways to contract *is* + *not* and *are* + *not* with pronouns. **Note:** We do not contract *am* + *not*.
(4) **I am** in the right class. → **Am I** in the right class? **He is** at work. → **Is he** at work?	Some **yes / no questions** are formed with *be*. To form a *yes / no* question in the simple present with *be*, switch the position of *am / is / are* and the subject: **Be (Am, Is, Are)** + **subject** + other information
(5) **Q:** Are they at work? **A: Yes, they are.**	For **short answers** to *yes / no* **questions**, use the simple present of *be*.
(6) **Q:** Is he in a band? **A:** No, **he's not**. / No, he **isn't**. ***Incorrect:*** Yes, ~~he's~~.	We use **contractions** in **negative short answers**. We don't use contractions in affirmative short answers.
(7) **When is** dinner? **Where are** you? **How is** it?	*Wh-* **questions** begin with *Who, What, When, Where, How (many)*, and *Why*. To form a *wh-* question with *be*, use: **Wh- word** + **be (am, is, are)** + subject
(8) **Who's** that? **How's** your job?	We often **contract** *wh-* words with *be* in speech and informal writing.
(9) **Q:** Where are your friends? **A: At the library.**	For **short answers** to *wh-* **questions**, we usually don't repeat the words from the question.

Affirmative statements		Negative statements	
I'm You're } at work. He's		I'm not You're not / You aren't } home. He's not / He isn't	

Yes / No questions	Short answers		
Am I in the right class?	Yes, **you are.**	No, **you're not.** / No, **you aren't.**	
Are you in the library?	Yes, **I am.**	No, **I'm not.**	
Is he in a band?	Yes, **he is.**	No, **he's not.** / No, **he isn't.**	

Wh- questions	Short answers	Long answers
When is lunch?	At 12:30.	It's at 12:30.
Where are you and Jack?	At the restaurant.	We're at the restaurant.
How are you?	Pretty good.	I'm pretty good.

See Appendix A on page A-1 for a list of contractions with **be**. *See Appendix B on page A-1 for more statements and questions with* **be**.

Grammar Practice

A Match the answers to the questions.

Questions

g **1.** Is your mother home?

_____ **2.** Are you and Kylie good friends?

_____ **3.** Where are your books?

_____ **4.** Am I in your list of friends?

_____ **5.** Who's this text from?

_____ **6.** When's the next meeting?

_____ **7.** Are your classes OK?

_____ **8.** How many of your friends are online now?

Answers

a. They're in my bag.

b. No, they're not.

c. Tomorrow.

d. Yes, we are.

e. Michael.

f. About 20.

g. No, she isn't.

h. Yes, you are.

B Rewrite the sentences with the pronouns. Use contractions. More than one correct answer may be possible.

1. Mr. Parker is our teacher.   (he)   *He's our teacher.* _____

2. Don and Suzie are married.   (they) _____

3. Cal and I are not from around here.   (we) _____

4. My phone number is 555-9921.   (it) _____

5. Her mother is not at home.   (she) _____

6. I am not online right now.   (I) _____

C Read the sentences. Rewrite them as questions with *be*. More than one correct answer may be possible.

	Yes / No questions	*Wh-* questions
1. My birthday is June 6.	*Is your birthday June 6?*	*When is your birthday?*
2. My classes are boring.	_____	_____
3. Class is at 10:00.	_____	_____
4. Mr. Perez is from Mexico.	_____	_____
5. That's my brother.	_____	_____
6. She is at work.	_____	_____
7. Their names are Emi and Jun.	_____	_____
8. I am at the library.	_____	_____

Grammar Focus 2 Present progressive

Examples	Language notes
(1) **Present** Past ——————— **XXX** ——————→ Future I'm **studying** for my chemistry final right now. It's **raining**—please hurry.	Use the **present progressive** to talk about actions happening right now, at the moment of speaking.
(2) He's **not sleeping** much these days. We're **playing** a lot of weddings on weekends.	We also use the present progressive for **longer actions** in progress now, but not necessarily at this exact moment.
(3) I'm **working** in a Japanese restaurant. The guy at the next desk **is snoring**. They're **designing** a new brochure.	To form the present progressive, use: subject + *be* + **base verb** + *-ing*
(4) **hire:** Business employers aren't **hiring** older workers. **get:** We're not **getting** much sleep these days. **try:** She's **trying** to get a new job.	The spelling of some verbs changes when *-ing* is added. • For verbs that end in a **consonant** + *-e*, drop the *-e* and add *-ing*. • For verbs that end in a **consonant** + **vowel** + **consonant**, double the last consonant and add *-ing*. ***Note:*** Don't double the last consonant if it is a *w*, *x*, or *y*.
(5) **Are** you **working**?	To form *yes / no* **questions** in the present progressive, use: *Be* + subject + **base verb** + *-ing*
(6) **Q:** Are you coming to our concert? **A: Yes, we are.**	For **short answers** to *yes / no* **questions**, use the simple present of *be*.
(7) **Where are** you **working**? **Who is** she **calling**?	To form *wh-* **questions** in the present progressive, use: *Wh-* **word** + *be* + subject + **base verb** + *-ing*
(8) **Who's calling** me now? *(Steve.)* **What's making** that noise? *(The computer.)*	If the *wh-* word is the **subject** of the question, use the **third person singular** form of the verb.

Affirmative statements	Negative statements
I'm She's ⎫ **quitting**. They're ⎭	I'm **not** She's **not** / She **isn't** ⎫ **working** at the café. They're **not** / They **aren't** ⎭
It's **getting** cold.	It's **not** / It **isn't getting** cold.
Yes / No questions	Short answers
Is he **playing** in a band? **Are** your classes **going** well?	Yes, **he is.** No, **they're not.**
Wh- questions	Short answers
How many classes **are** you **taking**? **What** kind of job **is** she **looking** for?	Five. A graphic design job.

See Appendices C and D on page A-2 for more statements and questions in the present progressive and for more examples of and spelling rules for -ing endings.

Grammar Practice

A Look at the picture. What are the people doing? Complete the sentences. Use the words from the box. Use the present progressive.

buy a newspaper   eat lunch   ~~listen to music~~   play basketball   ride a bike   wait for the bus

1. Pam _is listening to music_____.   4. Dan and Erik _____.

2. Kyle _____.   5. Amar _____.

3. Luisa _____.   6. Jennifer and Alicia _____.

B What are the people in Part A *not* doing? Use the words to write negative sentences.

1. She _isn't watching_____ (watch) TV.   4. They _____ (jog).

2. He _____ (drive) a car.   5. He _____ (read) a book.

3. She _____ (sit) on the bus.   6. They _____ (play) tennis.

C Unscramble the words to make questions. Then write short, true answers.

1. listening to music / you / right now / are / ?

   Q: _Are you listening to music right now?_____   A: _No, I'm not._____

2. wearing / today / what / your teacher / is / ?

   Q: _____   A: _____

3. classes / your / going / how / are / ?

   Q: _____   A: _____

4. these days / you / studying / are / a lot / ?

   Q: _____   A: _____

5. working / on weekends / your best friend / is / ?

   Q: _____   A: _____

6. right now / raining / it / is / ?

   Q: _____   A: _____

7. near you / sitting / is / who / ?

   Q: _____   A: _____

Listening

A 🎧 UNDERSTANDING MAIN IDEAS Listen to Maggie and her friends talking at a party. What do they talk about? Check (✓) the topics.

1. ☐ friends   ☐ family

2. ☐ school   ☐ work

3. ☐ food   ☐ shopping

4. ☐ movies   ☐ music

5. ☐ an apartment   ☐ an office

B 🎧 UNDERSTANDING DETAILS Listen again. Answer the questions. Write short answers.

1. Is Monica working in a clothing store?   _____

2. How many classes is Maggie taking?   _____

3. What is Maggie eating?   _____

4. Is Peter listening to a new song?   _____

5. What's Annie's place like?   _____

C AFTER LISTENING Talk with a partner. What kind of parties do you like? What topics do you like to talk about? What don't you like to talk about?

Speaking

A What are your classmates doing these days? Read the questions in the chart. Add two more.

These days, are you . . .	Name
reading a good book?	
watching a lot of TV?	
preparing for a trip?	
studying with a tutor?	
living at home?	
learning a language in addition to English?	
downloading a lot of music or movies?	
looking for a job?	
?	
?	

B   Walk around and ask the questions from the chart in Part A. When someone answers "yes," write the person's name. Ask a follow-up question. Look at the model.

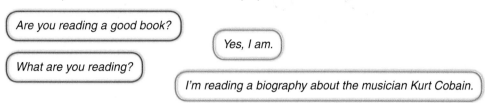

Are you reading a good book?

What are you reading?

Yes, I am.

I'm reading a biography about the musician Kurt Cobain.

C   Talk with a partner. Share information about your classmates.

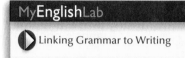

MyEnglishLab

▶ Linking Grammar to Writing

Writing

A   Think about what you're doing these days. Write a status update at the top of a piece of paper. Include your name or username.

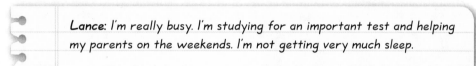

Lance: I'm really busy. I'm studying for an important test and helping my parents on the weekends. I'm not getting very much sleep.

B   Work in a group. Pass your update to the right. Write a response to your classmate's update. Try to use the grammar from the chapter.

Lance: I'm really busy. I'm studying for an important test and helping my parents on the weekends. I'm not getting very much sleep.

Ming: I'm sorry to hear that, Lance. I'm studying for a test, too. What test are you studying for? Is it English?

C   Continue passing and writing responses until your update comes back to you.

Lance: I'm really busy. I'm studying for an important test and helping my parents on the weekends. I'm not getting very much sleep.

Ming: I'm sorry to hear that, Lance. I'm studying for a test, too. What test are you studying for? Is it English?

skatergirl: Hey, Lance. Are you helping your parents at their restaurant? What are they paying you? LOL

MyEnglishLab

▶ Diagnostic Test

CHAPTER 2   Global Links

Getting Started

A   Do you ever share photos online? Do you write captions (short descriptions) for them? If so, what kind of information do you include?

B   Bianca is visiting her epal Lauren in London for the first time. Match the captions to Bianca's photos.

_____ 1.

_____ 2.

_____ 3.

_____ 4.

    a. I'm waiting in line for theater tickets. Lauren is taking the picture. She doesn't like lines!
    b. We love statues! I'm standing in front of a cool one here in Trafalgar Square.
    c. People are watching the Changing of the Guard ceremony. It happens every day at 11:30.
    d. Lauren is eating a chicken kebab on the street. I don't eat meat, so it doesn't look good to me.

C   Look back at the photo captions in Part B. Complete the tasks.

    1. Underline the examples of the **present progressive**.
    2. The **affirmative simple present** is formed with the base verb, with or without *-s* (*take / takes*). The **negative simple present** is formed with *do / does + not +* the base verb (*don't take / doesn't take*). Circle the examples.
    3. Look at the verbs you circled. What verbs follow *I, you, we,* or *they*? What verbs follow *he, she,* or *it*? Complete the chart.

	Follows *I, you, we, they*	Follows *he, she, it*
Affirmative simple present		
Negative simple present		

Reading

A WARM-UP Do you communicate in English outside of class? How? Where? Who do you communicate with? Discuss with a partner.

B SCANNING Scan the article. Where are the teachers? Write the countries. Then go back and read the whole article.

Mariko Setsuya: _____   Talya Demir: _____   Mariana Silva: _____

Ramon Gonzalez: _____   Alex Pierce: _____   Doug Lawson: _____

Connecting Classrooms

The world is truly getting smaller. Classrooms around the world are connecting more than ever before.

In Japan, English teacher Mariko Setsuya and her students are watching a video. The video shows English-language students in Mexico and their teacher, Ramon Gonzalez. The Mexican students are eating dinner in a local restaurant. One student is filming the dinner, and the others are describing in English the Mexican dishes on the table. Ms. Setsuya's students are listening, watching, and learning about a different culture. After the video, the Japanese students email the Mexican students questions such as, "What do you eat for breakfast in Mexico?" and "Do you eat dinner late in Mexico?" Then the Mexican students answer the emails.

In Turkey, Talya Demir and her English students are very interested in blogs from around the world. This week they're reading a blog by Alex Pierce's English students in the United States. Mr. Pierce's students update the blog every week. They write about their English classroom, discuss pop culture, and answer questions from students around the world. Some common questions are "What do you do after class?" and "Does your blog have readers from many countries?" Ms. Demir's students want to create their own class blog.

In Mariana Silva's English class in Brazil, students are talking to epals in Canada. They aren't talking on the phone; they're video chatting at computers in the classroom. The students in Canada are in Doug Lawson's English class. They're from all over the world, including Pakistan, France, Ghana, China, and Russia. Every week the two teachers give their students 10 minutes to talk to their epals. The students are learning about new cultures. They're also improving their speaking and listening. Everyone loves this part of the lesson, and many students also write or talk to their new friends outside of class.

C UNDERSTANDING DETAILS Match the classrooms to the activities. Some sentences have more than one correct answer.

Activities

_b, d_ **1.** Students answer questions.

_____ **2.** Students write questions.

_____ **3.** Students read a blog.

_____ **4.** Students write a blog.

_____ **5.** Students video chat.

_____ **6.** Students watch a video.

_____ **7.** Students make a video.

Classrooms

a. Mariko Setsuya's classroom

b. Ramon Gonzalez's classroom

c. Talya Demir's classroom

d. Alex Pierce's classroom

e. Mariana Silva's classroom

f. Doug Lawson's classroom

Grammar Focus 1 Simple present

Examples	Language notes
(1) **Present** Past ————X————→ Future It **takes** place every day. I **love** statues like this.	Use the **simple present** to talk about actions that are **repeated** or **usual**. We also use the simple present to talk about **facts** or **general truths**.
(2) **They write** about their daily lives.	To form simple present **affirmative statements** with *I*, *you*, *we*, and *they*, use the base verb.
(3) **She calls** and **talks** to her epal every week. Every night **he brushes** and **flosses** his teeth.	To form simple present **affirmative statements** with *he*, *she*, and *it* (third person singular), add -s to the base verb. For most verbs ending in *ch*, *o*, *s*, *sh*, *x*, or *z*, add -es.
(4) At night **she has** dinner, **does** her homework, and **goes** to bed early.	The verbs **have**, **do**, and **go** have irregular third person singular forms.
(5) We **don't have** a computer lab at our school. He **doesn't have** a computer.	In **negative statements** with *I*, *you*, *we*, and *they*, use: subject + *do not* + **base verb** With *he*, *she*, and *it*, use: subject + *does not* + **base verb** **Note:** The **contracted** form of *do not* is **don't**. The contracted form of *does not* is **doesn't**.
(6) **Do** you **text** your friends every day? **Does** he **belong** to any social networks?	For **yes / no questions** with *I*, *you*, *we*, and *they*, use: **Do** + subject + **base verb** With *he*, *she*, and *it*, use: **Does** + subject + **base verb**
(7) **Q:** Does your school have whiteboards? **A: Yes, it does. / No, it doesn't.**	For **short answers** to *yes / no* questions use the simple present of *do*.
(8) **What do** you **eat** for breakfast? **When does** it **start?**	For *wh-* **questions** with *I*, *you*, *we*, and *they*, use: **Wh-** word + *do* + subject + **base verb** With *he*, *she*, and *it*, use: **Wh-** word + *does* + subject + **base verb**
(9) **What happens** every Friday? *(A class field trip.)* *Incorrect:* What ~~does happen~~ every Friday?	If the *wh-* word is the **subject** of the question, use the **third person singular** form of the verb.

Affirmative statements		Negative statements	
He **makes** videos. They **discuss** pop culture.		He **doesn't make** podcasts. They **don't discuss** politics.	
Yes / No questions		Short answers	
Do you **eat** dinner late in Mexico? **Does** he **check** his email every day?	Yes, **we do.** Yes, **he does.**	No, **we don't.** No, **he doesn't.**	
Wh- questions	Short answers		Long answers
Where does he **go** after class? **How many** hits **do** you **get?**	Home. Hundreds.		He goes home. I get hundreds of hits.

See Appendix A on page A-1 for contractions with do. *See Appendices E and F on page A-3 for more statements and questions in the simple present and for spelling rules for* -s *endings.*

Grammar Practice

A Complete the message board. Use the simple present form of the verbs.

casey: What fun things do you do in your English class? On Tuesdays, our class
1. _____ (do) a video chat with a class in China.

junko: We **2.** _____ (listen) to an English pop song every Friday. Everyone
3. _____ (love) that!

pedro: That **4.** _____ (sound) fun. Our teacher **5.** _____ (not /
play) music, but she **6.** _____ (show) movies sometimes.

adam: We give group presentations once a month. They're fun, but the research
7. _____ (take) a long time.

anita: We **8.** _____ (not / give) presentations. How long **9.** _____
it _____ (take) to create one?

young-min: We **10.** _____ (do) creative writing in English. Our class
11. _____ (have) a webpage. It **12.** _____ (have) our stories.

oscar: 13. _____ anyone _____ (play) language games?
I **14.** _____ (not / like) them. I **15.** _____ (prefer) discussions.

fatima: We **16.** _____ (not / do) this in class, but our teacher
17. _____ (tell) us about language-learning message boards like this one!

B Unscramble the words to make *yes / no* and *wh-* questions.

1. social network / belong to / you / do / a / ? _____
2. have / your / does / class / a / whiteboard / ? _____
3. your best friend / do / you / text / ? _____
4. you / do / visit / what websites / ? _____
5. do / online friends / have / how many / you / ? _____
6. a lot / text / who / you / do / ? _____

C Work with a partner. Take turns asking and answering the questions in Part B. Give short answers. Look at the model.

Do you belong to a social network?

Yes, I do.

Grammar Focus 2 Simple present vs. present progressive

Examples	Language notes
(1) **Present** Past ———— **X** ————→ Future **Q:** When **do** you **check** your email? **A:** I **check** my email every morning. **Q: Do** you **have** an epal? **A:** Yes. He **lives** in Belarus.	Use the **simple present** to talk about **repeated** or **usual actions**, **facts**, and **general truths**.
(2) **Present** Past ———— **XXX** ————→ Future **Q:** What **are** you **studying** this semester? **A:** I'm **studying** history and economics. **Q: Are** you **studying** now? **A:** No. I'm **checking** my email now.	Use the **present progressive**, on the other hand, to tell about **actions happening now** and **longer actions in progress**.
(3) I **check** my email **every day**. He **sometimes posts** videos online.	With the **simple present**, we often use **time signals** such as *every day, often, always, sometimes, never, generally*, and *normally*.
(4) I'm **checking** my email **at the moment**. He's **posting** a lot of videos **these days**.	With the **present progressive**, we often use **time signals** such as *this _____ (month, etc.), currently, now, right now, at the moment, today, these days,* and *nowadays*.
(5) He **has** epals in both Ukraine and Thailand. That **tastes** good. Everyone **loves** this part of the lesson. I don't **believe** you. That computer **costs** $3,500.	We usually use the simple present—not the present progressive—with **non-action verbs** for these situations: **Possession** *belong, have* **Senses** *feel, smell, taste* **Emotions** *feel, hate, hope, like, love, prefer, regret, want, wish* **Mental activities** *believe, forget, know, think, remember, understand* **States of being** *be, cost, fit, include, look, mean, seem, sound*

Grammar Practice

 Complete the information. Use the simple present or present progressive form of the verbs.

These days Voice of America (VOA) **1.** _____ (reach) out to new audiences in

creative ways. Nowadays the radio and TV broadcasting service **2.** _____ (use)

Facebook to teach English lessons. The lessons **3.** _____ (be) part of

The Classroom, VOA's popular online learning program. Now more and more students

4. _____ (discover) this new way to learn and interact in English.

How **5.** _____ it
_____ (work)? The icon
on VOA's Learning English Facebook page
6. _____ (change) four times
a day. It **7.** _____ (show) that a
live, online class is in session. At that moment a teacher
8. _____ (teach) a free lesson.
Students never **9.** _____ (pay)!
Normally, students **10.** _____
(submit) questions as part of an interactive lesson.
The lesson **11.** _____ (include)
materials from The Classroom. Currently, thousands
of learners **12.** _____ (participate)
in these lessons.

B Find and correct the mistake in each conversation.

1. A: What are you doing? Are you reading the morning news?

   B: No, I'm not. I'm checking my email. I'm always checking my email in the morning.

2. A: I love this website. Do you know it?

   B: Yeah. I'm thinking it's very informative, but I prefer this one.

3. A: I text my friend Steve right now. Do you know him?

   B: Maybe. Does he belong to the Tech Club?

4. A: Do you do anything fun in class?

   B: Sure. We do some cool projects. For example, we're sometimes making videos.

5. A: This chicken isn't tasting good. What does that mean?

   B: It's probably bad. It belongs in the trash!

6. A: Normally I'm not doing video chats. I don't like them.

   B: I agree. I prefer face-to-face meetings.

Listening

A BEFORE LISTENING Work with a partner. Look at the pictures. What are the people doing? What time of day do you think it is in each place?

B 🎧 UNDERSTANDING MAIN IDEAS Listen to Angela and Ian's video chat. Order the pictures from *1* to *6*.

_____ a.

_____ b.

_____ c.

_____ d.

_____ e.

_____ f.

C 🎧 UNDERSTANDING DETAILS Listen again. Answer the questions. Write short answers.

1. What city is Angela calling from? _____

2. What time is it in London? _____

3. Who is Isabel? _____

4. What's Isabel doing this week? _____

5. What does Ian do for a living? _____

6. Where's Ian working now? _____

7. Who's teaching Angela the guitar? _____

8. When does Angela practice? _____

Speaking

A Read the questions. Complete the "You" column. Write short answers.

	You	Classmates
1. Are you spending a lot of time online these days?		
2. How many text messages do you receive every day?		
3. What computer or video games do you enjoy?		
4. How many social networks do you belong to?		
5. What do you like about social networking?		
6. What don't you like about social networking?		
7. Are you planning to get a new computer or phone soon?		
8. How are you using technology to learn English?		

B Work in groups of three. Discuss the questions in Part A. Take notes in the chart. Then discuss the chart with your group. What do you have in common? Look at the model.

> *We're all spending a lot of time online these days, especially Mariko.*
> *She has a food blog and writes in it every day.*

Writing

A Read and think about the questions.

- Where are you living now? Do you like it?
- Are you taking any classes? Which do you enjoy?
- Are you working? Where? Do you like your job?
- How do you spend your weekends?
- What don't you like about your schedule?

B What's your life like nowadays? Write an email to an old friend. Try to use the grammar from the chapter.

○ ○ ○

Hi Chen,
Everything is great here. I'm living in a dorm on campus right now. I really like it. I have a lot of friends on my floor. I'm taking six classes this semester. I really enjoy economics and psychology. I don't like history very much. I love my weekends. My friends and I often see movies or study together. Right now I'm not working. But I want a job! OK, I need to go. Write back soon.
Carmen

C Share emails with a partner. Ask and answer questions.

Grammar Summary

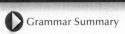

The verb **be** has three present forms (*am, is, are*). *Be* is often contracted with pronouns.

Affirmative statements	Negative statements
I am in class 2A. / **I'm** in class 2A. **He is** a student. / **He's** a student. **They are** pen pals. / **They're** pen pals.	**I'm not** in class 2B. **He's not** a teacher. / **He isn't** a teacher. **They're not** epals. / **They aren't** epals.

To form **yes / no questions with be in the simple present**, begin the sentence with the correct form of *be*. To form **wh- questions**, begin with a *wh-* question word such as *Who, What, When, Where, How (many)*, or *Why*.

Yes / No questions	Short answers	Wh- questions	Short answers
Am I in class A? **Is he** a teacher? **Are they** epals?	Yes, you are. No, he isn't. No, they're not.	**Who** are they? **What's** his name? **Where** is he?	My friends. Bill. In Canada.

Use the simple present form of *be* + base verb + *-ing* to form the **present progressive**. Use this form to describe actions happening now, either at the exact moment of speaking or for longer actions not necessarily at the exact moment of speaking.

Now: The moment of speaking	Now: Not necessarily the moment of speaking
I'm sending a text right now. **He's waiting** for you outside.	**I'm learning** Japanese. **He's working** at an Italian restaurant.

To form **yes / no questions with be in the present progressive**, begin the sentence with the correct form of *be*. To form **wh- questions**, begin with a *wh-* word. To ask a question about a subject, use *is*.

Yes / No questions	Short answers	Wh- questions	Short answers
Are you listening? **Is he** sleeping?	Yes, I am. No, he's not.	**What** are you doing? **Who's** calling me? [*wh-* word = subject]	Nothing. James.

Use the **simple present** to talk about actions that are routine, and for facts or general truths. Form the simple present with the base form of a verb after *I, you, we,* and *they*. Add *-s* to the base verb for *he, she,* and *it*. To make negative sentences, add *do not* (*don't*) after *I, you, we,* and *they*; add *does not* (*doesn't*) after *he, she,* and *it*.

I / You / We / They	He / She / It
I generally **prefer** email. I **don't like** texts.	He **writes** in his blog. He **doesn't keep** a journal.

To form **yes / no questions in the simple present**, begin the sentence with *Do* or *Does*. To form **wh- questions**, begin with a *wh-* word.

Yes / No questions	Short answers	Wh- questions	Short answers
Do you **study** every day? **Does** she **go** to the lab?	Yes, I do. No, she doesn't.	**How often do** you **study**? **When does** she **go** to the lab?	Every day. On Friday.

We use **non-action verbs** in the simple present to describe possession, senses, emotions, mental activities, and states of being.

Non-action verbs
Does this **belong** to you? It **looks** important. [possession] [state of being] I don't **like** peppers. I **think** they **taste** funny. [emotion] [mental activity] [sense]

Self-Assessment

A (5 points) Circle the correct words.

1. **A: Who's / Who are** that?   **B:** My friend Jessica.

2. **A:** When **is / are** your classes?   **B:** At 7:00 and 9:30.

3. **A:** Are you at home?   **B:** Yes, **I'm / I am.**

4. **A:** Are your parents in town?   **B:** No, they're **aren't / not.**

5. **A:** Is Mrs. Martin your teacher?   **B:** Yes, **she's / she is.**

B (6 points) Use the words to write sentences. Use the present progressive.

1. (I / download / a song)   _____

2. (he / play / video games)   _____

3. (I / not / live / at home / right now)   _____

4. (they / learn / web design / at night)   _____

5. (she / not / work / at the moment)   _____

6. (what / you / study / in class / ?)   _____

C (7 points) Find and correct the mistake in each sentence.

1. She doesn't belongs to a social network.

2. Do Maria have a computer?

3. It take a short time to upload photos.

4. He don't study very much.

5. What time do our video chat start?

6. He have three email messages.

7. What do your teacher do at the beginning of class?

D (7 points) Complete the sentences. Use the simple present or the present progressive form of the verbs.

1. What kind of computer _____ you _____ (prefer)?

2. _____ you _____ (work) on any interesting projects these days?

3. She _____ (not / take) any classes this semester.

4. I _____ (remember) my first day of school.

5. What _____ you _____ (do) with my phone? Please don't touch it.

6. What _____ this word _____ (mean)?

7. There's no one on the phone. I _____ (not / hear) anyone.

Unit Project: Class website

A Write about a classmate for the class website. Follow the steps.

1. Read the categories in the chart.
2. Think of and write questions in the chart.

	Questions	Notes
Name		
Birthday		
Current city		
School		
Major		
Classes		
Interests		
Important people		
Music		
Movies		
Favorite technology (cell phone, tablet)		
Languages		
Other		

3. Work in pairs. Interview a classmate. Take notes in the chart. Ask follow-up questions. Look at the model.

What's your name?

My name is Lucinda Martinez.

Do you have a middle name?

B Write an introduction of your classmate for a class website. Use your notes from Part A. Add other interesting information.

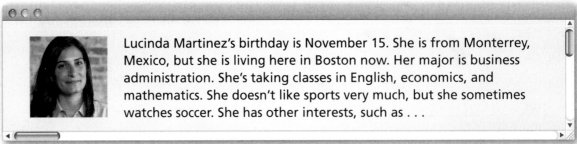

Lucinda Martinez's birthday is November 15. She is from Monterrey, Mexico, but she is living here in Boston now. Her major is business administration. She's taking classes in English, economics, and mathematics. She doesn't like sports very much, but she sometimes watches soccer. She has other interests, such as . . .

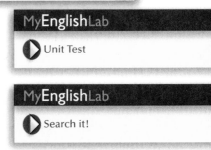

MyEnglishLab

Unit Test

MyEnglishLab

Search it!

UNIT 2

Achievements

OUTCOMES

After completing this unit, I will be able to use these grammar points.

MyEnglishLab

 What do you know?

CHAPTER 3

Child Prodigies

Getting Started

A A child prodigy is an unusually talented young child. Look at the pictures and read the questions. Then match the answers to the questions.

Questions

_____ 1. How many languages did Ung-Yong Kim read at age four?

_____ 2. When did Arran Fernandez begin his studies at Cambridge University?

_____ 3. What did singer Cleopatra Stratan achieve at the age of three?

_____ 4. What procedure did boy-surgeon Akrit Jaswal perform as his first surgery?

Answers

a. In 2010, this 15-year-old England native enrolled as an undergraduate student and became the youngest student since 1773.

b. This seven-year-old Indian doctor treated the burned hands of a girl.

c. This Korean prodigy knew Japanese, Korean, German, and English.

d. This Moldovan youngster made an album in Romanian and English.

B Which prodigy is most interesting to you? Compare answers with a partner.

C Look back at the questions and answers in Part A. Complete the tasks.

1. **Regular verbs** in the **simple past** end in *-ed*. Circle the examples in the answers.
2. **Irregular verbs** in the **simple past** don't end in *-ed*; they have different forms. Underline the examples in the answers.
3. Complete the chart with the examples from the questions. What do you notice about the helping verbs (also called *auxiliary verbs*)? What form are the main verbs?

Helping verbs	Main verbs
1. *did*	*read*
2.	
3.	
4.	

Reading

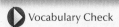
A WARM-UP Look at the picture in Part B. Circle the best caption.
Compare answers with a partner.

   a. A parent is helping a child with schoolwork.
   b. A child is enjoying playtime with a parent.
   c. A parent is preparing a child for a performance.

B SCANNING Scan the article. Underline two facts about child prodigies. Then go back and read the whole article.

What's the Truth about Raising Child Prodigies?

Why did Mozart start composing music at age four? Where did Chopin get his special abilities? How did Picasso become a painter? Many people—especially parents of young children—wonder where talent comes from. They wonder, *Is my child a prodigy?* Child prodigies are rare. And their special abilities show up early. They have talents that their peers don't. In fact, they often perform at the level of adults in language, mathematics, music, art, and other areas.

So is it possible to *make* your child into a little Einstein? Not exactly. Children are born super talented, or not. But the good news is that smart parental decisions can help child development, whether the child is a prodigy or just a regular kid.

In a University of Montreal study, researchers interviewed nearly 600 people between the ages of 6 and 38. Some of them were prodigies; some of them knew prodigies. The researchers asked, "Did the children love what they did?" "Did they study subjects they enjoyed?" According to the study, prodigies shared two features: independence and passion. Researchers found that prodigies were most successful under certain conditions: 1) The prodigies studied their favorite subjects. 2) They chose their own hobbies. 3) They determined their own practice schedules. In other words, the parents supported their independence and passion.

Of course, there are limits. For example, decisions about health and safety are still the parents' responsibility. But according to Ellen Winner, professor of psychology at Boston College and author of *Gifted Children*, parents need to listen to their children—and then let them do what they like to do. When isn't that good advice?

C UNDERSTANDING MAIN IDEAS AND DETAILS Write *T* for the true statements and *F* for the false statements.

_____ **1.** Child prodigies have talents that are clear at an early age.

_____ **2.** Often a child prodigy is not very good in music.

_____ **3.** Parents can do things to make their child a prodigy.

_____ **4.** Child prodigies value the freedom to choose.

_____ **5.** The three factors that help prodigies succeed can help regular children, too.

Grammar Focus 1 Simple past: Regular verbs

Examples	Language notes
(1) Past —— X —— Present ——→ Future Researchers **asked** people about prodigies.	We use the **simple past** to talk about **actions**, **situations**, **states of being**, and **events** that are finished.
(2) ***-d***: determine → determine**d** ***-ied***: study → stud**ied** ***-ed***: ask → ask**ed** seem → seem**ed** plan → plan**ned**	There are three endings for the regular simple past: ***-d***, ***-ied***, and ***-ed***. • Add ***-d*** if the **verb ends in -e**. • If the **verb ends in a consonant + *y*:** *y* → *i* + *-ed* • Add ***-ed*** to most other verbs. • **Double the consonant** if a verb ends in **a consonant + a vowel + a consonant**. ***Note:*** If the stress is on the first syllable, do not double the consonant: *visited*.
(3) /d/ → determin**ed** /t/ → help**ed** /ɪd/ → need**ed**	Regular simple past verbs end in three possible **sounds: /d/, /t/,** and **/ɪd/**.
(4) **I studied** English last year. **She studied** English last year. **They studied** English last year.	In the simple past, the verb form is the **same for all subjects**.
(5) He performed **yesterday**. I practiced a lot **last winter**. Lessons started **two months ago**. We enrolled **in August**. Our results posted **on Tuesday**. She graduated **at 15**.	Use **time signals** to explain when a past event occurred: ***yesterday; last*** _____ *(night, Tuesday);* _____ *(hours, days)* ***ago***. Use ***in*** with months and years; ***on*** with days and dates; and ***at*** with time and age.
(6) He **did not interview** 250 people.	To form **negative statements** in the simple past, use: subject + ***did not*** + **base verb**
(7) The parents **didn't help** their children.	The **contraction** of *did not* is *didn't*. We often use *didn't* in speech and informal writing.
(8) **Q: Did** they **enjoy** the class? **A: Yes, they did. / No, they didn't.**	For ***yes / no* questions** in the simple past, use: ***Did*** + subject + **base verb** For **short answers**, use the simple past of *do* (*did*).

Affirmative statements	Negative statements
I / She / They **started**.	I / She / They **didn't start**.
Yes / No questions	Short answers
Did she / you / they **learn** Latin?	Yes, she / I / they **did**. No, she / I / they **didn't**.

See Appendices G and H on page A-4 for more simple past statements and questions with regular verbs and spelling rules for -ed endings.

Grammar Practice

A Complete the sentences. Use the words from the box. Use the simple past.

enjoy	interview	need	play	share	study

1. Researchers _____ young and older adults.

2. Passion for a subject _____ an important role, the researchers learned.

3. All prodigies _____ this feature: passion for a subject.

4. Most of the children _____ subjects at home, not just in school.

5. At four years old, he _____ music and art.

6. He didn't like silence; he _____ music in order to create.

B Rewrite the sentences as *yes / no* questions. Then write short answers. (Look back at Part A on page 22 for the answers.)

1. Ung-Yong Kim discovered four new languages at four.

   Q: _____   A: _____

2. Akrit Jaswal performed his first medical procedure at 17.

   Q: _____   A: _____

3. Cleopatra Stratan recorded her first album at 13.

   Q: _____   A: _____

4. Arran Fernandez started classes at Harvard at 15.

   Q: _____   A: _____

C Complete the blog posting about a child prodigy. Use the simple past.

My Nephew, the Child Prodigy

Yesterday my four-year-old nephew Paul and I **1.** *visited* (visit) Lincoln

Center. I **2.** _____ (want) him to hear the beautiful music of my favorite

composer, Frédéric François Chopin. Suddenly, Paul **3.** _____ (start) tapping

his leg with his hand. His rhythm was perfect! I **4.** _____ (watch) his

expression as he listened. He **5.** _____ (close) his eyes, and his body

6. _____ (move) to the music. Even when the two-hour performance ended,

he **7.** _____ (not / hurry) to the exit. He remained in his seat, looking

thoughtful. But the most surprising thing **8.** _____ (happen) later. At home,

he went to the piano, but he **9.** _____ (not / play) his usual *Twinkle, Twinkle,

Little Star!* Instead, he **10.** _____ (start) playing, note for note, one of

Chopin's *Nocturnes*. Child prodigy? I think so!

Grammar Focus 2 Simple past: Irregular verbs

Examples	Language notes
	Many verbs are **irregular** in the simple past. These verbs do not have an -ed ending. They change in other ways.
(1) I **got** my love of music from my dad.	get → **got**
The girl **became** a doctor at 18.	become → **became**
He **knew** four languages.	know → **knew**
(2) She **didn't hear** him playing *Twinkle, Twinkle, Little Star.* **Incorrect:** She **didn't ~~heard~~** him playing *Twinkle, Twinkle, Little Star.*	For **negative** statements in the simple past, use: subject + *didn't* + **base verb**
(3) **Did** you **get** an A on the exam? **Did** he **know** all of the answers?	For *yes / no* **questions** with irregular verbs in the simple past, use: *Did* + subject + **base verb**

Affirmative statements	Negative statements
I He } **forgot.** We	I He } **didn't forget.** We
Yes / No questions	Short answers
Did { he / you } **take** violin lessons?	Yes, { he / we } **did.** No, { he / we } **didn't.**

See Appendices I and J on page A-5 for more statements and questions with irregular verbs and for a list of common irregular simple past verbs.

Grammar Practice

 A Read the conversation. Circle the irregular simple past verbs.

MyEnglishLab
Grammar Plus 2
Activities 1 and 2

DAD: Your book is so interesting! My wife and I (gave) our three kids everything: piano lessons, tennis classes, extra help after school. My wife and I always said, "Encourage them, but don't force them." They spoke, and we listened. But they didn't develop any great talents. Did we do something wrong?

AUTHOR: No! You taught them some important lessons. And you tried. That's what's important.

MOM: Thank you for sharing your amazing story! My daughter worked hard, saved money, bought her own guitar, took lessons, and began to play. Now, at 13, she's a great musician. I always told her, "Do the things you like!" That really helped her develop her skills.

AUTHOR: That's great. She sounds like a super hard worker— but not a prodigy. And that's fine!

B Complete the chart with the circled verbs from Part A. Then write the base forms.

Simple past form	Base form
1. *gave*	*give*
2.	
3.	
4.	
5.	
6.	
7.	
8.	
9.	
10.	

C Complete the paragraph. Use the simple past form of the verbs.

Maria Gaetana Agnesi was an 18th century Italian linguist, an expert on languages. According to sources, she **1.** _____ (write) the first book about calculus. From the beginning, people **2.** _____ (see) how smart she was. For example, by the age of five, she already **3.** _____ (know) French and Italian. When she was nine years old, she **4.** _____ (give) an hour-long speech in Latin. By the age of 15, she **5.** _____ (speak) Greek, Hebrew, Spanish, German, and maybe a few more languages. Historians say she also **6.** _____ (teach) her younger brothers.

D Answer the questions about Maria Gaetana Agnesi with short answers. Add explanations to negative answers.

1. Q: Did Maria Gaetana Agnesi write a book about cooking?

   A: *No, she didn't. She wrote a book about calculus.* _____

2. Q: Did she speak French and Italian by the age of four?

   A: _____

3. Q: Did she give a speech in French?

   A: _____

4. Q: Did she speak German by the age of 14?

   A: _____

5. Q: Did she teach her older brothers?

   A: _____

Grammar Focus 3 Simple past: *Wh-* questions

Examples	Language notes
(1) **Who did** she **write** for? **What did** she **sing**? **When did** she **perform**? **Where did** Chopin **get** his talent? **Why did** Mozart **start** composing at the age of four? **How long did** she **practice**?	To form *wh-* **questions** in the **simple past**, use: *Wh-* **word** + *did* + subject + **base verb**
(2) **Who composed** the music for *Don Giovanni*? (Mozart.) *Incorrect:* Who ~~did compose~~ the music for *Don Giovanni*?	If the *wh-* word is the **subject** of the question, use the **third person singular** (simple past) form of the verb.
(3) **Q:** What made her the ideal player? **A:** Her strength.	It's common to give **short answers** to *wh-* questions.
(4) **Q:** What did you do last weekend? **A:** We went to a party. **Q:** Why did you call her? **A:** I called her because I wanted to talk to her. / Because I wanted to talk to her.	Sometimes *wh-* questions require **detailed answers**. ***Note:*** In speech and informal writing, we often begin answers to *Why . . . ?* questions with ***Because . . .*** We don't repeat the main verb from the question.

Wh- questions		Short answers	Long answers
Who What When Where Why How How long	did { I **tell**? you **say**? he **quit**? she **go**? we **come** in? they **do**? it **take**?	Everyone. Many things. Last year. Down the hall. Because it's cold. Well. Forty minutes.	You **told** everyone. I **said** many things. He **quit** last year. She **went** down the hall. We **came** in because it's cold. They **did** well. It **took** 40 minutes.

See Appendix K on page A-5 for more wh- *questions in the simple past.*

Grammar Practice

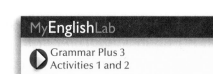

MyEnglishLab
▶ Grammar Plus 3
Activities 1 and 2

A Read the answers. Then complete the questions. Use the *wh-* words from the box. There's one extra word.

How long	What	When	Where	Who	Why

1. Q: _____ did Phiona Mutesi learn to play chess?

  A: Phiona Mutesi learned to play chess at the age of nine.

2. Q: _____ did Mutesi represent her country?

  A: She represented her country, Uganda, in the World Chess Olympiad in Russia.

3. Q: _____ made her a successful player?

A: Her instincts and talent made her a successful player.

4. Q: _____ did her fourth match last?

A: It lasted for more than three hours.

5. Q: _____ said that Mutesi was an excellent example for Ugandan children?

A: Her coach said Mutesi was an excellent example for Ugandan children.

B Complete the article. Use the words and the simple past form of the verbs.

 **ON SET**

Peter is a successful Los Angeles-based set designer. He began his work when he was just a child. Today, thousands of sets later, he's still very busy.

He took time from his busy schedule to talk about his influences and how he got his start.

INTERVIEWER: 1. _____ (When / you / create) your first piece of art?

PETER: I always loved playing with colors and creating as a kid. I have a stained glass window that I made in second grade. My parents still have it!

INTERVIEWER: 2. _____ (Who / influence) you the most?

PETER: My parents. They both have art backgrounds and were big influences on my work. They introduced me to art from the beginning of my life.

INTERVIEWER: 3. _____ (Why / you / start) your own design company?

PETER: Because I love design! I studied art in college and was always interested in it.

INTERVIEWER: 4. _____ (Where / you) study art?

PETER: At Cooper Union, in New York City. Then I worked as a carpenter to support myself.

INTERVIEWER: 5. _____ (How long / you / work) as a carpenter?

PETER: For about seven years. My set design company developed because it was a way for me to do what I liked—and support myself.

Listening

A BEFORE LISTENING Look at the picture in Part B. What sport is the woman dressed for? What do you know about this sport?

B 🎧 UNDERSTANDING MAIN IDEAS Look at the picture. Listen to the Q and A (question and answer). What does hockey player Jessica Mills talk about? Check (✓) the topics.

☐ sports   ☐ time management

☐ parents   ☐ study habits

☐ food   ☐ practice

☐ influences   ☐ goals

GUEST SPEAKER
JESSICA MILLS
Student Athlete

C 🎧 UNDERSTANDING DETAILS Listen again. Answer the questions. Write short answers.

1. Why did Jessica start playing hockey? _____

2. Did she like all sports? _____

3. Why did she like hockey the best? _____

4. Who influenced her? _____

5. When did she practice? _____

6. What three words are important to her? _____

Speaking

A Interview three classmates. Take notes.

	Name:	Name:	Name:
Did you play sports in school? If yes: What sports did you play? Where did you practice? How long did you practice?			
What did you study in school?			
Where and when did you study?			
Did you enjoy your studies? Why or why not?			

B Share your information with the class. Look at the model.

> In school, Alejandro played beach volleyball in Rio de Janeiro. He practiced every day after school and on weekends. . . .

Writing

MyEnglishLab

▶ Linking Grammar to Writing

A Think about an achievement or special experience from your childhood—for example, a musical performance, a trophy, or a good test result. Use the questions to help you. Write two more. Take notes.

- What happened?
- Why was it special?
- How did you feel?

- How old were you?
- _____
- _____

B Read about Reuben's experience. Then write a paragraph about your experience. Use your notes from Part A. Try to use the grammar from the chapter.

> When I was six years old, I had my first violin performance. I felt so nervous. I didn't like the violin. My mother made me study. She made me practice every day. But I didn't play very well, and I didn't want to play in front of people. I felt so uncomfortable. I wore a jacket and tie. I sweated a lot. But I played. When I finished, I looked at my mom. She had tears in her eyes. I realized that the performance was so important to her.

C Exchange paragraphs with a partner. Read your partner's paragraph. Write at least four *wh-* questions for your partner to answer.

> Why didn't you like the violin?
> What songs did you play?
> How long did your performance last?
> Did you have more lessons after that day?

MyEnglishLab

▶ Diagnostic Test

CHAPTER 4 Late Bloomers

Getting Started

A Do you know the expression *late bloomers*? They're people who realize their talents later in life. Read one late bloomer's timeline.

John and Carolyn McWilliams had a daughter on August 15, 1912, in Pasadena, California. Her name was Julia McWilliams.

She graduated from Smith College and worked for the United States OSS (Office of Strategic Services).

She was working in Sri Lanka when she met Paul Cushing Child.

They married in 1946, and Julia changed her name to Julia Child.

In 1948, they moved to Paris. Her husband was working for the U.S. embassy there.

While Julia Child was attending classes at Le Cordon Bleu, a world-famous cooking school, she met Simone Beck and Louisette Bertholle.

They started a cooking school, *L'Ecole de Trois Gourmandes* (The School of the Three Gourmands), in 1952.

In 1961, Julia Child published her first book, *Mastering the Art of French Cooking*.

In 1962, she starred in one of the first cooking shows, *The French Chef*.

She died in 2004. She introduced French cooking to the United States.

B What were two of Julia Child's achievements? How old was she? Complete the sentences.

1. She _____ when she was _____ years old.
2. She _____ when she was _____ years old.

C Look back at the timeline in Part A. Complete the tasks.

1. Underline the examples of the **past progressive**: *was / were* + base verb + *-ing* (*was working*).
2. Circle the examples of the simple past including the **simple past of** *be* (*was / were*).
3. Find and draw a rectangle around *when* and *while*.
4. Match the answers to the questions.

_____ 1. Which verb form shows continuous action in the past?   **a.** Simple past

_____ 2. Which verb form shows the completion of an action in the past?   **b.** *When / While*

_____ 3. Which words signal two or more actions in the same sentence?   **c.** Past progressive

Reading

A WARM-UP Do you know people who made big changes in their lives? What did they do before the change? What was the change? Discuss with a partner.

B PREDICTING Look at the headings in **bold** and the pictures. Check (✓) the ideas that you think will be in this article. Then go back and read the article to check your predictions.

☐ How to change the direction of your life ☐ Examples of people who changed paths later in life

☐ How to raise plants in the fall ☐ Tips for living longer

Who Says Achievement Has an Age Limit?

In an article that appeared several years ago in the *New Yorker* magazine, well-known author and speaker Malcolm Gladwell was asking readers to consider an important question: *why do we equate genius with precocity?* In other words, why do we believe talent must first show at a young age? He was raising an important point. Does creativity require youth? The truth is—and this is good news for many of us—it doesn't. He reminded us to look at people who did great things later in life; they are the so-called *late bloomers*.

What's a late bloomer?

The term *late bloomer* is actually a horticultural (farming) term used for plants that bloom late in their life. Here we are using it to describe a person whose talents become apparent *later*. Many of these people were doing one job and then changed to another job (sometimes a very different one) at some point in their adult lives.

Who are some late bloomers?

 For many years of his adulthood, French-born Eugène Henri Paul Gauguin (1848–1903) was working in banking and buying works of art. Painting was his hobby. At 35, he left his job in finance, started to paint, and became one of the most important painters of his time.

 While African-American Bessie Coleman (1892–1926) was painting fingernails as a manicurist, she was reading about airplanes and watching newsreels about flight. Then she met a man who encouraged her to get her pilot's license. At 29, she started her life as a pilot.

 Japanese author, dancer, and choreographer Kazuo Ohno (1906–2010) was teaching physical education when he started his formal dance lessons. He was 43 years old when he gave his first performance.

Gauguin, Coleman, and Ohno weren't average people. They were special. But they can teach all of us an important lesson: it's never too late to follow dreams. In fact, achievements have no age limit.

C UNDERSTANDING DETAILS Match the sentence halves.

A	B
_____ 1. *Precocity* refers to	a. a physical education teacher.
_____ 2. *Horticultural* refers to	b. a banker.
_____ 3. A *late bloomer* is	c. the growing of plants.
_____ 4. Before she became a pilot, Bessie Coleman was	d. unusually early development.
_____ 5. Before becoming a painter, Paul Gauguin was	e. someone who succeeds later in life.
_____ 6. Before he studied dance, Kazuo Ohno was	f. a manicurist.

MyEnglishLab

Reading Comprehension

Grammar Focus 1 Simple past: *Be*

Examples	Language notes
(1) He **was** 43 years old. They **were** late bloomers.	The **simple past of *be*** is *was* and *were*. Use *was* with *I, he, she,* and *it*. Use *were* with *we, you,* and *they*.
(2) She **was not** young when her career began. They **were not** different from other people.	The negative of *was* is **was not**, and the negative of *were* is **were not**.
(3) He **wasn't** a happy banker. They **weren't** young when they changed careers.	We often use the contracted forms **wasn't** and **weren't**, especially in speech and informal writing.
(4) **He was** a good writer at 70. → **Was he** a good writer at 70? **They were** talented people. → **Were they** talented people?	To form **yes / no questions** in the simple past with *be*, switch the position of *was / were* and the subject.
(5) **Who was** Paul Gauguin? **Where were** you?	To form **wh- questions** with *be* in the simple past, use: **Wh- word + *was / were* + subject**
(6) **Q:** Was she talented? **A: Yes, she was. / No, she wasn't.** **Q:** Were they child prodigies? **A: Yes, they were. / No, they weren't.**	For **short answers** to yes / no questions, use the simple past of *be*.

Simple past affirmative of *be*	Simple past negative of *be*
He **was** a late bloomer. They **were** successful later in life.	He **wasn't** a child prodigy. They **weren't** gifted children.
Yes / No questions	Short answers
Were you a child prodigy? **Was** he a great painter? **Were** their test scores high?	Yes, I **was**. / No, I **wasn't**. Yes, he **was**. / No, he **wasn't**. Yes, they **were**. / No, they **weren't**.
Wh- questions with *be*	Short answers
Who was Kazuo Ohno? **What was** her job? **When was** the performance? **Where were** they? **Why were** they late? **How long was** she a manicurist?	A choreographer. Waiting tables. Last night. At home. Because they had car trouble. For a few years.

See Appendix L on page A-6 for more statements and questions with the simple past of be.

Grammar Practice

MyEnglishLab

▶ Grammar Plus 1
Activities 1 and 2

A Complete the paragraph. Use *was, were, wasn't,* or *weren't*.

Angel **1.** _wasn't_ a successful young man. In fact, at 35, he **2.** _____
a father of three and had money problems. He **3.** _____ frustrated. He
4. _____ a waiter in a small restaurant in a town outside of Limon, Costa Rica. He
was able to save a little money, but Angel **5.** _____ happy. He **6.** _____
interested in healthy and natural food. Angel dreamed about leaving his small town and starting a
health food business.

At first, his brothers and sisters **7.** _____ supportive of his idea. Later, they helped him. He brought his family to Limon and started his business. His children and wife **8.** _____ happy to live in their new home.

Today Angel is 50, has many health food stores, and is a very successful businessman. He says, "This **9.** _____ once my dream. Now it is my reality."

B Unscramble the words to make *yes / no* and *wh-* questions with *be.* Then write short answers. (Find the answers in Part B on page 33.) More than one correct answer may be possible.

1. man / Paul Gauguin / French / a / was / ?

Q: _____   A: _____

2. happy / was / he / at the bank / ?

Q: _____   A: _____

3. art buyer / was / an / he also / ?

Q: _____   A: _____

4. his hobby / what / was / ?

Q: _____   A: _____

5. well-known / was / he / for his hobby / ?

Q: _____   A: _____

6. alive / he / was / in the 20th century / ?

Q: _____   A: _____

7. he / in 1898 / was / how old / ?

Q: _____   A: _____

8. late / he / why / bloomer / a / was / ?

Q: _____   A: _____

Grammar Focus 2 Past progressive

Examples	Language notes
(1) Past — XXX —— Present ——→ Future In the early 1900s, Bessie Coleman **was working** as a manicurist.	We use the **past progressive** to describe an **ongoing action** in progress at a specific time in the past.
(2) Early in his career, Paul Gauguin **was working** in a bank. He **wasn't painting** seriously.	To form the past progressive, use: subject + *was / were (not)* + **base verb** + *-ing* *Note:* See Chapter 1, Grammar Focus 2, for rules about spelling.
(3) He **was** a gym teacher **when** he **started** to dance professionally. She **was working** as a manicurist **when** she **became** interested in flying.	We often use *when* to introduce a clause in the simple past. The main clause can be in either the simple past or present progressive, depending on the order of events.
(4) **While** she **was living** in France, she **met** her cookbook co-authors. **While** he **was working** as a banker, he **was painting** as a hobby.	We often use *while* to introduce a clause in the **past progressive**. The main clause can be in either the simple past or present progressive, depending on the order of events.
(5) He **was** a banker. *Incorrect:* He ~~was being~~ a banker. She **heard** about flying planes. *Incorrect:* She ~~was hearing~~ about flying planes.	**Non-action verbs** are not usually used in the progressive. *Note:* See Chapter 2, Grammar Focus 2, for examples of non-action verbs.
(6) **Was** she **working** in 2011? **Were** they **studying** painting when they met?	To form *yes / no* questions in the past progressive, use: *Was / Were* + subject + **base verb** + *-ing*
(7) **Q:** Was he teaching while he was writing his book? **A:** Yes, he was. / No, he wasn't.	For **short answers**, use the simple past of *be*.
(8) **Why was** she **sleeping** while the music was playing?	To form *wh-* questions in the past progressive, use: *Wh-* word + *was / were* + subject + **base verb** + *-ing*
(9) **Q:** What was she doing in France? **A:** Cooking.	It's common to give **short answers** to *wh-* questions.

Affirmative statements	Negative statements
I **was learning** how to paint. We **were living** in Venice.	I **wasn't learning** how to sew. We **weren't living** in Paris.
Yes / No questions	*Short / Long answers*
Was she **studying** in 2009? **Were** you **working** when you learned to dance?	Yes, she **was**. / She **was studying** in 2009. No, I **wasn't**. / I **wasn't working** then.
Wh- questions	*Short / Long answers*
Why was she **taking dance**? **What were** you **studying**?	Because she enjoyed it. / She **was taking** dance because she enjoyed it. Marketing. / I **was studying** marketing.

See Appendix D on page A-2 for spelling rules for -ing endings. See Appendix M on page A-6 for more statements and questions in the past progressive.

Grammar Practice

A Complete the story. Use the simple past or past progressive. More than one correct answer may be possible.

Sabine Hueck was born and raised in São Paulo, Brazil. Sabine always **1.** _____ (love) food. But she never **2.** _____ (imagine) her future when she was younger.

While Sabine **3.** _____ (live) in Brazil, she **4.** _____ (help) in her grandmother's pastry shop. Later she **5.** _____ (move) to Peru and **6.** _____ (become) a schoolteacher. While she **7.** _____ (teach) during the week, she **8.** _____ (investigate) Peru's food culture on weekends.

A few years later, she **9.** _____ (decide) to move to Berlin. While she **10.** _____ (live) there, she **11.** _____ (work) in gastronomy, the study of food and culture. She **12.** _____ (travel) to other countries and **13.** _____ (take) many classes. While she **14.** _____ (study) gastronomy, she **15.** _____ (start) to develop her own style. Today she lives with her family in Berlin, Germany, and is a very famous chef, cooking teacher, and cookbook author!

B Read the answers. Then write *wh-* questions about the information in **bold**. Use the past progressive and information from Part A.

1. Q: *Where was Sabine living* _____? **A:** Sabine was living **in Brazil**.

2. Q: _____? **A:** She was helping **in a pastry shop**.

3. Q: _____ in Peru? **A:** She was **teaching**.

4. Q: _____? **A:** **On weekends**.

5. Q: _____ when **A:** **In Berlin**.
she started to develop her style?

C Read the blog post. There are six mistakes. Find and correct the mistakes.

Today was a wonderful day! I walked down the street when I suddenly was running into my friend Akira. While we drink coffee, he tell me about his painting class. Suddenly he was giving me an idea: to take an art class! I wanting a change in my life, and art is the answer.

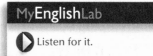
Speaking

A Do you know a late bloomer? Read the questions. Take notes. Then tell a partner about the person.

Questions	Notes
Who is / was the person?	
Where does / did the person live?	
What does / did the person do?	
What is an interesting event in this person's life?	
Was he / she successful? How?	
How did you learn about his / her achievements?	

B Tell your classmates what you learned from your partner. Look at the model.

> *Karima told me about her grandfather. He lived in Beirut, Lebanon, and owned a restaurant. When Karima's grandmother died, her grandfather was really sad. So he decided to learn how to paint. He was painting one afternoon when . . .*

Listening

A BEFORE LISTENING Do you know any artists? What kind of artwork do they do? What does a graphic designer do?

B 🎧 UNDERSTANDING MAIN IDEAS Listen to the interview. What does Antonio the graphic designer talk about? Check (✓) the topics.

People:

☐ artists   ☐ musicians   ☐ students

Experiences:

☐ owning a business   ☐ visiting museums   ☐ retiring

Things:

☐ graphic design   ☐ dreams   ☐ the Internet

C 🎧 UNDERSTANDING DETAILS Listen again. Answer the questions.

1. What was Antonio doing when he realized he wasn't a great artist?

_____

2. Were his classmates working?

_____

3. While he was working in his studio, who did he meet?

_____

4. What did he do when the computer arrived?

_____

5. Was he happy with his work?

_____

Writing

MyEnglishLab
▶ Linking Grammar to Writing

A Imagine that you suddenly have a talent. What talent is it?

B Now jump forward in time: Imagine it's 2020. Write an interview about your talent, looking back in time. Use the questions to help you. Try to use the grammar from the chapter.

• How did you discover this talent?
• Did you always like it?
• How did your life change?
• Did you move? Where?
• Did you quit your job?
• How did people react to your "new life"?

> **Q:** What was your talent?
>
> **A:** Music.
>
> **Q:** What were you doing when you realized your talent?
>
> **A:** I was working as a teacher.
>
> **Q:** How did you discover this talent?
>
> **A:** I was waiting in class for my students one day when I heard some beautiful guitar music. While I was listening, I became inspired! I always wanted to take guitar lessons, but I was working a lot, so I didn't have time. When I heard that beautiful guitar, I decided in that moment to take classical guitar classes. I started class and practiced all the time.
>
> **Q:** How did your life change?
>
> **A:** After I played in a concert one day, a man from the audience told me he wanted to record my music. That created a major change! I became very successful. I became a great musician at age 55! In fact, I have a new home on the beach, not far from Acapulco, Mexico . . .

C Share your interview with a partner. Ask and answer questions.

MyEnglishLab
▶ Diagnostic Test

Grammar Summary

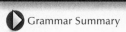

We form **regular simple past** verbs by adding *-d* or *-ed* to the verb. Some words have changes in spelling (*plan – planned / try – tried*). **Irregular simple past verbs** change in different ways. **Negative statements** use *did not / didn't* before the base verb. **Time signals** help explain when something happened.

Affirmative statements	Negative statements
I **talked** to many people **yesterday**. The teacher **said** nothing. We **worked** hard **last week**.	I **did not speak** with the artist. She **didn't say** many things. We **didn't miss** any classes **in February**.

To form **yes / no questions in the simple past**, use *Did* + subject + base verb. To form **wh- questions**, use a *wh-* word *(what, who, where, when, how,* or *why)* + *did* + subject + the base verb.

Yes / No questions	Short answers	Wh- questions	Short answers
Did he **study** music? **Did** we **practice** every day? **Did** they **do** the assignment?	Yes, he did. No, we didn't. Yes, they did.	**What did** she **do** today? **Where did** you **meet**? **When did** they **see** her?	Studied. In the library. Last night.

The verb **be in the simple past** has two forms: *was* and *were*. Use *was* with *I / he / she / it*, and *were* with *you / we / they*. To form negative statements, use the subject + *wasn't / weren't*.

Affirmative statements	Negative statements
I **was** the best student. You **were** my favorite student.	I **wasn't** a good athlete. You **weren't** my favorite student at first.

To form **yes / no questions with *be* in the simple past**, begin the sentence with *Was / Were* + subject. To form **wh- questions**, use *wh-* word + *was / were* + subject.

Yes / No questions	Short answers	Wh- questions	Short answers
Was he a late bloomer? **Was** she good at math? **Were** you talented musicians? **Were** they famous children?	Yes, he was. No, she wasn't. Yes, we were. No, they weren't.	**Who** was there? **What** was his talent? **Where** were the art students? **How old** was the painting?	Nobody. Karate. On the bus. Fifty years old.

Use the **past progressive** (*was / were* + base verb + *-ing*) to talk about an ongoing action in the past.

Questions	Answers
Was she **studying** last night at 6:00 P.M.? **What were** they **doing** last year?	No, she wasn't. She **was walking** home. They **were living** in France.

Use the **past progressive with the simple past** to talk about the order of events. Use **when** to introduce clauses in the simple past; use **while** to introduce clauses in the present progressive. The main clause can be in either the simple past or present progressive, depending on the order of events.

When	While
When the phone **rang**, I **jumped up** and answered it. **When** the new student **arrived**, the others **were taking** the test.	**While** I **was sleeping**, Tamiko **called**. **While** she **was teaching**, she **was writing** her novel.

Self-Assessment

A (7 points) Complete the sentences using the verbs from the box. Use the simple past.

decide	develop	happen	know	meet	teach	watch

1. She _____ him cross the street, but she didn't follow him.

2. _____ you _____ that woman? She looked familiar.

3. At the age of nine, she _____ to become a doctor.

4. Yesterday he _____ a very smart man.

5. What _____ to that man? He looked so surprised!

6. She wasn't a child prodigy; she _____ her skills later in life.

7. He _____ many subjects in the school.

B (6 points) Match the answers to the questions.

Questions	Answers
_____ 1. Was she a gifted child?	**a.** No, they weren't.
_____ 2. Did she become a famous writer at 50?	**b.** Medicine.
_____ 3. When did he learn to cook?	**c.** Yes, they did.
_____ 4. What was he studying his first year of college?	**d.** In 2010.
_____ 5. Were they successful?	**e.** Yes, she was.
_____ 6. Did they practice every day?	**f.** Yes, she did.

C (6 points) Find and correct six mistakes.

I was worked at the museum when I was meeting my husband Sami. We was coworkers. One day all the employees were talking about a concert. Sami asked me, "Did you went to the concert last night?" "No," I say. "I stayed home and studied English." Sami smiles. "Me, too," he said. "Do you need a study partner?" I said yes. And we are still partners today!

D (6 points) Unscramble the words to make sentences.

1. they / playing at a festival / they / were / when / met the other musicians / .

_____

2. her future husband / first saw / was Lira / where / living / when / she / ?

_____

3. she / while / Italian / she / learning / was / living / was / in Italy / .

_____

4. we / arrived / he / practicing / when / the drums / was / .

_____

5. called / were / doing / what / you / he / when / ?

_____

6. discovered / the cure / she / was / in a laboratory / working / when / she / .

_____

Unit Project: Timeline

A Research a prodigy or a late bloomer—someone who achieved something at an early or a late age. Follow the steps.

1. Choose someone in your family or someone you can research.
2. Take notes about the kinds of information in the list.

- Date of birth (and death, if applicable)
- Place of birth
- Hobbies
- Career
- Education

- Interesting facts about the person
- What was the person's achievement?
- How old was the person?
- Why did you choose this person?
- Where did you find the information?

3. Create a timeline for the person's life. Include the information in the list. Option: Include photos.

Juanita: A late bloomer

1950	
1955	**195?** Born in the Dominican Republic
1960	
1965	
1970	
1975	**1975** Married Ramon Calderon Vega
1980	
1985	**1976–1996** Raising children
1990	
1995	
2000	**1998** Hurricane George: Helped people in the community
2005	
2010	**2000–present** Raising grandchildren
2015	

Operating small restaurant **1990–2010**

Sold restaurant **2011**

B Present your prodigy or late bloomer to the class. Show the class your timeline. Tell about what you learned. Look at the model.

> *I chose my mother's friend, Juanita. She is probably the best cook in all of the Dominican Republic, and a wonderful woman. She was born in Sábana de la Mar, but she didn't tell me the year. When I was young, Juanita was always telling me the importance of eating healthy and fresh food . . .*

MyEnglishLab
▶ Unit Test

MyEnglishLab
▶ Search it!

Health and Fitness

MyEnglishLab

 What do you know?

CHAPTER 5 — Keeping Fit

Getting Started

A Work with a partner. What are some ways to stay fit and healthy? Brainstorm as many ideas as you can. Then compare ideas with another pair. How many of these things do you do?

B Look at the pictures. What do you think the fitness instructors are saying? Match the sentences to the pictures.

_____ 1.

_____ 2.

_____ 3.

_____ 4.

a. Let's all breathe in deeply. Hold it. Now raise your arms slowly over your head.

b. Roll forward and kick your feet quickly. How about straightening your arms?

c. Lift and hold. Now bring it down carefully. Why not increase the weight next time?

d. OK, fantastic job. Why don't we stop for the day? Get off your bikes. Don't forget to drink lots of water.

C Look back at Part B. Complete the tasks.

1. **Adverbs of manner** modify verbs and are usually formed by adding -ly to adjectives (*easy – easily*). Circle the examples.
2. **Imperative sentences** are used for giving commands, among other things. For affirmative commands, use the base verb. For negative commands, use *Don't* + the base verb. Underline the examples.
3. **Suggestions** are like commands, but "softened" by added language. Write the suggestions.

   Let's all breathe in deeply. _____

   _____ _____

Reading

A WARM-UP Look at the pictures in Part B. What are the benefits of each type of exercise? Which exercises look fun? Easy? Difficult? Discuss with a partner.

B SKIMMING Skim the flier. Write the class names. Then go back and read the flier again.

1. _____ 2. _____ 3. _____ 4. _____ 5. _____

Check Out the Latest Classes from Let's Pump Gym

Do you like to dance? How about shaking things up with the **Island Dance** class? Have fun and burn calories at the same time in this popular fitness class for women only. Dance the mambo, salsa, meringue, rumba, and the cha-cha. The music is different in every class, but the fun never stops. You don't dance well? Don't worry about it! Just listen to the music and move your way to a healthier you!

Why not get into shape with our **All-in-One** class? This class provides a full-body workout to reach every muscle group. Forget difficult exercise moves. Just follow the group leader and sweat! We start out slowly, but we move fast in no time! A quick two minutes of aerobic exercise is combined with two minutes of weightlifting for a toned body. Don't wait! This class fills up quickly.

Feeling out of shape? Why don't you get moving with our **Kickboxing** class? As a sport, kickboxing combines Eastern-style martial-arts kicks with Western-style boxing punches. Kickboxing, with separate classes for men and women, is very popular these days. Call or stop by immediately for your first choice of classes.

Are you tired of the treadmill? Why not try our group **Spinning** class? Bicycling is a great way to get in shape. Our instructors are always there to motivate you to work hard, but you are in control. Pedal fast or slow—you choose. Sit comfortably as the lights are turned low and the music is turned up, and pedal your way to fitness!

Do you prefer to take things slowly? Are you looking for a relaxing option to our more difficult classes? Don't look any further! Take our **Let's Stretch** class. It's important to stretch correctly, and we teach you how to do stretches for your neck, back, shoulders, arms, and legs. Stretching is important for any warmup or cooldown, but it's also a complete workout in itself.

C UNDERSTANDING INFERENCE What class are they talking about? Write the class name.

1. _____ "I took this class because I didn't want anything very difficult. It helped my neck and shoulders feel better after sitting at my desk all day." – *Hal*

2. _____ "Because I wanted something that worked all my muscles, I really enjoyed this class. I was tired after every class, but in a good way." – *Junko*

3. _____ "Our instructor was great, and I liked the music a lot. But, to be honest, this class was kind of boring. I didn't like sitting the whole time." – *Raul*

4. _____ "I don't know much about martial arts, but I learned a lot. It was great to work both my upper and lower body, too." – *Laura*

5. _____ "I don't like exercising, but this was fun. The music got my body moving." – *Ina*

Grammar Focus 1 Imperatives

Examples	Language notes
(1) Press this button. [instruction] Turn left. [direction] Always warm up. [advice or rule] Have a drink. [offer] Please join us for dinner. [invitation] Sit down! [command] Look out! [warning]	We use **imperative** sentences for **instructions**, **directions**, **advice** or **rules**, **offers**, **invitations**, **commands**, and **warnings**.
(2) **Be** careful. **Listen** to the music.	To form an imperative sentence, use: **base verb** + other information
(3) (You) **Have** fun.	In an imperative sentence, the **subject** is singular or plural *you*, but we usually don't say it. It is understood.
(4) **Always** drink water during your workout. **Never** exercise without warming up.	We often add *always* and *never* to advice or rules.
(5) **Don't worry** about it.	For **negative** imperatives, use: **Don't** + **base verb**
(6) **Please** call now. Don't wait, **please**.	Add *please* to make an imperative more polite.

Affirmative imperatives	Negative imperatives
Keep going! Always **follow** the group leader. **Take** a seat, please.	**Don't stop**! **Don't look** any further. Please **don't do** that!

Grammar Practice

MyEnglishLab
Grammar Plus 1
Activities 1 and 2

A Match the pictures to the imperatives. Use each picture twice.

a. b. c.

_____ **1.** Don't be afraid. Try to relax.

_____ **2.** Get those knees higher. Don't let up!

_____ **3.** Let's pull in those stomachs, ladies. Don't hold your breath.

_____ **4.** Don't stop. Now start running!

_____ **5.** Remember to point your toes. Keep your backs straight.

_____ **6.** Take a deep breath. Put your face in the water.

B Complete the list of rules. Use the verbs from the box. Add *Don't* for negative commands.

be	keep	return	show	wear
bring	limit	run	turn	wipe off

Let's Pump Gym

1. _____ your membership card when entering.

2. _____ proper shoes at all times.

3. _____ all personal items in the lockers.

4. Please _____ cell phones to vibrate mode.

5. _____ late for any classes, please.

6. _____ machines after each use.

7. _____ your time on any machine to 30 minutes if others are waiting.

8. _____ glass containers into the pool area.

9. _____ free weights to the proper storage area after each use.

10. Please _____ in the pool area.

C Think of and write more rules for Let's Pump Gym. Write imperative sentences.

1. _____

2. _____

3. _____

4. _____

5. _____

Grammar Focus 2 Suggestions: *Why . . . ?, Let's . . . ,* and *How about . . . ?*

Examples	Language notes
(1) **Try** this. [command] **Why don't you** try this? [suggestion]	**Suggestions** are less direct and more polite than commands. We usually use **"softer"** expressions when we want to make a suggestion.
(2) **Why don't you try** our Kickboxing class? **Why not try** our All-In-One class?	For a suggestion **to someone,** use: *Why don't you* + **base verb** *Why not* + **base verb**
(3) **Let's breathe** in. **Let's not take** a break. **Why don't we stop** for the day?	For a suggestion **to someone *plus* the speaker,** use: *Let's* + **base verb** *Let's not* + **base verb** *Why don't we* + **base verb** *Note: Let's* means *Let us.*
(4) **How about shaking** things up with the Island Dance class? (= *How about you shake things up with the Island Dance class?*) **How about taking** a class together? (= *How about you and I take a class together?*)	For a suggestion **to someone *or* to someone plus the speaker,** use: *How about* + **gerund** (**base verb** + *-ing*)

(5) **Q:** Why don't we get ice cream?
    A: Great idea. / OK. [agreeing]
 	
    Q: Let's take the bus.
    A: I'd rather not. [refusing]
 	
    Q: How about walking in the mornings?
    A: That's an interesting suggestion. [neutral]
	We can **respond to suggestions** in a variety of ways.

Suggestions with *Why . . . ?*	Suggestions with *Let's . . .*
Why don't you **Why don't we** } **stay** home? **Why not**	**Let's** **Let's not** } **go out** for dinner.
	Suggestions with *How about . . . ?*
	How about going to the gym?

Grammar Practice

MyEnglishLab

Grammar Plus 2
Activities 1 and 2

 A Read the conversation. Underline the suggestions.

KEVIN: Let's do something active this weekend.

LACEY: Great idea! Why don't we go hiking?

KEVIN: Let's not do that. We did that last weekend. How about going for a bike ride?

LACEY: That sounds fun. Do you want to rent the bikes from Rent-A-Bike?

KEVIN: No, they're too expensive. Why don't we rent from Outdoor Rentals?

LACEY: OK. I'll call them. Hand me my cell phone, please.

KEVIN: Why don't you check their website first? Here, search their company name . . .

B Complete the conversations. Write the correct words.

1. **A:** I feel so out of shape.

   B: _____ (Why don't you / How about) take a dance class or something?

2. **A:** _____ (Let's / How about) going rollerblading?

   B: That's a great idea.

3. **A:** _____ (Why not / Let's not) go to the gym today. I'm too tired.

   B: No problem. So, what do you want to do?

4. **A:** The buses aren't running today. How do I get to class?

   B: _____ (How about / Why not) walk? It's not very far.

5. **A:** _____ (Why don't we / Why don't you) play tennis later?

   B: Thanks, but I need to do my homework. How about tomorrow?

6. **A:** I'm going to the beach. Do you want to join me?

   B: Sure. _____ (Why don't / Let's) go!

C Match the sentence parts.

A	B
_____ 1. I'm getting fat. How about	**a.** you take a yoga class?
_____ 2. It's beautiful today. Let's	**b.** go to bed early?
_____ 3. I'm really tired. Why don't we	**c.** going on a diet with me?
_____ 4. Our gym fees are due. Let's	**d.** not forget.
_____ 5. You sound stressed. Why don't	**e.** take a walk on the beach.

Grammar Focus 3 Adverbs of manner

Examples	Language notes
(1) **deep:** Breathe in **deeply.** **slow:** Move your arms **slowly.** **quick:** Come **quickly.** **speedy:** Change positions **speedily.** **comfortable:** Sit **comfortably.**	**Adverbs of manner** describe action verbs. They answer the question *How?* To form most adverbs of manner, use: **adjective + -ly** *Note:* For adjectives that end in *y*, change *y* to *i*. For adjectives that end in *e*, drop the *e*.
(2) Stretch **correctly.**	An adverb of manner **follows** the verb it describes.
(3) **Kick** your feet **quickly.** *Incorrect:* Kick ~~quickly your feet.~~	When there is a **direct object**, use: **verb** + direct object + **adverb of manner**
(4) We start out **slowly.** [formal] We start out **slow.** [informal]	Some adverbs have **two forms:** one with *-ly* and one **without -ly.** Examples include *slowly / slow, loudly / loud,* and *quickly / quick.* The form without *-ly* is common in informal speech.
(5) Our instructors are **hard** workers. [adjective] Our instructors work **hard.** [adverb] She signed up for the **late** class. [adjective] I got up **late** this morning. [adverb] The dance class has 20 students. There's **hardly** enough room to move. [adverb—*almost not*] I haven't been to the pool **lately.** It's been a busy summer. [adverb—*recently*]	Some adverbs and adjectives have the **same form.** Examples include *early, fast, hard,* and *late.* *Note:* The adverbs *hardly* and *lately* have different meanings from the adverbs *hard* and *late.*
(6) You're a **good** dancer. [adjective] You dance **well.** [adverb]	*Well* is the adverb form of the adjective *good.*
(7) I had a **lovely** time. [adjective] Everyone here is so **friendly.** [adjective]	Not all words that end in *-ly* are adverbs. Some are **adjectives** such as *friendly, ugly, lonely,* and *lovely.*

Informal / Formal	Same form as adjective
deep → deeply different → differently loud → loudly slow → slowly quick → quickly	early far fast hard late

Grammar Practice

MyEnglishLab

Grammar Plus 3
Activities 1 and 2

A Write the adverb forms of the adjectives. Some words have two adverb forms. Write both forms.

1. careful _____

2. quick _____

3. easy _____

4. fast _____

5. hard _____

6. late _____

7. slow _____

8. good _____

B Rewrite the sentences. Use adverbs.

1. You're a slow eater.   *You eat slowly.* _____

2. She's a beautiful dancer.   _____

3. We're fast learners.   _____

4. They're good teachers.   _____

5. I'm a hard worker.   _____

6. He's a careful driver.   _____

C Find and correct the mistake in each conversation.

1. **A:** You dance beautifully. Was it difficult to learn those steps?

   B: Not at all. You can learn them easy. Do you want me to show you quickly?

2. **A:** On the treadmill I start out slowly, but then I try to run fastly. Is that good?

   B: Yes, but it's also a good idea to run slowly at the end, or walk. It's called cooling down.

3. **A:** My friend is training for her first marathon. She's working very hardly.

   B: My brother just ran one successfully. He completed it easily.

4. **A:** My personal trainer motivates me and explains everything good. And she's so friendly.

   B: That's great. Can I get her number? I haven't felt motivated at all lately.

D Complete the instructor's advice. Use the adverb form of the words from the box.

careful	easy	fast	hard	regular	slow	smooth

Before we start our workout, I have a few important reminders. First, we know that
stretching is important, so make sure that you stretch your whole body. Hold each stretch
position for about 10 seconds. Don't rush and go **1.** _____. That's dangerous.
Instead, stretch **2.** _____ and **3.** _____. Your body will thank
you, and your workout will go **4.** _____. Now, during our workout, give
yourself plenty of room so you can move **5.** _____. And be sure to drink
water **6.** _____. Don't wait until the end of the workout. Finally, work
7. _____, but remember to have fun. Exercise needs to be enjoyable.

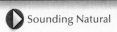
Speaking

A Work with a partner. Look at the pictures and read the descriptions. Each partner chooses three exercises to demonstrate. Study them for five minutes. Look at the model.

> *Let's divide them up randomly.*

> *OK. Why don't you take Leg Extension, Side Bend, and Cross Arm?*

B Now close your book. With your partner, take turns instructing how to do the exercises. Can you follow each other's instructions? Look at the model.

> *First, press your back firmly against your chair.*

> *Like this?*

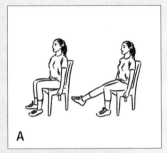

A

Leg Extension Press your lower back firmly against the back of the chair. Hold the edges of the seat lightly. Straighten your right leg slowly with your toes pointed out. Don't straighten your knee forcefully. Do 10 repetitions. Then repeat with your left leg.

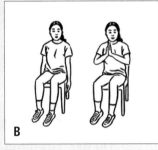

B

Hand Press Sit upright. Put your hands together in front of your chest and press them together firmly. Make sure you continue to breathe normally. Hold for 10 seconds. Then relax for 10 seconds. Do this 5 times.

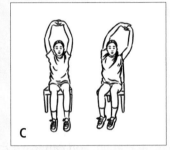

C

Side Bend Sit upright at the edge of your chair. Interlace your fingers with your palms facing away and raise arms overhead. Pull arms to the left. Don't bend your back. Hold for 5 seconds. Then pull arms to the right. Repeat.

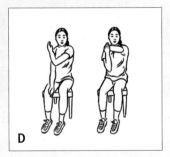

D

Cross Arm Sit upright. Bring your left arm across your upper body. Cup your left elbow in your right hand. Pull your right arm gently across your chest. Hold for 3 seconds. Don't lift your shoulders. Repeat with your right arm. Do 5 repetitions.

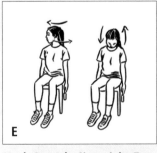

E

Neck Stretch Sit upright. Turn your head slowly to the right as far as you can comfortably. Hold for 3 seconds. Then turn your head slowly to the left as far as you can comfortably and repeat. Next, let your head fall gently to your chest. Do 5 repetitions.

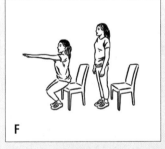

F

Chair Squat Push off carefully from sitting position until your hips are just over the chair. Keep your arms out for balance. Hold for 3 seconds and then stand up slowly. Sit back down and repeat 10 times.

Listening

A 🎧 UNDERSTANDING MAIN IDEAS Listen to the talk show interview with athletic trainer Rachel Lewis. Who do athletic trainers work with? Check (✓) the correct answers.

☐ teachers ☐ doctors ☐ sports teams ☐ the military

☐ university staff ☐ animals ☐ health club members ☐ police

☐ athletes ☐ patients ☐ dancers ☐ firefighters

B 🎧 UNDERSTANDING DETAILS Listen again. Answer the questions.

1. What's another term for *athletic trainer*? _____

2. What do athletic trainers do at high schools and universities? _____
_____

3. What does the trainer say about getting a job with a sports team? _____
_____

4. What is an athletic trainer's goal when working with a business or organization?
_____

5. What is the basic qualification to be an athletic trainer? _____

6. How much will this profession grow in the next 10 years? _____

C AFTER LISTENING Work with a partner. How would you describe the job of an athletic trainer? Does this kind of work interest you? Why or why not?

Writing

A Read the online post and response. What is your advice? Share ideas with a partner.

I hope someone can help me. My doctor says I'm out of shape and need to exercise more. The problem is I hate to exercise. I find it really boring. And I don't feel motivated to start. What can I do? Any ideas? –LAZY D

Lazy D - I know how you feel. I don't really like to exercise either. Why don't you do something with a friend? Here's an idea. How about going for walks in the morning? I do this with my roommate. We walk slowly at first, but later we increase our speed. Do this three or four times a week. It's important to do any exercise regularly.

B Write your own response. Try to use the grammar from the chapter.

C Work in a group. Share your writing. Did you give similar advice?

CHAPTER 6

Push it to the limit!

Getting Started

A Look at the pictures in Part B. How are they different? Describe them to a partner.

B Read what Carrie was like a year ago, and what she's like now. Then circle the correct answers.

One year ago, Carrie wasn't very healthy. She ate junk food every day. Her body was often stiff because she hardly ever exercised. She couldn't even touch her toes! She felt terrible, so she decided to start an exercise program. At first, she wasn't able to run for very long. But she worked hard and didn't give up.

Carrie is much healthier now. She never eats junk food, and she goes to the gym three or four times a week. She often runs on a treadmill. She can run for over an hour. Carrie's dream is to run a marathon. She thinks she'll be able to qualify for the Chicago Marathon next year. And, of course, now she's able to touch her toes!

1. Carrie's body was stiff because she _____.
    a. ate a lot of junk food
    b. hardly ever exercised

2. She felt terrible, so she decided to _____.
    a. see a doctor
    b. start an exercise program

3. These days she never _____.
    a. eats junk food
    b. goes to the gym

4. Carrie's dream is to _____.
    a. touch her toes
    b. run a marathon

C Look back at the readings in Part B. Complete the tasks.

  1. Adverbs and expressions of frequency tell how often something is done (*always, sometimes, never*, etc.). Circle the examples.

  2. We express **ability** with *can / could (not)* and *be (not) able to*. Underline the examples.

  3. What time period do the examples of ability you underlined refer to? Complete the chart.

Past ability	Present ability	Future ability
She couldn't even touch her toes.		

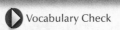

Reading

A WARM-UP Work with a partner. Read the following description. Which race would be the most difficult for you? What do you think the training is like? Why do you think people compete in competitions like this?

An Ironman competition is a series of three races. There's a 2.4-mile (3.8-km) swim, a 112-mile (180-km) bike ride, and a 26-mile (42-km) marathon, in that order and without a break. The most famous Ironman is in Kailua-Kona, Hawaii.

B SCANNING Scan the interview and add the questions from the box. Then go back and read the whole interview.

Do you ever break your routine?	How do you motivate yourself?
How did you get interested in all this?	How often do you train?

Ironman in Training

Local businessman Jake Mercer is training for his first Ironman competition. Lisa Rhodes of Sports Today asks him about it.

Lisa Rhodes: _____

Jake Mercer: I train four or five days a week. I train for a minimum of 20 hours and a maximum of 30 hours. That doesn't include weekends.

LR: Wow, so you always train at least 20 hours a week. That's amazing. Do you always swim, run, and bicycle on each training day?

JM: No, I hardly ever do that. I usually do a combination of two things, such as swim and run, or bike and swim.

LR: _____

JM: Sometimes I get worn out, and I take a day off.

LR: Is there anything you don't like about training?

JM: Well, I can't control the weather. Rain can be miserable. And I'm often worried about dogs and cars.

LR: _____

JM: A friend of mine was training for a marathon, and I started running with him. I couldn't run very fast at first, but I got better. We then started biking. I was able to keep up with him better on the bike.

LR: And what about swimming?

JM: It's funny, I wasn't able to swim well as a kid. I can swim pretty fast now, though. I swim with my wife.

LR: Oh, is she also training?

JM: No, but I hope she does. We'll be able to train together.

LR: _____

JM: Hip-hop music helps. I can't live without my mp3 player.

LR: Any advice for readers who are interested in training for an Ironman?

JM: Not everyone can do an Ironman. It takes a lot of discipline. It also takes a lot of time, and not everyone has that. But everyone can exercise and adopt a healthy lifestyle.

C UNDERSTANDING DETAILS Complete the sentences.

1. Jake trains _____ hours a week.
2. He hardly ever _____.
3. He sometimes _____.
4. He is often _____.
5. He couldn't _____ as a kid.
6. He can _____ now.
7. He hopes he and his wife _____.

Grammar Focus 1 Ability: Modals and expressions

Examples	Language notes
(1) I **can** swim. I **couldn't** finish the race. She**'s able to** touch her toes. We **weren't able to** train yesterday.	We can **express ability** with the **modal verbs** *can* and *could* (the past of *can*), and with **be able to.**
(2) She **can** dance. [more common] She**'s able to** dance. [less common]	**Present:** • For **present** ability, use *can* and **be able to.** *Can* is more common in everyday speech than *be able to.*
(3) She **could** swim well <u>as a child</u>. I **was able to** swim the butterfly <u>at four</u>. I **was able to** finish my first marathon. *Incorrect:* I ~~could~~ finish my first marathon.	**Past:** • For **past** ability, use *could* or *was / were able to.* A <u>time signal</u> is often used with past ability. • For **affirmative** sentences about past **one-time events**, use **be able to.** Don't use *could.*
(4) I **can** meet you after the race. Soon she**'ll be able to** run a mile in four minutes.	**Future:** • For **future ability** with plans, use *can.* • For **future achievement**, use **will be able to.**
(5) I **can** swim. She **can** swim. When Charlie was our boss, we **could leave** early.	For **affirmative** sentences with *can*, use: subject + *can* + **base verb** *Note:* *Can* and *could* never change form.
(6) They **cannot work** out today. I **could not hear** the instructor. I **am not able to go.** She **was not able to finish** the race.	For **negative** sentences, use: subject + *can / could* + *not* + **base verb** subject + *be* + *not* + *able to* + **base verb** *Note:* *Can* + *not* becomes one word.
(7) I **can't** swim. I **couldn't** go yesterday.	The contracted form of *cannot* is **can't.** The contracted form of *could not* is **couldn't.**
(8) **Can** he **swim?** **Could** you **run** fast as a child?	To form **yes / no questions** with *can*, use: *Can / Could* + subject + **base verb**
(9) **Are** you **able to work out** every day? **Were** they **able to finish** the marathon?	To form **yes / no questions** with **be able to**, use: *Be* + subject + *able to* + **base verb**
(10) **Why couldn't** he **swim** very far? **How far can** you **run?**	To form **wh- questions** with *can*, use: *Wh-* **word** + *can / could* + subject + **base verb** *Note:* Adverbs such as *far, long,* and *well* are often added to *wh-* questions about ability.
(11) **How far are** you **able to run?** **Why wasn't** he **able to swim** very far?	To form **wh- questions** with **be able to**, use: *Wh-* **word** + *be* + subject + *able to* + **base verb**

Questions	Answers
Can / Could you **swim** well? **Are / Were** you **able to swim** well? **Is / Was** he **able to swim** well? **What do** you **do** well? **How** well **could** you **swim** as a kid?	Yes, { I **can / could.** / I **am / was.** / he **is / was.** No, { I **can't / couldn't.** / I'm **not / wasn't.** / he **isn't / wasn't.** Dance. / I **can dance** well. Not very well. / I **couldn't swim** very well.

Grammar Practice

A Compete the paragraphs. Use *can*, *can't*, *could*, or *couldn't*.

One year ago, I was afraid of the water. I **1.** _____ swim at all. Then I decided to

take swimming lessons. I **2.** _____ take them near my house, so I drove 40 miles

(64 km) every weekend for lessons. It was worth it! Now I **3.** _____ swim really

well. I **4.** _____ do the backstroke and the butterfly stroke.

My friend and I saw some Olympic events in 2012. Unfortunately we **5.** _____

get any tickets for the gymnastics events. But we **6.** _____ get some tickets for

some other interesting events, such as fencing and tae kwon do. They were awesome! I hope we

7. _____ go again someday!

Stephanie loves the gym. She **8.** _____ go in the mornings because she starts

work at 6:00 A.M., so she goes after work. She especially loves lifting weights. At first she

9. _____ only lift about 40 pounds (18 kg). Now she **10.** _____ lift

45 pounds (20 kg) easily. It's helping her tone her muscles. She **11.** _____ really see

the difference.

B Complete the conversations. Use the correct form of *be able to* and the verbs.

1. A: I'm sorry you hurt your foot. _____ (play) soccer this weekend?

    B: I don't think so. It's really painful.

2. A: I heard Craig tried to climb Mount Kilimanjaro. _____ (do) it?

    B: No, _____ (not / finish) the climb. He got altitude sickness.

3. A: I don't understand the rules of cricket. _____ you _____

    (understand) them?

    B: Not really. But Ian _____ (explain) them at the match tomorrow.

4. A: I heard you went bungee jumping on your vacation.

    B: Actually, _____ (not / jump). I got scared. I'm embarrassed about it.

5. A: I have tickets to the game, but _____ (not / go). Do you want them?

    B: Sure. Thanks so much!

C Check (✓) the sentences that can be expressed in a different way. Then rewrite them.

☐ **1.** I'm not able to understand this math problem. _____

☐ **2.** They couldn't go to their son's soccer match. _____

☐ **3.** I'll be able to speak German fluently soon. _____

☐ **4.** He can hike up and down that mountain in a day. _____

☐ **5.** Could you go swimming alone as a child? _____

☐ **6.** She was able to win her first bike race last year. _____

Grammar Focus 2 Frequency: Adverbs and expressions

Examples	Language notes
(1) He **usually** goes jogging at night. He goes jogging **several times a month**. He's **occasionally** too busy to go.	**Adverbs** and **expressions of frequency** describe *how often* we do something.

(2) **100%**   always
             almost always
             usually
   50%   often / frequently
             sometimes / occasionally
             rarely / seldom
             hardly ever / almost never
   0%   never
	Adverbs of frequency range from **always** to **never**.

(3) • **every** _____ (day, Friday, week, weekend, month)
 	
   • _____ (once, several times) a _____ (day, week, year)
 	
   • **from time to time**
   • **once in a while**
	Expressions of frequency also include some **time signals**.

(4) I **am sometimes** late for class. I **never sleep** past 6:00 A.M. **Sometimes** we're too tired to work out.	For sentences with **adverbs of frequency**, use: subject + *be* + **adverb of frequency** subject + **adverb of frequency** + **verb** *Note:* We can also place *usually* and *sometimes* at the **beginning** of a sentence.
(5) They **were** at the gym **every morning**. We **exercise seven days a week**. **Every Friday** she **works out** on the treadmill. He **goes** hiking **once in a while**.	For sentences with **expressions of frequency**, use: subject + *be* + **expression of frequency** subject + **verb** + **expression of frequency** *Note:* We can also place expressions of frequency at the **beginning** or **end** of sentences.
(6) Are you **sometimes** late for class? Do you **ever** lift weights at the gym? Why am I **always** tired? Where do you **usually** work out?	We use affirmative adverbs of frequency (*always, often, usually, sometimes*) in **questions** more commonly than negative adverbs of frequency. Use: *Be* + subject + **adverb** *Do / Does* + subject + **adverb** + base verb *Wh-* word + *be* + subject + **adverb** *Wh-* word + *do / does* + subject + **adverb** + base verb *Note:* We use the adverb *ever* in *yes / no* questions; it means "at any time."

(7) **Q:** Is he **always** early?
    A: Yes, **always**. / No, **not usually**.
 	
Q: **How often** do you play soccer?
    A: We play **once a week**.
 	
Q: Do you **ever** stretch?
    A: Sure, **sometimes**. / **Once in a while**.
	For **short answers** to questions with **adverbs of frequency**, we can use adverbs of frequency.
	
	For short answers to questions that ask *How often . . . ?* use expressions of frequency.
	
	For short answers to questions with *ever*, use either adverbs or expressions of frequency.

Grammar Practice

A Read the answers. Then write questions with *Are you ever . . . ?*, *Do you ever . . . ?*, or *How often . . . ?*

1. Q: _____   **A:** I go jogging every weekend.
2. Q: _____   **A:** I play basketball twice a week.
3. Q: _____   **A:** No. I never lift weights.
4. Q: _____   **A:** Yes. I'm sometimes late for practice.
5. Q: _____   **A:** Yes. I often go to health food stores.

B Rewrite the sentences. Use the adverbs and expressions of frequency.

1. Kayla goes bowling on Mondays, Wednesdays, and Fridays.

    (three times a week) _____

2. David almost never exercises.

    (hardly ever) _____

3. Hank and Chloe run every Saturday at 8:00.

    (always) _____

4. Sun-hee and Jason occasionally play tennis together.

    (from time to time) _____

5. William is frequently at the gym on weekends.

    (often) _____

C Read the descriptions. Insert the words in the correct places.

                    always   **never**
1. Paul is a gym rat. He is at the gym. He eats junk food.
                every night   **hardly ever**
2. Tina is a sports nut. She watches sports on TV. She misses a game.
            twice a day   **several times a year**
3. Pam is a fitness freak. She swims laps. She competes in marathons.
            almost always   **seldom**
4. Larry is a couch potato. He is in front of the TV. He exercises.

D Unscramble the words to make questions. Then write short, true answers.

1. TV / watch / you / do / on / ever / golf / ?

    Q: _____   A: _____

2. you / sometimes / do / breakfast / skip / ?

    Q: _____   A: _____

3. does / in / class / how / teacher / often / your / sing / ?

    Q: _____   A: _____

4. play / often / you / how / do / basketball / ?

    Q: _____   A: _____

Speaking

A How healthy and fit are you? Interview a partner. Circle the answers. Take turns. Look at the model.

> How often do you exercise?

> Once or twice a week. What about you?

HOW HEALTHY ARE YOU?

1. How often do you exercise?
   a. Every day.
   b. Once or twice a week.
   c. Um, does surfing the Internet count?

2. How often do you eat regular meals?
   a. Almost always.
   b. I usually try to.
   c. I eat when I feel like it.

3. Describe your diet.
   a. Very healthy.
   b. I try to eat healthy food when I can.
   c. I can eat whatever I want, and I do.

4. Do you ever do flexibility training, such as stretching or yoga?
   a. Yes, I often do.
   b. I try to stretch when I can.
   c. The TV remote control is never far away.

5. Do you ever lift weights or do exercises such as leg lifts or push-ups?
   a. Sure. I do them a lot.
   b. Sometimes I do.
   c. No, hardly ever.

6. Do you ever participate in aerobic activities, such as running or biking?
   a. Absolutely. I love to get my blood flowing!
   b. I do from time to time.
   c. Rarely. I prefer to watch TV.

7. How often do you try a new sport or activity?
   a. Very often—maybe several times a year.
   b. Occasionally.
   c. Not that often.

8. How important is fitness to you?
   a. Very important. It's my health, after all.
   b. Somewhat important.
   c. Not that important. I'm still young!

9. Which of these activities do you do at least twice a month? Check (✓) them.
   ☐ go running   ☐ play tennis
   ☐ play soccer   ☐ play softball or baseball
   ☐ do aerobics   ☐ play table tennis
   ☐ go skating   ☐ lift weights
   ☐ go bowling   ☐ go bicycling
   ☐ go swimming   ☐ do martial arts
   ☐ play volleyball ☐ do yoga
   ☐ go dancing   ☐ take an exercise class

B Work in a group. Score your partner's answers and share the results with the group. Do you agree with the interpretation? Why or why not?

For questions 1–8, give: 2 points for each "a" answer 1 point for each "b" answer 0 points for each "c" answer **For question 9, give:** 1 point for each checked (✓) activity	TOTAL: 21–32 points: Fantastic! You're in great shape! 11–20 points: Very good. You have very good habits, but you can always improve them. 0–10 points: You can improve your fitness level. Why not start today?

Listening

A BEFORE LISTENING Work with a partner. Look at the pictures of extreme sports. What seems dangerous about each one? Do you want to try any of them? Why or why not?

B 🎧 UNDERSTANDING INFERENCE Listen to the webcast and look at the pictures of extreme sports. Number the pictures in the order you hear about them (*1* to *4*).

_____ **a.** cliff diving _____ **b.** ice climbing _____ **c.** kite surfing _____ **d.** sand boarding

C 🎧 UNDERSTANDING DETAILS Listen again. How often does each person do the sport? What are the dangers? Complete the information.

How often	Dangers
1. _____	_____
2. _____	_____
3. _____	_____
4. _____	_____

Writing

A Think about something you learned to do. Consider the questions.

- What did you learn to do?
- How well can you do it?
- Could you do this when you were young?
- How were you able to learn it?
- Was it difficult to learn? Why or why not?
- Will you be able to do it even better in the future?

B Write a paragraph about the thing you learned. Try to use the grammar from the chapter.

> I learned how to slackline last year. It's like tightrope walking and dancing. I couldn't keep my balance at first. But I can move pretty well now. I was able to learn . . .

C Share your paragraph with a partner. Ask questions about your partner's experience.

Grammar Summary

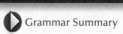

Use **imperatives** to give instructions, directions, advice or rules, offers, invitations, commands, and warnings. We can add *always* and *never* to affirmative advice and rules. Add *please* to be more polite.

Affirmative: Base verb	Negative: *Don't* + base verb
Try! Always **stretch**. Never **skip** the warm-up. Please **stay**.	**Don't go.** **Don't worry.** **Don't be** late, please.

There are several ways to make and respond to **suggestions**.

Why don't we / you + base verb	*Let's (not)* + base verb
A: Why don't we / you see a movie? **B:** OK.	**A:** Let's (not) go out. **B:** Great idea.
Why not + base verb	*How about* + gerund (base verb + *-ing*)
A: Why not order a pizza? **B:** That's an interesting suggestion.	**A:** How about watching TV? **B:** I'd rather not.

Adverbs of manner help describe actions. Many are formed by adding *-ly* to adjectives. Some adverbs have the same form as adjectives. Some have two forms, the one without *-ly* being more common in informal speech. The adverb form of *good* is *well*.

Adjective	Adverb	Verb + adverb	Verb + direct object + adverb
bad	bad**ly**	They <u>sang</u> **badly**.	They <u>sang</u> the song **badly**.
easy	easi**ly**	She <u>scored</u> **easily**.	She <u>scored</u> the goal **easily**.
fast	fast	We <u>finish</u> **fast**.	We <u>finish</u> tests **fast**.
slow	slow**ly** / slow	I <u>drove</u> **slowly**.	I <u>drove</u> my car **slowly**.

We express **ability** with *can* and *be able to*. Like all modals, *can* and *could* are followed by the base verb. They have the same form for all subjects. Use *was / were able to* (not *could*) to talk about past one-time events in the affirmative. Use *can* for future ability to describe plans. Use *will + be able to* to describe future achievements.

Past	I **could play** the piano at the age of 12. I **couldn't play** the piano at the age of five.	How **was** I **able to play** the piano at age 12? I **wasn't able to play** the piano at age five.
Present	**Can I run** a mile in six minutes? I **can't run** a mile in four minutes.	I'm **able to run** a mile in six minutes. I'm **not able to run** a mile in four minutes.
Future	Where **can** I **pick** up the tickets tomorrow? I **can't pick** up the tickets Friday.	**Will** I **be able to speak** French in one year? I **won't be able to speak** French in one week.

Adverbs and expressions of frequency describe how often we do something. Adverbs of frequency come after *be*, but before regular verbs. *Usually* and *sometimes* can also go at the beginning of a sentence. Time signals that express frequency can go at the beginning or end of a sentence, and after all verbs.

Adverbs of frequency		Examples	Frequency expressions
100% │ 50 │ 0%	always almost always usually often / frequently sometimes / occasionally rarely / seldom hardly ever / almost never never	I am **always** at work by 6:00. Do you **usually** work weekdays? Is he **often** late? **Sometimes** I work weekends. Why is she **never** here?	**Every day** I stretch. I play tennis **once a week**. I go swimming **from time to time**. I'm lazy **once in a while**.

Self-Assessment

A (4 points) Find and correct the mistake in each sentence.

1. Don't to forget to stretch before your workout.

2. Let's go not to the movies this weekend. I want to see a concert.

3. Why don't we playing basketball later?

4. How about take a short break?

B (10 points) Write the adverb form of the adjectives in the box. Then insert the adverbs into the sentences in **bold**.

careful: _____	fast: _____	hard: _____
easy: _____	good: _____	

1. **She plays the violin.** She has years and years of experience.

2. **She ran on the treadmill.** Now she's slowing down.

3. **They finished the race.** They had no problems.

4. **Please read the gym membership contract.** It's important.

5. I finally finished my essay. **I worked.**

C (5 points) Rewrite the sentences. Use the words from the box.

always   frequently   hardly ever   occasionally   twice a week

1. I often work out with my friend Marta.

   _____

2. Blake almost never takes vitamins.

   _____

3. Nora never jogs without her mp3 player.

   _____

4. Ronnie and I go bowling from time to time.

   _____

5. Tara does aerobics on Tuesday and Thursday.

   _____

D (6 points) Complete the voicemail message. Circle the correct words.

Hi Rox! It's Adam. Listen, Erik and I **1. can't / couldn't** come over now to help you pack up your stuff. Sorry. I **2. 'm not able to / couldn't** start my car this morning. And I **3. could / 'm not able to** take it to the garage now because it's closed. Also, Erik is at work. He tried, but he **4. couldn't / 'll be able to** get the day off. We **5. can / couldn't** come on Saturday, though. How early will we **6. be able to / could** start? I have to work at noon. Can you let us know, please?

Unit Project: Sports presentation

A Work with a partner. Research a sport you don't know much about. Follow the steps.

1. Choose a sport from the list or think of one on your own.

American football	floorball	hockey	netball	rugby
cricket	futsal	hurling	polo	shinty
curling	handball	lacrosse	rounders	water polo

2. Research your sport. Use the questions to help you.

- Where is the sport popular?
- How often can you see it on TV?
- Is this sport similar to any other sport?
- What is the history of the sport?
- How many players are there?
- Can anyone play the sport?

- What are some of the rules?
- How do you win?
- What are some expressions used by the fans?
- Do people ever play it in your home country?
- How is the sport changing?

3. Create a poster of your sport. Include pictures and any illustrations to make your poster more interesting.

B Present the information to the class. Answer any questions. Look at the model.

> Our sport is netball. It's very popular in Australia, New Zealand, England, and Singapore. You hardly ever see it on TV, but it is getting more popular. It's similar to basketball, but there are some differences. There are two teams of seven players. Men can play, but it's mostly played by women.

> You win by scoring goals. As in basketball, players pass the ball and try to make it into the other team's goal ring. But a player can take no more than one step before they pass the ball. Fans shout expressions such as, "Pass the ball!" and "Shoot!"

> It is not an Olympic sport right now, but many people are trying to change this. Someday, I think we will be able to watch netball at the Olympics.

MyEnglishLab
▶ Unit Test

MyEnglishLab
▶ Search it!

The World of Travel

OUTCOMES

After completing this unit, I will be able to use these grammar points.

CHAPTER 7

Grammar Focus 1
Future: *Will* and *be going to*

Grammar Focus 2
Future: Questions

Grammar Focus 3
Possibility: Modals and expressions

CHAPTER 8

Grammar Focus 1
Future: Simple present and present progressive

Grammar Focus 2
Future real conditional

MyEnglishLab

 What do you know?

Ecotourism

Getting Started

A Look at the picture. What are the people in the focus group talking about?

> Next summer we might take an ecotourism trip to Costa Rica to see leatherback turtles. Or we may help clean up the Gulf of Mexico. That could be interesting.

> In the future, I will fly less. I promise! I'm going to find "green" ways to travel—like biking!

> I just bought a monthly train pass. So, starting tomorrow, I'm going to take the train—an environmentally friendly kind of transportation.

> We are going to see more effects of global warming, I predict. This is just the tip of the iceberg. Soon we will discover other forms of environmental damage.

B Work with a partner. Circle the correct answers.

1. Ecotourism is . . .
   a. for people who are tired of city life.
   b. a trip that takes you far from home.
   c. travel that doesn't cause damage.

2. Environmentally friendly transportation . . .
   a. causes pollution.
   b. avoids damaging the air, water, and earth.
   c. is close to home.

3. Green travel is . . .
   a. gentle to the environment.
   b. what people in tropical climates use.
   c. the least expensive way to travel.

4. The *tip of the iceberg* refers to . . .
   a. something that is very cold.
   b. a small example of a greater problem.
   c. something that is going to melt.

C Look back at the comments in Part A. Complete the tasks.

1. We use *will* and *be going to* to talk about **future actions**. Complete the chart with examples.

Prediction	
Plan	
Intention / Promise	

2. Look for verb forms that express **future possibility**. Underline the three examples.
3. We often use time signals when we talk about future events (*tomorrow, next month*). Circle the examples.

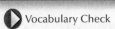

Reading

A WARM-UP Look at the pictures. Which forms of travel and recreation do you think damage the environment? Tell a partner.

B SKIMMING Skim the article. Check (✓) the sentence that expresses the main idea. Then go back and read the whole article.

☐ 1. Soon we'll travel in spaceships.

☐ 2. We won't use planes any more.

☐ 3. We need to be more environmentally conscious.

☐ 4. In the future, fewer people will travel.

The Future of Travel

Travel is fun, we all agree. Unfortunately, as travelers, we damage the environment. And until something changes, we are going to continue to harm the earth. Consider this:

- Cruise ships dump up to 170,000 gallons (643,520 li) of waste into the sea each day.
- An average golf course uses at least 528,344 gallons (2 million li) of water a day.
- A large hotel creates over 7 tons of waste per day. Up to 60 percent of this waste is recyclable.

And that's just the tip of the iceberg! There are countless other bad environmental practices happening around the globe today. What's the answer? One solution might be *ecotourism*: travel that respects the local environment and its people. Another may be greener transportation.

So how are we going to make these possibilities become realities? Here are some "best practices," and we at *We're Off!* magazine are going to commit to them today:

1. We will always respect our destination and its people.
2. We will try to reduce our waste.
3. We will make sure that we use greener kinds of transportation.
4. We will conserve water and reduce our use of electricity during our trip.
5. We won't travel by plane as much. When we do, we will pack less.

What more could you do to protect this planet and the welfare of its residents? We all could do plenty!

C UNDERSTANDING INFERENCE Write *T* for the true statements and *F* for the false statements.

_____ 1. Dumping waste into the ocean may harm ocean life.

_____ 2. Tourists prefer green golf courses.

_____ 3. Ecotourism is mainly about the traveler's comfort and needs.

_____ 4. The magazine wasn't very "green" in the past.

_____ 5. Green travel practices could help protect the environment.

MyEnglishLab
Reading Comprehension

Ecotourism **67**

Grammar Focus 1 Future: *Will* and *be going to*

Examples	Language notes
(1) Past ———— Present ┤ X ——→ Future She **will** travel to Selous Game Reserve next month. She**'s going to** travel to Selous Game Reserve next month.	We use *be going to* and *will* to talk about actions and events in the **future**.
(2) She**'ll** arrive after rush hour. She**'s going to** take the 7:10 train.	We can use *will* or *be going to* to present **facts**.
(3) People **will** travel differently in the future. We**'re going to** discover new energy sources. **Look—no clouds! It's going to be** a beautiful day! *Incorrect:* Look—no clouds! It'll be a beautiful day.	We can use *will* or *be going to* to make **predictions** or **guesses** about the future. *Note:* Use *be going to* (not *will*) when the sentence follows **a fact that helps us make a prediction**.
(4) He**'s going to** go India next summer. He already bought his ticket.	Use *be going to* to talk about already made **plans**.
(5) That's the phone. I**'ll** get it! That idea sounds great! I**'ll** go with you! My bus is leaving. I**'ll** write more later!	Use *will* for a **decision** made at the moment of speaking, and for **intentions** and **promises**.
(6) He **is going to travel** by airplane. They **are going to leave** tonight.	For statements with *be going to*, use: subject + *be* + *going to* + base verb *Note: Be* is in the simple present and matches the form of the subject.
(7) She**'s not going to** waste energy. For example, she **isn't going to** take taxis everywhere.	In **negative** statements with *be going to*, we often use the contracted forms.
(8) We **will protect** the environment. I**'ll walk** to the museum.	*Will* never changes form. But it is often contracted with the subject when the subject is a pronoun. Use: subject + *will* + base verb
(9) We **won't** stay at that hotel again. It was terrible.	For **negative** statements with *will*, we usually use the contracted form of *will not*: **won't**.
(10) She's going to take a bike trip **next month.** **In the future** our trees will be taller!	We can use future time signals at the beginning or at the end of a sentence. Examples include **soon, tomorrow, next** _____ (week, month, year), and **in the future**.

Affirmative and negative statements			
will		*be going to*	
I You She We They	will (won't) **stay** there again.	I'm You're She's We're They're	(not) **going to pack** a big bag.
It	will (won't) **take** a lot of gas.	It's	(not) **going to help** the environment.

See Appendix A on page A-2 for contractions. See Appendices N and O on page A-7 for more statements with will *and* be going to.

Grammar Practice

A Complete the conversation. Use the correct form of the words. Use contractions.

SOFIA: That documentary was inspiring! *I'm* going to be a greener traveler. I
1. _____ (be going to / ride) my bicycle more. As a result,
I **2.** _____ (will / not / drive) as much.

JULIE: Good thinking! That way, you **3.** _____ (will / protect) the
environment and get exercise!

SOFIA: Right. What about you?

JULIE: Well, my sister and I **4.** _____ (be going to / research) cruise lines.

SOFIA: Sounds interesting. How will you choose?

JULIE: We **5.** _____ (will / not / use) environmentally unfriendly companies.

SOFIA: That's smart. Hey, after work tomorrow, Pat and I
6. _____ (be going to / go) to the library to get some information
on ecotourism. Join us!

JULIE: Great idea. I **7.** _____ (will / see) you there!

B Complete the conversations. Circle the correct words.

1. A: Hey, look out! **You're / You'll** going to hit that car!

   B: Oh! Sorry—I'll be more careful!

2. A: Going by taxi **will / be going to** cost $40, the driver said.

   B: Right. Let's walk.

3. A: I can't wait! Fran is going to visit us next weekend!

   B: Sorry, but her plans changed. Now she **isn't going to / won't** come.

4. A: When are you going to start your essay about green travel?

   B: Soon! I promise. **I'm going / I will** do it!

C Write the future verb forms you circled in Part B. Then match the reasons to the forms.

Form	Reason
_b_ **1.** *will*	**a.** Fact
____ **2.** _____	**b.** Prediction or guess
____ **3.** _____	**c.** Already-made plans
____ **4.** _____	**d.** Decision made in the moment

D Write true statements with *will* and *be going to*. Use the time signals.

1. (soon) _____

2. (tomorrow) _____

3. (next month) _____

4. (in the future) _____

Grammar Focus 2 Future: Questions

Examples	Language notes

(1) What **will** the hotel cost? [fact]
Is the travel program **going to** start soon? [fact]
Will people travel differently in the future?
  [prediction / guess]
The phone is ringing. **Will** you get it? [request]
Look—clouds! **Is** it **going to** rain? [prediction /
  guess following fact]
Are you **going to** go to Africa next summer?
  [plans]
	We use **will** and **be going to** in **questions** in the same situations as statements:
	
	both: facts; predictions / guesses
	
	will: in-the-moment requests (willingness)
	
	be going to: predictions / guesses that follow facts; plans

(2) **Will** you **travel** using environmentally friendly modes of transportation? **Is** he **going to take** a hiking trip?	To form **yes / no questions**, use: **will** + subject + **base verb** **be** + subject + **going to** + **base verb**

(3) **Q:** Will they help us?
  A: Yes, they will. / No, they won't.
 	
  Q: Is she going with them?
  A: Yes, she is. / No, she isn't. No, she's not.
 	
  Incorrect: A: Yes, ~~they'll~~.
        A: Yes, ~~she's~~.
	For **short answers** to yes / no questions with **will**, use *will* or *won't*.
	
	For **short answers** to yes / no questions with **be going to**, use the simple present of *be*.
	
	Note: Don't use **contractions** in **affirmative** short answers.

(4) **When will** the train **arrive** in Milan? **What are** you **going to pack**?	To form **wh- questions**, use: **Wh- word** + **will** + subject + **base verb** **Wh- word** + **be** + subject + **going to** + **base verb**

Yes / No questions	Short answers	
Will you **buy** a ticket for me? **Will** it **be** cold there?	Yes, I **will** Yes, it **will**.	No, I **won't**. No, it **won't**.
Are we **going to fly**? **Is** it **going to be** a "green" trip?	Yes, we **are**. Yes, it **is**.	No, we **aren't**. / No, we're **not**. No, it **isn't**. / No, it's **not**.
Wh- questions	Short answers	
What will she **do about** the environment? **When are** they **going to take** their next trip?	Use her car less. Next month.	

See Appendices N and O on page A-7 for more questions with will *and* be going to.

Grammar Practice

A Match the answers to the questions.

Questions

_____ 1. Will he fly there?

_____ 2. Are they going to take a taxi just two blocks?

_____ 3. How will you conserve water?

_____ 4. When is she going to take her trip?

_____ 5. Is she going to ride her bike to school?

_____ 6. What is he going to take with him on the trip?

_____ 7. Will you go on an environmentally friendly trip with me?

_____ 8. How is she going to be a "green" traveler?

Answers

a. She'll walk more.

b. Next month.

c. Yes, she is.

d. One carry-on bag.

e. I'll take short showers.

f. Yes, they are.

g. No, he won't.

h. Yes, I will.

B Read the questions. Then write *T* for the true statements and *F* for the false statements.

1. ANA: Luisa, is it going to rain?

_____ Ana wants Luisa to make a prediction.

2. SUNNY: Nelson, will you promise to stop flying so much?

_____ Sunny is asking about a fact.

3. LUISA: Ana, are you going to France next summer?

_____ Luisa wants to know Ana's plans.

4. PADMA: Nav, will you grab my bag, please?

_____ Padma is making a request in the moment.

5. FREDERIC: Nancy, are you going to be here tomorrow?

_____ Frederic is asking for a promise.

C Find and correct the mistake in each conversation.

1. A: Will you tries to use green transportation in the future?

   B: Yes, I will.

2. A: How much will be the ticket?

   B: Around $20.

3. A: Is Johan going travel to the Balkans next fall?

   B: No, he isn't.

4. A: How are they go to be greener?

   B: They're going to walk to work, for example.

5. A: Is she going to bring a carry-on bag?

   B: Yes, she's.

Grammar Focus 3 Possibility: Modals and expressions

Examples	Language notes
(1) They **might** travel to Easter Island soon. *(They're thinking about it.)* She **may** visit Machu Picchu next year. *(It's an option she's considering.)* She **could** spend some time in Chichen-Itza, Mexico. *(She'll already be in Mexico, so it's a possibility.)*	We use the **modal verbs** *might*, *may*, and *could* to talk about **future possibility**. *Note:* We also use *might*, *may*, and *could* for permission. See Chapter 13.
(2) He **might ride** his bike more. It **may use** less energy. She **could take** the train instead.	To form a statement, use: subject + ***might / may / could*** + **base verb** *Note:* Like other modals, *might*, *may*, and *could* **never change form**.
(3) We **might not take** the cruise. We **may not visit** Barbados soon. We **could not** see the tortoise yesterday. *Incorrect:* We ~~could not~~ see the tortoises tomorrow.	For **negative** statements, use: ***might / may*** + ***not*** + **base verb** *Notes:* • Don't contract *may* or *might* with *not*. • Don't use ***could not*** to indicate possibility in the future; it indicates impossibility in the past.
(4) **Might** you **visit** the Grand Canyon on your next trip? **Could** we **fly** home on a Friday?	For ***yes / no questions*** about future possibility, use: ***Might / Could*** + subject + **base verb** *Notes:* • ***Might . . . ?*** is considered very formal. • We sometimes ask about future possibility with ***Do you think*** + subject + ***might*** + base verb.
(5) **Q:** Do you think you might visit the Monterey Bay Aquarium? **A:** Yes, I might. / I may. / I could.	For affirmative **short answers** to *yes / no* questions about **future possibility**, use *might*, *may*, or *could*.
(6) **When might** you **leave**? **Where could** we **go** on our next trip?	For *wh-* questions about future possibility, use: ***Wh- word*** + ***might / could*** + subject + **base verb**

Affirmative statements	Negative statements
I You He She { **might** **may** **could** } **visit** a volcano in Costa Rica. We They	I You He She { **might not** **may not** } **travel** by plane. We They
It **might / may / could be** expensive to drive there.	It **might / may not cost** much to go by train.

Grammar Practice

A Rewrite the sentences. Use the words.

1. They're possibly not going to France next year.

   (may / not) _____

2. She's thinking about visiting the pyramids in Egypt.

   (could) _____

3. He's considering seeing the ruins in Corfu.

   (might) _____

4. We don't think we'll go to the mountains next month.

   (might / not) _____

5. It's a possibility that I will fly to Mongolia after my visit to China.

   (could) _____

6. There's a chance you won't see penguins in Antarctica.

   (may / not) _____

B Read the travel plans. Then complete the chart. Check (✓) the correct answers.

I'm making plans for my next trip. I'm going to travel to Angkor Wat in Cambodia next year. I might stop in London on my way, but I won't stop in Paris. Once I arrive in Cambodia, of course I am going to visit the famous temple. I'll respect its condition: I won't damage any of the area, and I will be careful where I walk and what I touch. I could hire a tour guide, but I may not—I'll decide when I get there. I'm definitely going to bring my camera. My friend Diana may come with me, but Susannah isn't going to join us. I will write about the trip in a special Angkor Wat trip blog—and I may post videos, too. I can't wait!

	Yes (definitely)	Maybe (possibly)	No
1. Travel to Angkor Wat			
2. Stop in London			
3. Stop in Paris			
4. Respect the condition of the temple			
5. Damage the area			
6. Hire a tour guide			
7. Bring my camera			
8. Have my friend Diana with me			
9. Have my friend Susannah with me			
10. Write about the trip			
11. Post videos of the trip			

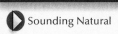

Speaking

A Are you a green traveler? Read the questions and choices to a partner. Circle his or her responses. Add up the points.

What will you do?

---

1. Your boss gives you next Friday and Monday off. What will you do with your long weekend?
   a. Find the cheapest online flight and just go! (2)
   b. Take a local train to a nearby resort. (0)
   c. Study travel brochures and pick something. (1)

2. You are in Cartagena, Colombia. The forecast says it's going to be muggy and warm tomorrow. What will you do?
   a. Wear cool clothes, drink lots of fluids, and read in the shade. (0)
   b. Run the air-conditioner all day and stay inside. (2)
   c. Spend the day at the pool listening to music on my mp3 player. (1)

3. You call to reserve a hotel room in Tanzania. The clerk says she'll give you a discount on a room with a self-composting toilet (one that uses less water). What will you tell the clerk?
   a. "No way. I want a 'regular' toilet." (2)
   b. "OK. But I may not like it!" (1)
   c. "Sure, I'll try it!" (0)

4. You want to go somewhere to enjoy the water tomorrow. Choose a plan.
   a. I'm going to take a day-long cruise. (1)
   b. I'm going to rent some jet skis. (2)
   c. I'm going to go canoeing on a nearby river. (0)

5. You and a friend are in Istanbul. It'll be dinnertime soon. What sounds good?
   a. We'll eat in the hotel restaurant and order a hamburger and fries. (2)
   b. We'll try one of the places suggested in our guidebook. (1)
   c. We'll walk around the city and get dinner at a street cart. (0)

6. You and your neighbor plan to attend the Garlic Festival downtown this weekend. You live 30 blocks away. How will you get there?
   a. I'll drive and she'll drive—we each have errands to run afterwards. (2)
   b. We'll share a taxi both ways. (1)
   c. We'll bicycle there and home. (0)

Total points: _____

Key: 0: You are an ecotourist! 1–8: You could be greener! 9+: What might you do to be a greener traveler?

B Work in a small group. Discuss your scores and answers. Who is the greenest? Who is the least green? What changes in behavior might you make? Look at the model.

> *My partner won't use a self-composting toilet on this trip, but he might on the next one!*

C Discuss the results as a class.

Listening

A 🎧 UNDERSTANDING MAIN IDEAS Listen. Circle the correct answers.

1. The information is _____.
   a. an academic talk
   b. a commercial
   c. a radio show
   d. a classroom guest speaker

2. Go Green is _____.
   a. a trip-planning service
   b. an online chat group
   c. a student camping tour
   d. an environmental education group

B 🎧 UNDERSTANDING DETAILS Listen again. Answer the questions.

1. How will travelers learn to protect the environment? _____

2. Who can afford to travel with Go Green? _____

3. How will travelers meet local people with Go Green? _____

4. Why do travelers with Go Green return home fitter? _____

5. What doesn't Go Green allow? Why? _____

C AFTER LISTENING Work with a partner. Do you believe the claims in the Go Green ad? Which claims appeal to you? Which Go Green feature do you like best?

Writing

A How can you help the environment—both at home and when you travel? Think of three things you will definitely do, and three things you might do. Take notes.

Definitely	Possibly
1.	1.
2.	2.
3.	3.

B Write about your plans. Use your notes. Try to use the grammar from the chapter.

> *Here's what I plan to do at home: I'll use public transportation more. I won't drive my car as much. Instead, I'll walk. I might ask my family to waste less and reuse more. . . .*

C Share your writing with a partner. What other ideas can you give your partner?

CHAPTER 8 Your Travel Personality

Getting Started

A What types of travelers are there? What type of traveler are you? Check (✓) the description(s) that fit you. Compare answers with a partner.

☐ **1.** I'm going on vacation next month, and my suitcase is already packed.

☐ **2.** I'm leaving on a trip in a few hours, but my backpack is still in the closet.

☐ **3.** My vacation starts next June. I bought train tickets and made room reservation last July!

☐ **4.** The bus departs at 3:00 this afternoon. I'll be at the bus station by 2:55.

☐ **5.** My train leaves at 10:00 tonight. I'm at the train station now—three hours early.

B Look at the pictures. Read about the different types of travelers. Then match the descriptions to the pictures.

_____ 1.

_____ 2.

_____ 3.

_____ 4.

a. If there's adventure, she'll be there!
b. She'll travel anywhere if people are in need.

c. If her friend plans a trip, she won't miss out!
d. She'll go to the beach if she needs alone time.

C Look at Parts A and B. Complete the tasks.

1. We can use the **simple present** to talk about future scheduled events. Underline the examples.

2. We can use the **present progressive** to talk about future plans. Circle the examples.

3. We use the **future real conditional** to talk about a future situation that _will_ happen _if_ something else happens. Write the number(s) or letter(s) of the sentences in the future real conditional. _____

Reading

A **WARM-UP** Look at the headings in Part B. What do you think they mean? Which one sounds like you?

B **SKIMMING** Skim the article. Choose and write the best title. Then go back and read the article again.

Customize your next vacation   The best type of travel partner

People to avoid while traveling   What kind of traveler are you?

Title: _____

Where are you going on your next vacation? What are you doing while you're there? Are you eating in local restaurants and visiting historic sites—or hiking in the mountains? Are you traveling alone, or with a friend, family, or group? In her new book *You Are How You Travel*, travel writer Mary Levin presents six traveler types. Here's a look at what she says:

The Foodie For you, the food is the focus! Your plane leaves Egypt in two hours—but you take one last chance to go to the Khan el-Khalili spice market in Cairo before you depart.

The Adventurist You enjoy rock climbing and skydiving. You don't use a map and don't need a compass. Your train departs in two hours, but you spend the last hours of vacation climbing the amazing rocks of Meteora, Greece.

The History Buff You're passionate about the past and do your homework. If you don't do your research, you aren't going to have a good time.

The Groupie Your friends plan to rent a beach house. This is your dream vacation. If your friends go, you're going to go, too! And the opposite is true —if they don't go, you won't go either! (But if you can talk at least one person into it, you might still go!)

The Volunteer or Service Traveler A huge community service project starts next year. You have your ticket already! You enjoy everything from building playgrounds to teaching English in places from Alaska to Zambia. You'll go if there's a place that needs your help!

The Easygoing Type You like down time. The only thing you need is the perfect spot and some time. If you have these, you'll figure out the rest! You *don't* like to make plans when you travel. If you can sit on the beach and enjoy a cold drink, you'll have a great time.

In conclusion, the way you travel should fit your personality. Finding yourself is sometimes the goal of a trip. But knowing yourself beforehand may be even more important!

C **APPLYING INFORMATION** Which type of traveler made the statement? Write the types.

1. "Did you know that this house was built during the Revolutionary War? They found cannon balls in the front yard!" _____

2. "We realized that these children didn't have paper or crayons. When we gave them supplies, they created beautiful pictures!" _____

3. "The bigger the mountain, the better for me!" _____

4. "The smells, colors, tastes . . . I love trying them all." _____

5. "Just give me the sun, a beach, and a towel, and I'll be happy!" _____

6. "Sharing travel moments with my friends is the best." _____

Grammar Focus 1 Future: Simple present and present progressive

Examples	Language notes
(1) Her flight **leaves** tomorrow. When does the train **leave**? We**'re visiting** friends in California next month. **Are** they **coming** to the party tomorrow?	In addition to *will* and *be going to*, we can also use the **simple present** and the **present progressive** to talk about the future.
(2) **Are there** any good upcoming concerts? We **arrive** tomorrow at 7:45. The conference **begins** Monday. When **does** the next train **depart**?	We can use the **simple present** to talk about future events that are **scheduled**. We commonly use verbs such as *(There) is / are, arrive, begin, depart, end, leave,* and *start*.
(3) Frank **is coming** for dinner tonight. She**'s going** to the doctor tomorrow. What **are** you **doing** this weekend? She**'s visiting** her mom next week.	We can use the **present progressive** to talk about future **plans** and **intentions**. We use this form especially when talking about personal arrangements.
(4) The plane arrives **at 5:00 P.M.** Does he start his new job **on Wednesday**? She begins her volunteer position **in a month**. We're leaving **in two weeks**. What are you doing **this afternoon**? **Next year** they're opening a tourism office downtown. She has a test **tomorrow**. *Incorrect:* They ~~tomorrow leave~~.	We often add **time signals** that refer to the future, including: *at* _____ (time) *on* _____ (day of the week) *in* _____ (month, year) *in* _____ (minutes, hours, days, weeks) *this* _____ (*morning, afternoon, evening*) *next* _____ (*week, month, year*) *tonight, tomorrow* *Note:* Time signals can go at the **beginning or end** of statements. They go at the **end** of questions.

Grammar Practice

MyEnglishLab

Grammar Plus 1
Activities 1 and 2

 A Dana and her friend Bill are traveling to Zurich tomorrow. Read Dana's notes. Then circle the correct words. Answer the questions with information from Dana's notes.

1. **Q:** **Is there** / **Is** a flight from New York to

    Zurich tomorrow?

    A: _____

    _____

2. **Q:** What time **does** / **is** the flight depart for Zurich?

    A: _____

    _____

3. **Q:** When **does the flight arrive** / **does the flight arriving** in Zurich?

    A: _____

4. **Q:** Who **is printing out** / **prints out** the tickets in the morning?

    A: _____

Tomorrow:
Flight LX 017 from
   New York (JFK) to Zurich (ZRH)
- departs: 5:50 P.M.
- arrives: 8:05 A.M. (next day)
*Bill – print out tickets in A.M.

B Complete the sentences. Use the simple present or present progressive form of the verbs.

1. The prime minister _____ (arrive) in a few minutes. The tourists are ready!

2. Fran is taking an environmental studies class this semester. It _____ (end) on June 26.

3. Guess what? Sylvia and Javier _____ (get) married on the beach next year!

4. I have to run to the train soon! The last one _____ (leave) at 1:15 A.M.!

5. Sorry, but I can't take you. I _____ (not / have) time this morning.

6. There's a party at Dan's tomorrow night, but I _____ (not / go).

7. We _____ (meet) our friends tomorrow morning at 7:00 for the tour.

C Write about your upcoming plans. Use the time expressions and the present progressive.

1. (this evening)   _____
2. (this afternoon)   _____
3. (tonight)   _____
4. (tomorrow)   _____
5. (next weekend)   _____
6. (in a few weeks)   _____

D Work with a partner. Ask and answer questions about your upcoming plans. Use the present progressive and the information from Part C. Look at the model.

> What are you doing this evening?

> I'm cooking dinner for a friend.
> What are you doing this evening?

> I'm studying for a history test.

Grammar Focus 2 Future real conditional

Examples	Language notes
(1) If you spend a week on the beach, you're going to be happy. [future real conditional] You won't be happy if you stay home all week. [future real conditional] If I sleep on an airplane, I get a headache. [habitual present]	We use the **future real conditional** to talk about something that's likely to happen in the future if certain circumstances are true. *Note:* We use the **habitual present** (*if* + simple present + simple present) to talk about things we usually do or that usually happen.
(2) **If** he **has** time, he **will go**. **If** your friends **go**, you **are going to go**. **If** you **go** snorkeling, you**'ll probably see** some beautiful coral.	A future real conditional sentence has two clauses: an **if-clause** (the possible situation) and the **main clause** (the future result). Use: *if-clause* = *if* + subject + **simple present** + **main clause** = subject + **will / be going to** + **base verb** *Note:* We can also use *probably* in the main clause to indicate future probability.
(3) **If I go snorkeling in the ocean,** I won't remove shells from the coral reef. **I won't buy shells taken from the reef** if someone tries to sell them to me.	We can **begin** future real conditional sentences with the **if-clause** or with the **main clause**. Use a **comma** between the two clauses when the *if*-clause comes first.
(4) If she **doesn't go** to Paris, she'll spend more time in Aix-en-Provence. If they visit Las Vegas, they **aren't going to have** time for the Grand Canyon. If we **don't go** shopping today, we **won't have** a chance to buy souvenirs.	To form the **negative** in the future real conditional, use: *If*-clause (**negative**), main clause (positive) *If*-clause (positive), main clause (**negative**) *If*-clause (**negative**), main clause (**negative**)
(5) You **might have** more fun if you go with friends. They **may see** some wild animals if they get up early. If she goes on that small boat, she **could get** seasick.	When we are **less sure** about the future result, we can use these **modals** in the **main clause**: *might* + **base verb** *may* + **base verb** *could* + **base verb**
(6) **Q: If it snows,** are they going to stay home? **A:** Yes, they are. / No, they aren't. **Q:** What will we do **if the hotel is full**? **A:** We'll drive to the next town.	**Questions** in the future real conditional can begin or end with the *if-clause*.

Grammar Practice

A Complete the sentences. Use the future real conditional. More than one correct answer is possible.

1. If you _____ (walk) a lot on your trip, you _____ (not / gain) weight.

2. You _____ (not / get) your visa if you _____ (not / get) those shots.

3. I _____ (not / take) my bike on the trip if the forecast _____ (be) bad.

4. If she _____ (do) a good job as our tour guide, she _____ (get) a promotion.

5. If we _____ (not / hurry), we _____ (not / get) there in time.

6. If we _____ (not / catch) this train, we _____ (take) the next one.

B Write sentences with the words. Use the future real conditional. More than one correct answer is possible.

1. the weather / be good / tomorrow   we / go to the park

   _____

2. they / go to Morocco / next year   they / visit Marrakech

   _____

3. my friend / invite me to Brazil   I / be so happy

   _____

4. she / probably miss the train   she / not / hurry

   _____

5. there not be / cheap flights to Europe   we / not spend the weekend in Geneva

   _____

C Complete the sentences. Use your own ideas. Then compare answers with a partner.

1. We'll have a great time on the trip if _____.

2. If our friends don't want to take the boat, _____.

3. _____ if we don't catch the train.

4. _____ if he stays an extra day in Los Angeles.

5. We could have a great meal if _____.

6. She might not enjoy the bus ride if _____.

7. I may go to Barcelona if _____.

8. If I don't have enough money to take that trip, _____.

Listening

A BEFORE LISTENING Have you ever been on a city tour? If so, when and where? If not, when might you take one?

B 🎧 UNDERSTANDING MAIN IDEAS Listen to the New York City tour guide. Number the activities in the order the tourists will do them (*1* to *6*).

_____ a.

_____ b.

_____ c.

_____ d.

_____ e.

_____ f.

C 🎧 UNDERSTANDING DETAILS Listen again. Answer the questions.

1. What time are they meeting? _____

2. If the weather is bad, where will they go? _____

3. If they have extra energy after shopping, what will they do? _____

4. Where will they take pictures if it's nice at sunset? _____

5. Where will they go for dinner? _____

Speaking

A Imagine that tomorrow you are leaving on vacation. Read the questions and think about your answers.

1. Where are you going? Why?
2. If you want ideas for places to eat, who will you ask?
3. Where will you get directions if you need them?
4. What will you do if you have a problem?
5. If the weather's bad, how will your plans change?
6. If you're not having a good time, what will you do?

B Discuss the questions in Part A with two classmates. Take notes in the chart. Look at the model.

> What will you do if the weather is bad?

> If it's really bad, I'll do something indoors, like see a play.

	Classmate 1	Classmate 2
1.		
2.		
3.		
4.		
5.		
6.		

C Work with a new partner. Talk about the classmates you interviewed. What types of travelers are they? Do they seem like good travel partners? Why or why not?

Writing

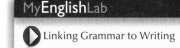

MyEnglishLab

Linking Grammar to Writing

A A friend is coming to visit. Think about the questions in the list.

- What kinds of activities will you do?
- If the weather is nice, what will you do outside? If it rains (or snows!) what will you do?
- What will you cook if your friend wants to eat at home?
- If your friend wants to shop, where will you go?
- Where will you and your friend go if you want to sightsee?

B Write a one-paragraph email about activities you'll enjoy with your friend. Try to use the grammar from the chapter.

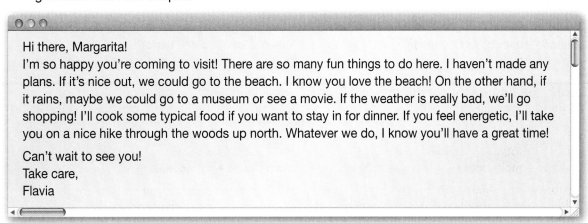

Hi there, Margarita!
I'm so happy you're coming to visit! There are so many fun things to do here. I haven't made any plans. If it's nice out, we could go to the beach. I know you love the beach! On the other hand, if it rains, maybe we could go to a museum or see a movie. If the weather is really bad, we'll go shopping! I'll cook some typical food if you want to stay in for dinner. If you feel energetic, I'll take you on a nice hike through the woods up north. Whatever we do, I know you'll have a great time!

Can't wait to see you!
Take care,
Flavia

C Share your paragraph with a partner. Answer any questions.

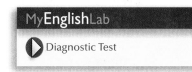

MyEnglishLab

Diagnostic Test

Grammar Summary

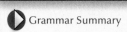

We use *will* and *be going to* to talk about facts and make predictions about the future. We also use *be going to* to talk about something already planned or decided. We use *will* when we're making a decision or a promise in the moment of speaking. For the negative form of *will*, we usually use the contracted form *won't*.

Will and *be going to*	
affirmative statements	**negative statements**
I'**ll** join you! You'**ll** do great on the essay tomorrow. She'**s going to** visit Spain in March. They'**re going to** sail to the Caribbean.	I **won't** have time tomorrow. We **won't** stay there again. He'**s not going to** go out tonight. It's raining. They'**re not going to** have the parade today.
questions	**short answers**
Will you **get** me a soda, please? **Will** we **have** time to eat before leaving? **Is** she **going to be** OK? **Are** we **going to take** the bus? **How will** they **get** here? **Where are** we **going to stay**?	Yes, I **will**. No, I **won't** (will not). Yes, you **will**. No, you **won't** (will not). Yes, she **is**. No, she **isn't**. / No, she'**s not**. Yes, we **are**. No, we **aren't**. / No, we'**re not**. By taxi. At a hostel.

We use the **modals** *might*, *may*, and *could* to talk about possible events in the future. For negative statements, use *not* after *might* and *may*. Use *might* and *could* in questions.

Statements	Questions
They **might go** to Dubai. We **may take** a cruise. It **could rain** all weekend. They **may not** have enough time. We **might not** go to Italy.	**Might** we **see** you there? **Could** we **visit** the museum? **When might** he **call**? **Where could** we **get** a good meal?

We can use the **simple present** and the **present progressive**, along with **time signals** (*tomorrow, tonight, on Friday, next week*, etc.) to talk about the future. We typically use the simple present with schedules and the present progressive with plans.

Statements	Questions
The train **leaves** at 7:00 tonight. She'**s starting** her new job tomorrow.	When **does** the plane **depart**? What time **are** we **going** to the party?

We use the **future real conditional** to talk about something that's probably going to happen in the future if certain circumstances are true. Use the simple present in the *if*-clause, and *will* or *be going to* in the main clause. If something is less likely to happen, use *might*, *may*, or *could* in the main clause.

If-clause + main clause	Main clause + *if*-clause
If you visit next winter, we'll ski. **If the water gets rough**, we may get seasick.	We'll go to the beach **if you visit in July**. We could have fun **if the seas are calm**.
Negative statements	**Questions**
If you don't fix the tire, you might have problems. **If he drives,** we won't get there in time.	Will they visit the Louvre **if they go to Paris**? Where will they stay **if the campground is closed**?

Self-Assessment

A (5 points) Match the answers to the questions.

_____ 1. Will you carry my suitcase, please?   **a.** No, he isn't.

_____ 2. Is he going to sleep at the campground?   **b.** Yes, I will.

_____ 3. Are they going to stay in Costa Rica?   **c.** I'm sorry, I'm busy.

_____ 4. Is their mom going to go, too?   **d.** Yes, they are.

_____ 5. Will you join me for lunch?   **e.** Yes, she is.

B (5 points) Read the sentences. Write *P* (possibility) or *D* (definite plan).

_____ 1. He might travel to Italy next month.

_____ 2. She's going to go to Warsaw tonight.

_____ 3. We may not take a trip to Honduras next year.

_____ 4. They won't travel to Trinidad and Tobago this year.

_____ 5. You could visit Covent Garden in London.

C (5 points) Complete the sentences about Joanne's upcoming plans. Use the simple present or the present progressive. More than one correct answer may be possible.

1. Joanne _____ (fly) to Las Vegas on Thursday.

2. Her flight _____ (leave) at 10:00 A.M.

3. She _____ (present) her company's new product at the conference.

4. Joanne _____ (stay) in a hotel near the conference.

5. She _____ (not / have) time to do any sightseeing.

D (10 points) Complete the sentences. Use the future real conditional. More than one correct answer may be possible.

1. If we _____ (not / have) time tomorrow, we _____ (visit) the Taj Mahal the next day.

2. If the conference _____ (be) in Montreal this year, I _____ (make) plans to see old friends at McGill University.

3. If they _____ (be) in Seattle an extra day, they _____ (go) shopping in Pike Place Market.

4. We _____ (go) scuba diving in the Cayman Islands if the cruise ship _____ (stop) for long enough.

5. They _____ (have) great stories to tell if they _____ (cross) the ocean in a sailboat!

Unit Project: Travel brochure

A Work in a small group. Create a travel brochure. With your brochure, give your readers a clear picture of a famous city. Tell them what they'll see, what they could do, what they might eat, etc. Follow the steps.

1. Choose a city from the list, or come up with your own idea.

Athens	Luxor	Prague	Seoul
Cape Town	Naples	Puerto Vallarta	Sydney
Edinburgh	Osaka	Rio de Janeiro	Vancouver
Hong Kong	Paris	San Juan	Zurich

2. Research the city. Use the topics in the list to help you. Take notes.

- Top 3 things to see
- Geography
- Climate and weather conditions
- Best time to visit

- Entertainment
- Food that the area is known for
- Arts and culture (museums, landmarks, etc.)
- Languages, local dialects

3. Use your notes to write and design your brochure. Use photos, maps, and other images to illustrate it.

B Present your brochure to the class.

Welcome to Ouro Preto

What you'll do if you come to Ouro Preto

If you come to Ouro Preto, Brazil, the first thing you'll want to do is drink a coffee near Tiradentes Square. There you'll notice amazing buildings. Then you might want to walk around the city on the beautiful cobblestone streets. You could visit some stores and museums. If you're hungry, you may want to try pão de queijo, cheese bread . . .

MyEnglishLab
▶ Unit Test

MyEnglishLab
▶ Search it!

UNIT 5

The Power of Music

CHAPTER 9

Music and Social Change

Getting Started

A The title of this unit is "The Power of Music." In what ways do you think music can be powerful? What are some things that music can do?

B Read about a program that uses music for social change. What are the youth of Venezuela learning from the program *El Sistema*?

El Sistema, originally called Social Action for Music, is a music education program in Venezuela. Economist and musician José Antonio Abreu founded the program in 1975.

For nearly four decades the program has given free music training to over 800,000 children. Of these children, 90 percent have come from poor backgrounds. The music lessons have changed the lives of these children. In addition to music, the program has emphasized the learning of teamwork, responsibility, and mutual respect.

Abreu has directed *El Sistema* since he started the program. It now has 30 orchestras in Venezuela. One of the orchestras, the Simón Bolivar Youth Orchestra, has performed all over the world.

El Sistema has produced some extremely talented professionals, including Edicson Ruiz. In 2003, at the age of 17, Ruiz became

the second youngest member in the history of the Berlin Philharmonic. Another success story is world-famous conductor Gustavo Dudamel. He has served as music director of the Los Angeles Philharmonic since 2009.

Abreu feels music is an effective agent of social development. He said, "It is evident that music has to be recognized as an element of socialization . . . because it transmits the highest values—solidarity, harmony, mutual compassion."

C Look back at the reading in Part B. Complete the tasks.

1. The **present perfect** is formed by *have / has* + the past participle of a verb (*said, performed, been*). Underline the examples.
2. Circle the regular past participles. (These take the same forms as the simple past.) Draw a rectangle around the irregular past participles. (These take forms different from the simple past.)
3. We often use time signals beginning with *for* and *since* with the present perfect. Find the examples and write them in the chart.

Used with a length of time	Used with a time clause	Used with a point of time
for _____	since _____	since _____

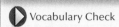

Reading

A WARM-UP Work in a group. Discuss the questions.

- Do you ever go to concerts? Where?
- Do you prefer to listen to music indoors or outdoors? Why?
- What are some reasons for having a concert? Is it just to make money?
- What famous international musicians can you name?

B PREDICTING Look at the pictures. Check (✓) the words you think could describe the Festival in the Desert. Then read the article and check your predictions.

☐ expensive   ☐ international   ☐ modern   ☐ tolerant   ☐ unique   ☐ unwelcoming

The Festival in the Desert

Since 2001, the Festival in the Desert in northern Mali has been one of the most unique world music concerts in the world. Held every January, it's inspired by the traditional celebrations of the Tuareg people. The Tuareg have gathered in the area around Timbuktu for many years. During these meetings they exchange ideas and try to address problems. These social gatherings are what the festival is built upon.

The origins of the festival go back to 1996, when 3,000 guns were burned in Timbuktu. There was fighting at the time among different communities of the southern Sahara. This public act marked the end to the fighting and the beginning of the reconciliation between the various communities. This has proved to be an example of how to manage conflicts. It has inspired countless people around the world.

Today, about 30 artistic groups come together for three days of music and artistry in one of the most inhospitable places in the world. The festival has always been a mix of the modern and the traditional. It has helped preserve the cultures of the desert and at the same time has exposed the people to the outside world. For some this has meant being listened to and recognized. For others it's meant discovering the desert through the tolerant, friendly, and welcoming nature of the local people.

Many famous local and international musicians have played at the festival since it began, including Oumou Sangaré and Ali Farka Touré from Mali, Jimmy Buffet from the United States, and Led Zeppelin's Robert Plant from the U.K. In 2003, Plant said, "It's one of the few honest things I have been part of in a long, long time. It's amazing to play out in the sand. There are no doors, no gates, and no money. It reminded me of why I sang in the first place."

C UNDERSTANDING MAIN IDEAS Match the main ideas to the paragraphs in the reading. Write *1* for the first paragraph, *2* for the second paragraph, and so on.

_____ **a.** The festival combines the old and new, and means different things to different people.

_____ **b.** Musicians from Mali and other countries have played the festival.

_____ **c.** The Tuareg gatherings in northern Mali inspired the festival.

_____ **d.** The idea for the festival came about because of a public reconciliation of people in the area.

MyEnglishLab

▶ Reading Comprehension

Grammar Focus 1 Present perfect

Examples	Language notes
(1) **Present** Past ———— X|x ————→ Future Many musicians **have played** at the festival. Music **has changed** their lives.	We use the **present perfect** to talk about a **past event that happened at an unspecified time**—the exact time is unknown or unimportant. The event may have happened once or more.
(2) I **have traveled** abroad. I **have not had** Ethiopian food.	We can also use the present perfect to talk about **general experiences**. The point is that we have (or have not) had the experience, not when.
(3) He **has broken** his leg. *(He can't ski now.)* They **have left** for the show. *(They aren't here now.)*	We can also use the present perfect to describe a **single action in the past** that **impacts** the present.
(4) We **have enjoyed** the concert. It **has been** a great experience.	To form the present perfect, use: *I, you, we, they* + **have** + **past participle** *he, she, it* + **has** + **past participle**

(5)   **Base** **Simple** **Past**
           past   **participle**
Regular: close closed closed
Irregular: feel   felt   felt
         be   was / were been
         go   went   gone
	Regular past participles have the same form as regular verbs in the simple past: **base verb + -ed**
	
	Irregular past participles have various forms, sometimes the same as irregular verbs in the simple past, sometimes not.

(6) We**'ve enjoyed** the trip. It**'s been** great. I **haven't spoken** to him. He **hasn't called**.	In statements, we often **contract** the subject with *have* or *has* ('ve, 's). The **negative** contraction of *have* is *haven't / hasn't*.
(7) **Have** you **been** to Africa?	For **yes / no questions**, use: ***Have / Has*** + subject + **past participle**
(8) **Q:** Have you been to New Zealand? **A:** Yes, I **have**. / No, I **haven't**, but my aunt **has**.	For **short answers**, use **have / has**.
(9) **Q:** Has she **ever skied**? **A:** No, she **hasn't ever skied**. / No, she's **never skied**. / No, she **never has**.	To emphasize that you are asking about the entire past, add **ever** before the participle. There are several ways to answer in the **negative**.
(10) **Where have** you **traveled**? **Who has been** to Mali? *(Akane has.)*	For **wh- questions**, use: **Wh- word** + **have / has** + subject + **past participle** *Note:* If the *wh-* word is the **subject**, use *has*.
(11) I **have always wanted** to visit Mali. *Incorrect:* I ~~always have~~ wanted to visit Mali. He **has attended** the festival **twice**.	Place **adverbs of frequency** after *have / has*. Place **time signals** at the end.

Affirmative statements	Negative statements	Contractions
I**'ve visited** Morocco. He**'s recorded** a new single.	I **haven't visited** Mali. He **hasn't recorded** an album.	I've = I have he's = he has
Questions and answers		
Q: **Have** you ever **flown**? **A:** No, I **haven't**. **Q:** **Has** he **learned** a language? **A:** Yes, he **has**.	**Q:** **Where have** you **traveled**? **A:** Mexico. **Q:** **What** language **has** he **learned**? **A:** Thai.	

See Appendix A on page A-1 for contractions with have. *See Appendix J on page A-5 for a list of irregular past participles. See Appendix P on page A-8 for more statements and questions in the present perfect.*

Grammar Practice

A Complete the paragraph about the accomplishments of musician, activist, and humanitarian Elton John. Use the present perfect form of the verbs.

Elton John **1.** _____ (chart) over 50 Top 40 songs during

his career. He **2.** _____ (have) seven consecutive number

one albums, second only to the Beatles. John and his songwriting partner, Bernie

Taupin, **3.** _____ (work) together on more than 30 albums.

In fact, John **4.** _____ (sell) more than 250 million albums

in all and **5.** _____ (win) many awards. He

6. _____ (be) very active in raising money for his charities as well. The

Elton John AIDS Foundation **7.** _____ (raise) over $200 million. He

8. _____ (receive) a knighthood from Queen Elizabeth II, making him

Sir Elton John.

B Complete the conversations. Use the present perfect form of the verbs.

1. A: _____ you _____ (ever / be) to a rock concert?

   B: Actually, no. I _____ (never / be) to one.

2. A: How many times _____ you _____ (see) Shakira in concert?

   B: We _____ (go) to three of her live shows.

3. A: _____ Lady Gaga _____ (ever / have) a number one song?

   B: Yes, she _____. In fact, she _____ (have) several.

4. A: _____ you _____ (finish) downloading the album?

   B: No, I _____. It's taking a long time.

C Complete the article using the words from the box. Use the present perfect.

appear	(not) decide	express	give	play	(not) record	win	write

Teen Band Wins Award

A teenage band named Project Music **1.** _____ this year's Social Change Award.
Organizers of the award **2.** _____ the band $10,000 in prize money for their efforts in
fighting neighborhood violence with their anti-violence lyrics. The three members—brothers
David and Robert King, and friend Haley Adams—**3.** _____ on weekends at various
neighborhood youth centers around the city and **4.** _____ on numerous TV and
radio shows. They **5.** _____ more than 12 songs—mostly talking about the dangers
of violence and the importance of mentoring—but **6.** _____ an album. Michael
Adams, Haley's father and the band's manager, said a record company **7.** _____
interest in signing them to a contract for their first album. They **8.** _____ what to do
with the prize money, but Robert says, "We know we want to do something good with it."

Grammar Focus 2 Present perfect: *For* and *since*

Examples	Language notes
(1) The Tuareg **have gathered** in the area around Timbuktu for many years.	We also use the **present perfect** to talk about a situation that began in the **past**, continues to the **present**, and will *probably* continue into the **future**.
(2) Dudamel **has been** the music director of the Los Angeles Philharmonic **for several years.** **Since 2009** they've **supported** the Los Angeles Philharmonic.	With the present perfect, we often use **time signals** beginning with *for* and *since* to indicate an amount of time.
(3) I've been a fan of world music **for a long time.** **For 20 years** the band has had the same members.	To describe **how long** something has been occurring, use: *for* + **a length of time** Time signals with *for* can go at the beginning or end of a sentence.
(4) **Since last year** the band has played more than 100 concerts. I've been a fan of world music **since 1995.**	To describe when something **started**, use: *since* + **a point in time** Time signals with *since* can go at the beginning or end of a sentence.
(5) Abreu has directed *El Sistema* **since he started the program.** **Since I was a teenager,** I have been a fan of world music.	We also use *since* to form a **time clause.** Use a comma if the time clause is at the beginning.

Examples	Time signals with *for*	
I've lived here **for six months.** She's been a singer **for several years.** They've performed together **for a long time.**	five minutes three days a week	months several years a long time
Examples	**Time signals with *since***	
I haven't seen you **since 2009.** The song has been on the charts **since June.** We've known each other **since we were kids.**	yesterday last week I was a teenager	June high school she graduated from college

 ## Grammar Practice

MyEnglishLab

▶ Grammar Plus 2
Activities 1 and 2

A Complete the sentences. Use *for* or *since*.

1. Steve has been a musician _____ seven years.

2. He's won several awards _____ 2009.

3. We've practiced this song _____ two hours.

4. I haven't heard that song _____ I was in college.

5. I've had weekly guitar lessons _____ the past two years.

6. My favorite band has performed in four different cities _____ last week.

7. Maria has been in line for tickets _____ 45 minutes.

8. I have loved reggae music _____ I was in high school.

B Complete the sentences. Use your own information.

1. I have been in this class for _____.

I have been in this class since _____.

2. I have been awake today for _____.

I have been awake today since _____.

3. I have lived in my current home for _____.

I have lived in my current home since _____.

4. I have studied English for _____.

I have studied English since _____.

5. I have known my best friend for _____.

I have known my best friend since _____.

6. I have had this hairstyle for _____.

I have had this hairstyle since _____.

C Read the story. There are five mistakes. Find and correct the mistakes.

I've lived in Portland, Oregon, since one year. I like it here, but it rains a lot. My roommate Sheri has been here for she was a kid, so it's normal for her. It's mid-November now, and for early October it's rained every single day. I'm kind of sick of it. But Sheri says that she misses the rain when she visits hot, dry places like Arizona or New Mexico. In fact, she hasn't traveled anywhere since a long time because she likes it so much here. Everyone says that with time, I'll enjoy the weather. One thing I've already learned to like is coffee. I've had a cup every morning since the past few weeks. Actually, since the rain started, I haven't gone without! I think I'm becoming a local.

Listening

A BEFORE LISTENING Write the past participle forms.

1. cut _____   **6.** learn _____   **11.** refuse _____

2. deny _____   **7.** live _____   **12.** see _____

3. do _____   **8.** make _____   **13.** start _____

4. forget _____   **9.** plant _____   **14.** tell _____

5. kill _____   **10.** pollute _____

B 🎧 UNDERSTANDING MAIN IDEAS Listen to the song by West African band Koffi and the Awutes. Check (✓) the best title.

☐ "Where Have You Been?"   ☐ "Who Have You Spoken To?"

☐ "Look What We Have Done"   ☐ "I Haven't Made Up My Mind"

C 🎧 UNDERSTANDING DETAILS Listen again.
Write the past participles of the verbs from Part A.

Grandfather said to his grandchildren,

I've **1.** _____, and I've

2. _____.

I have **3.** _____ so much—much about life.

But there's one thing I will never forget.

Look at what we've **4.** _____ to our world.

Look at what we've done to our land.

Look at what we've done to the universe.

It's time to stop what we've done to the earth.

For so many years, we've **5.** _____ the trees.

Since I was born, we've **6.** _____ the animals.

For so many years, we've **7.** _____ the sea.

We have been blinded by our greed.

We have **8.** _____ what's plain to see.

We have **9.** _____ to admit the truth.

We have **10.** _____ to do what is right.

So now look at what we have done to the earth.

Have you already **11.** _____ up your mind?

Already **12.** _____ trees?

Already told the world to stop cutting trees?

Have you already **13.** _____ your friends to stop killing animals?

Have they all **14.** _____ cleaning the air?

Look at what she's done to our world.

Look at what he's done to our land.

Look at what they've done to humanity.

It's time to stop what we've done to our world.

Now let us stop what we've done to our world.

It's time to stop what we've done to the earth.

Speaking

A   Read the chart. Add three more things. Then walk around the classroom. Find someone who has done each thing. Write the person's name. Look at the model.

> *Have you ever bought a vinyl record?*

> *Yes, I have. I bought a used copy of . . .*

Have you ever . . .			
1. bought a vinyl record?		6. been on the radio or TV?	
2. been to a hip-hop concert?		7. given money to charity?	
3. sung in a karaoke bar?		8.	
4. gone to an outdoor concert?		9.	
5. performed in a band?		10.	

B   Share your information with the class.

Writing

A   Look at the timeline of the rock band U2. Think about which accomplishments are most impressive.

1976   The band forms in Dublin, Ireland. (It has the same four members today.)
1980   The band releases its first album.
1982   Lead singer Bono marries Alison Stewart. (They are still married.)
1988   The band wins its first Grammy Award. (They now have a total of 22.)
1992   The band releases the song "One," with proceeds going to AIDS research.
1999   Bono acts in his first movie. (His fourth and last performance was in 2007.)
2001   Bono and Alison have their fourth child. (The first was born in 1989.)
2005   The band becomes members of the Rock and Roll Hall of Fame.
2008   The band signs a 12-year deal with Live Nation, a concert events company.
2009   The band releases its 12th album.
2010   Eight of their songs make *Rolling Stone's* "The 500 Greatest Songs of All Time."
2013   The band releases its 13th album.

U2 lead singer Bono

B   Write about some of U2's accomplishments. Try to use the grammar from the chapter.

> The band U2 has been together for over 35 years. The same four members are still together. They haven't changed. The band has released 13 albums since 1980. Their lead singer Bono and his wife have been married for over 30 years. They have . . .

C   Exchange paragraphs with a partner. How are your paragraphs different?

Chapter 10   How Music Helps

Getting Started

A How do different types of music make you feel? Write a type of music, or the name of a particular song. Then compare with a partner.

Music that ...

relaxes me _____

energizes me _____

makes me sad _____

cheers me up _____

makes me angry _____

makes me miss the past _____

B Read the conversation. Why does Chloe feel so good?

BRYAN: You look happy.

CHLOE: I am. I've just come from the doctor's office, and I have a clean bill of health. It's funny. I haven't changed my diet recently, but I feel healthier. My doctor thinks it's because of music. I've had lots of stress lately.

BRYAN: Interesting.

CHLOE: I read an article about music and stress last month. After that I started listening to soft music after work. It's already made me feel better.

BRYAN: Has it helped you physically?

CHLOE: It has! It's already lowered my blood pressure. Have you ever used music to relax?

BRYAN: Actually, I have. Last night I played some heavy metal before bed.

CHLOE: Heavy metal? I'm not sure that's very relaxing.

BRYAN: Yeah, maybe not. Hey, speaking of health, have you had lunch yet?

CHLOE: No, not yet. Let's go somewhere.

C Look back at the conversation in Part B. Complete the tasks.

1. Read the words. Then find and underline them in the dialogue. Which verb form are they used with? Write *SP* (**simple past**) or *PP* (**present perfect**).

_____ just   _____ lately   _____ after work   _____ before bed

_____ recently   _____ last month   _____ already   _____ yet

2. When do we use these words with the present perfect? Match.

_____ **1. just**   **a.** With an action that has happened earlier than expected

_____ **2. already**   **b.** With an action that has not happened, but is expected to

_____ **3. yet**   **c.** With an action that has happened only a short time ago

Reading

A WARM-UP Work with a partner. Read this quote from cellist Yo-Yo Ma. He believes that music can heal. Do you agree? If so, how does it heal?

"Healing? I think that is what music is all about. Don't you?"

B SCANNING Scan the article for the meaning of "Broca's region." Why is this area important? Then go back and read the whole article.

THE HEALING POWER OF MUSIC

Music can relax us, excite us, and comfort us. Many of us start our days with music, listen to it at the gym, and even study to it. We are aware of the benefits of music, but did you know that music actually heals? These three patients have all benefited from music therapy.

■ Patient X has recently had a brain injury. He hasn't been able to recall memories from before the 1970s. Researchers have just found that music from this period helps him remember. When he talks about or plays music from the 1970s, he can talk about what he was doing then.

■ Patient Y has just suffered a stroke. She's lost the ability to speak. Therapists have discovered that her favorite music "reminds" her of forgotten words and grammar. She hasn't regained all her former abilities yet, but music has already helped her access some of these pathways for language.

■ Several years ago Patient Z lost his ability to recognize everyday objects, such as dishes and clothes. This made it impossible for him to do simple tasks. Doctors have found that he can perform daily routines if they're organized in song. They've already developed songs for bathing, dressing, and eating.

After years of research, one finding stands out. The areas of the brain involved in music are also active in processing language, memory, attention, and motor control. Music can activate these systems and drive patterns of interaction among them. For example, whether a person processes a challenging musical piece or a difficult grammar problem, the same part of the brain is activated. This area is called *Broca's region*. Scientists have speculated that this important part of the brain supports timing, sequencing, and the knowledge of rules that are necessary for music, speech, and movement.

Music is a complex auditory language. Research has shown that it's useful for retraining some injured brains. It has been the one thing that has truly helped some patients recover.

C UNDERSTANDING FACTS AND OPINIONS Write *F* for fact and *O* for opinion.

_____ **1.** Music can heal people.

_____ **2.** Patient Y will regain all her lost abilities.

_____ **3.** Patient Z's situation is the most serious.

_____ **4.** Broca's region is active when processing a grammar problem.

_____ **5.** Music is a kind of language.

_____ **6.** Music is the most useful tool for retraining all patients with injured brains.

MyEnglishLab

▶ Reading Comprehension

Grammar Focus 1 Present perfect: *Just, already, yet*

Examples	Language notes
(1) Research **has shown** that music is useful for retraining brains. Many patients **have credited** music therapy for their recovery.	We often use the **present perfect** in news reporting and academic writing to report on **recent developments and findings**.
(2) Roger has **just** arrived. What has the patient **already** learned? Have you eaten **yet**?	We often use the **indefinite time adverbs** *just*, *already*, and *yet* with the present perfect.
(3) She **has just suffered** a stroke. *(She suffered a stroke very recently.)* She **just suffered** a stroke. [simple past]	Use *just* to show that an action or situation happened only **a short time ago**. Use: subject + *have* + *just* + **past participle** *Note:* In American English, people commonly use *just* + the simple past.
(4) It **has already lowered** my blood pressure. *(It's only been one week.)* They **have left already**. *(It's early.)*	Use *already* to show that an action has happened previously, often **earlier than expected**. It's only used in the affirmative. Use: subject + *have* + *already* + **past participle** *Note:* *Already* can go at the end of a sentence, but it's less common.
(5) They **haven't arrived yet**. She **hasn't regained** her former abilities **yet**.	Use *not* with *yet* to show that an action has not happened but is **expected** to. In statements it's only used in the negative. Use: subject + *have* + *not* + **past participle** + *yet*
(6) **Q: Have** you **already eaten**? *(It's only 5:00 P.M.)* **A:** Yes, I have. / No, I haven't. **Q: Have** they **arrived yet**? **A:** Yes, they have. / No, they haven't. / Not yet.	In **questions**, use *already* to express **surprise**. Use *yet* to ask if something has happened. *Have* + subject + *already* + **past participle** *Have* + subject + **past participle** + *yet* For short answers, use **have / has**. A common negative **short answer** to questions with *yet* is *Not yet*.

	Affirmative statements	Negative statements	Yes / No questions
just	He **has just left**.	—	—
already	He **has already left**.	—	Has he **already left**?
yet	—	He **hasn't left yet**.	Has he **left yet**?

Grammar Practice

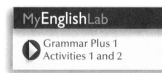

A Read the first sentence. Then write *T* for the true statements and *F* for the false statements.

1. She has already returned from the doctor's office.

_____ She came back from the doctor's office earlier than I expected.

2. Have they started the treatment yet?

_____ I'm sure they haven't started the treatment.

3. He's just graduated from college.

_____ He is going to graduate from college very soon.

4. We haven't been able to visit you yet.

_____ We plan to visit you in the future.

5. Has the movie started already?

_____ I am not surprised the movie has started.

6. Many people have already benefited from this research.

_____ The research is probably recent.

B Complete the conversations. Use the present perfect form of the verbs. Write the adverbs in the correct place.

1. A: I _____ (already / see) that movie. Can we watch something else?

   B: Sure. What looks good?

2. A: Do you want a sandwich?

   B: No, thanks. I _____ (just / eat).

3. A: Sorry, I'm late. Is Marco still here?

   B: No, he _____ (already / leave).

4. A: _____ you _____ (yet / be) to the market

    _____?

   B: No, not yet. Do you want something?

5. A: _____ the repairman _____

    _____ (yet / come)?

   B: Yes, he _____ (already / be) here.

6. A: I _____ (just / hear) the great news! _____ you

    _____ (already / tell) your parents?

   B: No, I _____ (yet / not / call) them _____. Can

    you believe it? I'm getting married!

C Craig has a busy weekend. Look at his "to do" list. Write sentences using _already_ and _not yet_.

1. _Craig has already bought groceries._

2. _____

3. _____

4. _____

5. _____

6. _____

To do
- ☑ buy groceries
- ☐ call Aunt Lucy
- ☐ clean the house
- ☑ do the laundry
- ☑ get a birthday present for Kim
- ☐ finish the report

Grammar Focus 2 Present perfect vs. simple past

Examples	Language notes
(1) Past ——— X|x ———→ Future (Present) I **have worked** at the travel agency for two years. *(I still work here.)* Past ——— X ———→ Future (Present) I **worked** at the travel agency for two years. *(I don't work there anymore.)*	The **present perfect** and **the simple past** both refer to past events, but **they treat the past in different ways.** Use the **present perfect** to talk about actions that began in the **past**, continue to the **present**, and may or may not continue into the **future**. Use the **simple past** to talk about **completed actions** that have no relationship to the present.
(2) She **has lost** the ability to speak. *(We don't know exactly when this happened, or when isn't important.)* She **lost** the ability to speak **in 2011**. *(The speaker knows the time it happened and chooses to include it in the sentence.)*	Use the present perfect to talk about actions that happened at an **unspecified** time in the past. Use the simple past to talk about actions that began and ended at a **specific** time in the past.
(3) Patient Y **has just suffered** a stroke. **Have** you **had** lunch **yet?** Patient X **has recently had** a brain injury. I played some heavy metal music **last night**. He published his research article **in 2009**. **When he was young**, Patient Z lost his ability to recognize everyday objects.	Common **time signals** with the **present perfect** include *ever, just, already, (not) yet, lately, recently, so far,* and *until now.* Common **time signals** with the **simple past** include *yesterday, last night, in 2010, (several years) ago, from _____ to _____,* and clauses beginning with *when . . . .*
(4) I **have been** at the doctor's office **for an hour**. *(I'm still here.)* I **have been** at the doctor's office **since 2:00**. *(I'm still here.)* I **was** at the doctor's office **for an hour**. *(I'm not there now.)* **Incorrect:** I ~~was~~ at the doctor's office **since 2:00**.	We often use **for** and *since* with the **present perfect** for actions that **continue in the present**. We can use **for** with the **simple past** for **completed actions**. We cannot use *since* with the simple past.

Grammar Practice

MyEnglishLab

Grammar Plus 2
Activities 1 and 2

A Complete the information. Use the present perfect or simple past form of the verbs.

When Jenna **1.** _____ (be) 10 years old, she **2.** _____ (take) piano

and violin lessons. She **3.** _____ (practice) hard, **4.** _____ (play)

in the school band, and **5.** _____ (perform) in music recitals. She

_____ always **6.** _____ (love) music and still does. But when she

7. _____ (be) in high school, she **8.** _____ (decide) she didn't want

a career in music. Instead she **9.** _____ (choose) nursing as her career path.

In 2003, Jenna **10.** _____ (begin) nursing school. Four years later she

11. _____ (graduate) with a B.S.N. degree and **12.** _____ (start)

working as a nurse in a large hospital. But lately Jenna **13.** _____ (start) to miss music.

She thinks it would be great to combine her love of music with her career in nursing.
She **14.** _____ (recently / start) playing the piano and violin again.

Last month Jenna **15.** _____ (read) an article about music therapy and right
away **16.** _____ (feel) this would be perfect for her. So a couple of weeks ago
she **17.** _____ (apply) for a M.S. degree program at a local university. She
18. _____ (not / hear / yet), but she's confident they will accept her. She
19. _____ (already / make) plans to reduce her hours at the hospital so she can
study and work at the same time.

B Read the article. There are eight mistakes. Find and correct the mistakes.

Research on the effects of music on learning was in progress for decades. When research on the Mozart Effect—the theory that listening to Mozart's music improves performance—has became popular in the late 1950s, parents everywhere have begun to expose their children to classical music. As with most theories, critics' opinions on the Mozart Effect have been controversial. But what wasn't controversial is that music education helps children in a variety of ways—including overall academic performance.

In 2010, a Canadian research group has compared two groups of children between the ages of four and six. In the study, one group took music lessons, and the other has had no musical instruction. The results showed that the children with musical instruction have performed above their peers in memory skills, math, and literacy. And according to the National Association for Music Education, students with a musical background who took the SAT scored higher than the non-musical students—56 points higher on the verbal portion and 39 points higher on the math portion. So far, research of this kind was very encouraging. In addition, other advocates of music instruction have recently suggested other non-musical benefits including greater self-esteem, mental concentration, and physical coordination.

Listening

A 🎧 UNDERSTANDING DETAILS Listen to the interview with Dr. Warrens. Then circle the correct answers.

1. What is asthma?
   a. It's a respiratory disease. People have no feeling in their chest.
   b. It's a respiratory disease. People have trouble breathing.

2. Is there a cure for asthma?
   a. Yes. Research has shown that music cures asthma.
   b. No. No one has discovered a cure for asthma yet.

3. Have hospitals ever used music to help people in pain?
   a. Yes. They've used music in this way for a long time.
   b. Yes. They have recently started using music in this way.

4. What is an inhaler?
   a. It's something someone with asthma uses. It helps the person relax with music.
   b. It's something someone with asthma uses. It helps the person breathe.

5. Why is playing a woodwind instrument helpful to someone with asthma?
   a. It helps the person stay calm.
   b. It helps control the person's breathing.

B 🎧 UNDERSTANDING INFERENCE Listen again. Check (✓) the information that you can infer.

☐ **1.** Dr. Warrens is on *Health Talk* to talk about her recent book.

☐ **2.** In the future, there will be more than 9 million children in the United States with asthma.

☐ **3.** An inhaler plus classical music can help many people with asthma.

☐ **4.** Playing a guitar might help someone with asthma.

C AFTER LISTENING Work with a partner. Discuss the questions.

• Do you know anyone with asthma? How does the person treat it?
• What else besides music could help people with asthma relax?
• How do you think woodwind instruments help people?
• Would you ever consider music therapy? Why or why not?

Speaking

A Complete the questions. Use the past participle of the verbs and your own ideas.

1. Have you _____ (speak) to _____ today?
   name of person

2. Have you _____ (see) the movie _____?
   name of new movies

3. Have you _____ (have) _____ today?
   meal

4. Have you _____ (play) _____?
   name of new video game

5. Have you _____ (hear) the song _____?
   name of new song

6. Have you _____ (watch) _____?
   name of new TV show

B Work with a partner. Take turns asking your questions from Part A. Include in your answers *just*, *already*, and *(not) yet*. Add additional information. Look at the model.

> Have you spoken to Jamie today?

> Not yet. I'll probably talk to her tonight.

Writing

A Think of a goal or something you are trying to achieve. Use one of the ideas in the list or think of your own. Think about these questions: What steps have you already taken to achieve your goal? What haven't you done yet?

Goals: find a job   improve grades   meet new people

            get into shape   learn a new skill   save money

B Write about your goal and the steps involved in reaching it. Try to use the grammar from the chapter.

> I have always wanted to buy a car. I have just gotten a part-time job in order to save some money. I haven't saved very much yet, but I have saved about $400 so far. As a hobby, I make jewelry. Last month I sold some pieces and made an extra $100.

C Share your writing with a partner. Ask and answer follow-up questions.

> Have you decided on the type of car yet?

> No, not yet. I'm still looking.

Grammar Summary

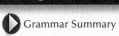

We use the **present perfect** in a variety of circumstances, including the following:

Actions that happened at an unspecified time in the past	Many musicians **have played** at the festival.
Experiences	He **has been** to Europe. He **hasn't been** to Africa.
Single actions in the past that have an impact on the present	I **have lost** my concert ticket. (*I can't attend the show.*)
Actions that began in the past and continue to the present, and will *probably* continue into the future. Notice the use of *for* and *since*.	She **has lived** in the same house <u>for a long time</u>. [*for* + length of time] She **has lived** in the same house <u>since 1990</u>. [*since* + point in time] She **has lived** in the same house <u>since she was a girl</u>. [*since* + past time clause]
Recent developments and findings	There **has been** a huge increase in the number of music downloads.

To form the present perfect tense, use *have* or *has* + the past participle of a verb. We often contract subject pronouns with *have* or *has* in statements.

Affirmative statements	Negative statements	Contractions
I**'ve eaten** breakfast. You**'ve lived** in New York. He**'s texted** me twice. She**'s told** the truth. It**'s been** a bad day. We**'ve read** the book. They**'ve learned** piano.	I **haven't eaten** lunch. You **haven't lived** in Chicago. He **hasn't called** me. She **hasn't told** a lie. It **hasn't been** a good day. We **haven't seen** the movie. They **haven't learned** violin.	I've = I have you've = you have he's = he has she's = she has it's = it has we've = we have they've = they have
Questions	**Short answers**	
Have you ever **been** to Brazil? **Has** she **seen** the beach? **Who have** you **traveled** with? **What** languages **have** you **studied**?	Yes, I **have**. / No, I **haven't**. Yes, she **has**. / No she **hasn't**. Friends. English and French.	

We often use the **indefinite time adverbs** *just*, *already*, and *yet* with the present perfect. Use *just* with an action that has happened very recently, *already* with an action that has happened previously, often earlier than expected; and *yet* with an action that is expected to happen.

Statements	Questions and short answers
I **have just left** the concert. I **have already left** the concert. I **haven't left** the concert **yet**.	**Q:** Have you **already** left? **A:** Yes, I have. / No, I haven't. **Q:** Have you left **yet**? **A:** Yes, I have. / Not yet.

We use the **present perfect** to talk about past events and experiences that connect to the present and possibly the future, and use the **simple past** to talk about past actions that have no relationship to the present. **Time signals** can provide additional clues. Common time signals with the **present perfect** include *ever*, *just*, *already*, *(not) yet*, *lately*, *recently*, *so far*, and *until now*. Common time expressions with the **simple past** include *yesterday*, *last year*, *in 2010*, *ago*, *from . . . to . . .* and clauses beginning with *when . . . .*

Present perfect vs. simple past, with time expressions	
He **has recently been** to Asia. (*He has traveled to Asia—when isn't important.*)	He **went** to Asia **last year**. (*He traveled to Asia last year—we know when it happened.*)

Self-Assessment

A (5 points) Read each sentence. Then write a sentence with the same meaning. Use the words.

1. I got here a minute ago. (just / arrive) _____

2. Pam had lunch earlier than expected. (already / eat) _____

3. We got here three hours ago. It's 4:00 now. (since / be) _____

4. Frank lived in Dallas from March 2008 to March 2010. (for / live) _____

5. Mike isn't here, but I'm expecting him. (yet / come) _____

B (8 points) Which sentences have mistakes? Write *M* (mistake) or *NM* (no mistake). Then rewrite the incorrect sentences.

_____ 1. I just have gotten your message. _____

_____ 2. We haven't eaten yet dinner. _____

_____ 3. Have you finished your homework already? _____

_____ 4. Sherry didn't come yet home from class. _____

_____ 5. Where has your sister been? _____

_____ 6. I've graduated six months ago. _____

_____ 7. Wendy has lived in Sydney for a year. _____

_____ 8. Hank played the guitar since he was eight. _____

C (12 points) Complete the conversation. Use the simple past or present perfect form of the verbs.

A: 1. _____ you ever _____ (listen) to classical music?

B: Of course. I mean, I 2. _____ (listen) to CDs, but I
3. _____ (never / be) to a live concert.

A: 4. _____ you _____ (use) classical music to help you study?

B: To study? No.

A: Well, research 5. _____ (show) that it's really useful. It's really relaxing, and it can help some people with their grades. I 6. _____ (try) it last night, and today I 7. _____ (get) an A on my history test.

B: Really? Where 8. _____ you _____ (read) this research?

A: In an article. I 9. _____ (find) it at the library. I'll give it to you. There 10. _____ (be) a lot of research on this topic lately.

B: Interesting. Say, 11. _____ you _____ (have) lunch yet? I'm starving.

A: Yeah, sorry. I 12. _____ already _____ (eat).

Unit Project: Awareness raising

A Many singers and bands have started charities or foundations. Work with a partner. Give a presentation on a charity or foundation. Follow the steps.

1. Choose a charity or foundation from the list, or think of your own.

Jon Bon Jovi   **Madonna**   **Mariah Carey**   **Ricky Martin**

- Jon Bon Jovi - The Jon Bon Jovi Soul Foundation
- Madonna - Raising Malawi
- The Dave Matthews Band - Bama Works Fund
- Britney Spears - Britney Spears Foundation
- Jack Johnson - Johnson Ohana Charitable Foundation
- Incubus - Make Yourself Foundation
- Jennifer Lopez - The Maribel Foundation
- Mariah Carey - Camp Mariah
- Sting - The Rainforest Foundation
- Ricky Martin - Ricky Martin Foundation

2. Research the charity or foundation. Use the questions to help you.

- What is the goal of the foundation? What exactly does it do?
- When did . . . found it? Why?
- How much money has . . . raised?
- How much of the money goes to the foundation?
- What has the foundation achieved?
- Has there been any criticism of the foundation?
- How involved is . . . ?
- What is your opinion of the musician and the charity?

3. Find photos, songs, or other items to use in your presentation. Then prepare your presentation. Decide how you will divide up the presentation with your partner.

B Give your presentation to the class. Answer any questions. Look at the model.

> The goal of Camp Mariah is for young people in cities to explore educational and career options. They do this while they have fun at a summer camp. Many of these people have never been to a summer camp, so it's something new and exciting for them.

> The camp was founded in 1994. It has been very popular since then. It has helped hundreds of young people. They . . .

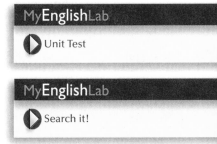

MyEnglishLab
▶ Unit Test

MyEnglishLab
▶ Search it!

Education

CHAPTER 11   Today's Classrooms

A What do you remember about your first days of school? What concerns did you have? What about your parents?

B Read the conversation. Who are they? What are their concerns?

> SAMANTHA: Hey, Charles! Can you believe it's September and the first day of school already? Is Nina excited?
>
> CHARLES: All summer she talked about starting sixth grade at Lincoln Middle School! The school looks good, including this new gym. But I'm worried about some things.
>
> SAMANTHA: I'm concerned, too. You know, Brendan is in seventh, and his classes are huge.
>
> CHARLES: I know! There are just too many kids in the classes.
>
> SAMANTHA: Yeah—and not enough books for all of them.
>
> CHARLES: It seems like the kids just don't get enough attention in school. And often they have too much homework!
>
> SAMANTHA: I know. And I don't always have enough time to help. I really wish I had time.
>
> CHARLES: I'm with you. We need more teachers.
>
> SAMANTHA: Right! I know teachers often don't make enough money, but they have great schedules. Hey—weren't you a teacher? How about volunteering at Lincoln? . . .

C Look back at the conversation in Part B. Complete the tasks.

1. **Count nouns** are common nouns that have singular and plural forms, and can be counted (*day – days, school – schools, child – children*). Circle the plural count nouns.
2. **Noncount nouns** have only one form and cannot be counted (*time, energy, money*). Underline the noncount nouns.
3. The **quantifiers** *many*, *much*, and *enough* tell about amounts and modify nouns. Complete the chart with the examples.

	Used with count nouns	Used with noncount nouns
many	*kids*	
much		
enough		

4. Which sentence **expresses desire** for a specific change?

_____

Reading

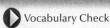
A WARM-UP Read the quotation. What does it mean? Discuss with a partner.

"A teacher affects eternity; he can never tell where his influence stops."

— *Henry B. Adams, novelist and academic*

B SKIMMING Skim the editorial. Circle the main idea. Then go back and read the article again.

a. There are many problems but also many possible solutions.
b. Not enough teachers are available these days.
c. There are too many students in the classes.

Our Current Education Situation

"I wish things were different!" Public school teachers around the globe have made this statement many times. Their first wish? That all students stayed in school. They also wish they had more classrooms, and that each one came with up-to-date technology. Although devoted, motivated, and eager to teach, teachers often face too many obstacles—things that prevent them from creating an adequate learning environment. There's been too much talk and not enough action. How can we, members of the community, help? Is it possible for us to make positive changes to our current educational systems? Of course! But first, we need to determine what the problems are. Here's a starter list:

Overcrowded classrooms There are too many students in each classroom. In many places, there aren't enough chairs and desks to go around—sometimes because there's not much room.
School dropouts Because of the current economic situation, many children are forced to leave school and go to work at a young age.
Shortage of supplies Schools around the globe don't have enough supplies. Many schools lack the basics: books, writing utensils, whiteboards, and more.
Lack of technology Though we've come a long way, we need more computers and technological training for our children.
Lack of training for teachers We have enough teachers; we just don't have enough *educated* teachers. Also, teachers need ongoing education and support for both teaching and classroom management, including discipline.
Lack of funding in general Basically, more money is needed to improve every aspect of education.

In order to solve these problems, we need community, business, and family involvement. Companies, why not donate funds for buying computers? We can also target capable local people who may be interested in the improvement of our schools. Families, how about getting involved?

Yes, we global citizens wish things were different. It's time to look forward. We need to find the way to solve our many problems with the educational system, and make positive and long-lasting changes.

C UNDERSTANDING PROBLEMS AND SOLUTIONS Read the sentences. Does the sentence state a problem (P) or a solution (S)? Write *P* or *S*.

_____ **1.** Many obstacles prevent teachers from creating a good learning environment.

_____ **2.** Classrooms have too many students in them.

_____ **3.** Many children drop out of school and go to work.

_____ **4.** Teachers can be trained to deal with discipline problems.

_____ **5.** Local businesses can donate funds for computers.

Grammar Focus 1 Count and noncount nouns

Examples	Language notes
(1) Molly is an **instructor**. [singular] The **parents** were supportive. [plural]	**Count nouns** are things that can be counted individually. They can be **singular** or **plural**.
(2) He is **a student**. I work in **this office**. Where is **your school?** **The cafeteria <u>is</u>** small.	**Singular count nouns** • often follow **determiners** such as *a*, *an*, and *the*; singular demonstrative adjectives (*this, that*); and possessive adjectives (*my, your, her,* etc.). • take a <u>**singular form verb**</u> when the subject. *Note:* See Chapter 12 for more about possessive adjectives.
(3) **Some students** don't have desks. How old are **these computers?** **Their stories** were interesting. **Universities** charge out-of-state students more. **The hallways <u>are</u>** dark.	**Plural count nouns** • usually end in **-s**. • often follow **determiners** such as *the* and *some*; plural demonstrative adjectives (*these, those*); and possessive adjectives. • take **no determiner** (∅) when used in generalizations. • take a <u>**plural form verb**</u> when the subject.
(4) **Education** is important. **The information** is available to all. **That homework** was difficult. I need **help**. [generalization] **Our training <u>begins</u>** on Tuesday. *Incorrect:* Our training ~~begin~~ on Tuesday.	**Noncount nouns** are things that cannot be counted individually. They • have only **one form**. • can follow *the*, singular demonstrative adjectives, and possessive adjectives. • take **no determiner** (∅) when used in generalizations. • take a <u>**singular form verb**</u> when the subject.
(5) You need to improve your **attitude**. She's interested in **geology**. A teacher must earn the students' **respect**. Schoolchildren shouldn't have access to **candy**. The **team** has a new coach. The **weather** has been really nice!	**Noncount nouns** can be identified by **category**. • **abstractions**: *attitude, education* • **areas of study**: *geology, math* • **emotions**: *respect, love* • **masses** (foods, drinks): *candy, soda* • **groups of people and things**: *team, money* • **natural events and things**: *weather, skin*

Count nouns	Noncount nouns
student(s), teacher(s), book(s), school(s)	education, work, technology, information

See Appendix Q on page A-8 for more count and noncount nouns.

Grammar Practice

A What kind of noun is each word? Write *SC* for singular count nouns, *PC* for plural count nouns, or *NC* for noncount nouns.

_____ 1. problems   _____ 8. oxygen   _____ 15. children

_____ 2. money   _____ 9. ocean   _____ 16. rain

_____ 3. computer   _____ 10. assignments   _____ 17. salt

_____ 4. information   _____ 11. work   _____ 18. news

_____ 5. desks   _____ 12. idea   _____ 19. employees

_____ 6. teacher   _____ 13. people   _____ 20. mail

_____ 7. bread   _____ 14. knowledge

B Circle the correct words.

1. Around the world, **the / Ø** students appreciate good teachers.

2. Listen, everyone. Foster has **a / some** great idea!

3. That assignment **was / were** easy.

4. I bought **this / these** backpack last fall.

5. Her classes **seem / seems** difficult.

6. They told us **a / some** stories over lunch.

7. Do you need **help / helps**?

8. His attitude **is / are** very good.

9. Can I give you **an / my** advice?

10. We don't like **a / Ø** math.

Students in Egypt

C Find and correct the mistake in each sentence.

1. Do you understand this homeworks?

2. I went to movie with friends last night. It was a comedy.

3. Some person think it's rude to text in class.

4. A history is one of my favorite subjects.

5. Some dormitories allow the animals.

6. Were that information helpful?

Grammar Focus 2 Quantifiers

Examples	Language notes
(1) We have **many issues** to resolve. There weren't **many students** at that school. **Are there many students** in your class? **How many parents** attended the meeting?	Use the quantifier *many* with **plural count nouns** in: • affirmative statements • negative statements • *yes / no* questions • *How . . . ?* questions
(2) We don't have **much time**. **Do** those teachers have **much training**? **How much time** do you need? There's still **much work** to be done. We have **a lot of homework**.	Use the quantifier *much* with **noncount nouns** in: • negative statements • *yes / no* questions • *How . . . ?* questions **Note:** *Much* is very formal in affirmative statements. We commonly use **a lot of**.
(3) There are **too many students** in the classroom, and teachers give students **too much homework**.	**Too many / too much** means more than necessary. Often the meaning is negative.
(4) There are **enough computers** for everyone. There aren't **enough computers** here. We have **enough homework** already! You don't have **enough homework**. Did we order **enough books**? Did you have **enough time**?	Use the quantifier *enough* in: • affirmative and negative statements with **plural count nouns** • affirmative and negative statements with **noncount nouns** • *yes / no* questions with *both* **plural count nouns** and **noncount nouns**
(5) There isn't **enough interest** in computer training, and there aren't **enough instructors** anyway.	**Not enough** means less than needed.

Quantifiers with count nouns	Quantifiers with noncount nouns
Do you have **many** books to work with? I told her that **too many** times! There are **not enough** pens.	How **much** homework do you have? She doesn't have **too much** time today. He had **enough** training to do the job.

Grammar Practice

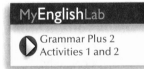
MyEnglishLab

▶ Grammar Plus 2
Activities 1 and 2

A Circle the correct words.

1. Try not to make **too many / too much** noise.

2. **How much / How many** time do they want?

3. I don't like studying in Boston. There are **too many / too much** tourists.

4. I want to take classes there, but it costs **much of / a lot of** money.

5. There are **many / much** problems at that school.

6. Are there **enough / too much** computers in your classroom?

7. Come on! We don't have **many / much** time.

8. Is **too much / many** training possible?

B Complete the speech by Principal King to his faculty. Use *too many*, *too much*, *enough*, or *not enough*.

Good morning, faculty! Welcome back to school. We need to talk about four key issues as we begin the new school year.

There are **1.** _____ students in the hall after the bell rings. They have **2.** _____ time to get to class in a timely manner—they're just fooling around.

When I walk by some classrooms, I hear way **3.** _____ silence! There should be more discussion. I know your students have a lot to say—they are always complaining that there isn't **4.** _____ time to discuss important issues! Teachers, use that energy!

If you think that there are **5.** _____ students in your classroom, let's discuss it. I want to work with you so that the class size is fair. Are you giving each student **6.** _____ attention?

Finally, remember that balance is key. Homework is important, but **7.** _____ homework can be counterproductive. Also, if you are spending **8.** _____ hours grading every weekend, let's talk.

C Match the sentence parts.

A	B
_____ **1.** Does he have too many	**a.** homework?
_____ **2.** How much	**b.** classes this semester?
_____ **3.** You look tired. Did you get enough	**c.** math tutors available.
_____ **4.** Is $20 too much	**d.** sleep?
_____ **5.** How many	**e.** students have laptops?
_____ **6.** There aren't enough	**f.** money for a used textbook?
_____ **7.** Do your teachers give a lot of	**g.** homework do you have?

Grammar Focus 3 Desires: Expressions with *wish*

Examples	Language notes
(1) She **wishes** (that) she had time to study. I **wish** (that) we were at the same school.	We use *wish* to talk about things that we want to be different.
(2) Teachers **wish** <u>(that) they had smaller classes</u>.	To form wish statements, use: subject + *wish* + <u>noun clause</u> *Note:* The *that* at the start of noun clauses is often dropped.
(3) I **wish** <u>I **earned** a lot of money</u>. *(I don't earn a lot now.)* She **wishes** <u>she **were** with him</u>. *(But she's not.)* We **wish** <u>we **were studying** in college now</u>. *(Instead, we're working now.)*	To express desire about a **present** situation, use: subject + *wish* + **simple past** subject + *wish* + **past progressive** with *were* *Note:* In <u>noun clauses with *be*</u>, use *were*, not *was*.
(4) I **wish** <u>it **weren't** raining</u>. *(But it is.)*	Add *not* to make the statement negative.
(5) I **wish** the train **left** at noon. *(But it leaves at 1:00.)*	As we saw in Unit 4, we can use various forms to talk about the future. For **future scheduled events**, use: subject + *wish* + **simple past**
(6) I **wish** she **weren't leaving** tomorrow! *(She's leaving tomorrow.)* I **wish** we **were going to go** to the same school next year. *(We are going to different schools.)* We **wish** Dale **would come** to the party. *(He doesn't want to.)*	For **future plans and commitments**, use: subject + *wish* + **past progressive** with *were* subject + *wish* + **were going to** + base verb subject + *wish* + **would** + base verb *Note:* Here *would* is the past form of *will*.
(7) She **wishes** her school **could participate** in the summer conference. *(It can't.)*	For **future possibility**, use: subject + *wish* + **could** + base verb *Note:* Here *could* is the past form of *can*.
(8) He wishes he had more time to read **these days**. *(He doesn't have time to read now.)* They wish they were studying at East Academy **next year**. *(They're going to study at Northfield next year.)*	Add **time signals** to clarify *when*. Examples include *these days, next year, right now, soon,* etc.

Questions with *wish*	
present situations	future situations
Does he **wish** he **were** in school? **Don't** you **wish** you **had** the summer off? **Do** they **wish** they **were living** here?	**Do** they **wish** the bus **left** later this morning? **Does** he **wish** he **were graduating** in the spring? **Do** they **wish** the game **were going to be** on Sunday? **Don't** you **wish** it **would snow** tomorrow? **Does** she **wish** she **could go** to the party?

Grammar Practice

A Complete the sentences. Use the correct form of words. Sometimes more than one correct answer is possible.

1. I _____ (wish / I / go) to the beach tomorrow.

2. He _____ (wish / he / be) tall and thin.

3. We _____ (wish / we / travel) together next month.

4. My mother _____ (wish / I / not / study) abroad next semester.

5. The community _____ (wish / all students / have) up-to-date technology.

B Look at the pictures. Complete the wishes. Add time expressions when possible.

There aren't computers for all the students.

1. She wishes *there were computers for all the students this year* _____.

We don't have an umbrella!

2. They wish _____.

She is talking loudly.

3. We wish _____.

I can't eat ice cream.

4. She wishes _____.

C What things do you wish were different now? In the future? Write a list of wishes. Then compare with a partner.

NOW	FUTURE
I wish I were an excellent singer.	
I wish it weren't raining.	

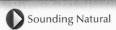
Speaking

A Work with a partner. What was school like for you? What about your parents? Ask about the topics in the list below. Use *many* and *much*. Look at the model.

- Technology
- Discipline
- International students
- Parental involvement
- Dropouts
- Teachers with professional training
- Homework
- Bilingual classes
- (Your idea) _____

> Was there much technology when you were a student in high school?

> No, there wasn't much. For example, we didn't have computers. But teachers did use things like slide projectors to show pictures.

B Discuss the results with the class.

Listening

A 🎧 UNDERSTANDING MAIN IDEAS Many schools have an organization called the PTA (Parent-Teacher Association). Members often discuss problems and solutions at PTA meetings. Listen to the meeting. Check (✓) the things the people wish for.

☐ a bowling league   ☐ budget cuts   ☐ smaller classrooms

☐ more time with their kids   ☐ computers, books, school supplies   ☐ more space

B 🎧 UNDERSTANDING DETAILS Listen again. Circle the correct answers.

1. How would an after-school bowling league help?
   a. It would keep students active after school.
   b. Students could earn extra money.

2. Why are students in Mrs. Lewis's class sitting on the floor?
   a. Because there are too many students in one room.
   b. Because they are being punished.

3. What is an example of a task a mentor might do?
   a. Help a student with homework.
   b. Help build a new classroom.

4. Why is the local lumber company mentioned?
   a. It could donate building supplies.
   b. It could provide construction workers.

C AFTER LISTENING What changes are needed at your school? With a partner talk about the things you wish were different. Look at the model.

> I wish the school had a nice coffee bar.

> I agree. I wish we were sitting in it right now!

Writing

MyEnglishLab
▶ Linking Grammar to Writing

A Read the problems in the list. Circle the problems in your local schools. Add your own ideas. What are some solutions?

not enough respect for teachers	not enough funding for sports
not enough pay for teachers	too many students in each classroom
too much tardiness	not enough activities

B Read the message board posting. Then write a message about one of the issues from Part A. Try to use the grammar from the chapter.

> I've been thinking about the teens in my community. We have too many kids and not enough jobs! I wish there were a kind of job search center to help them find work. I also wish we had a training program to help them develop some job skills.

C Share your writing in a small group. What advice do you have for your classmates?

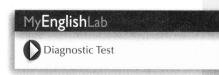
MyEnglishLab
▶ Diagnostic Test

CHAPTER 12 Mission Possible!

Getting Started

A Do you set personal goals? What are they like? How do you achieve your goals? Check (✓) the statements that are true for you. Compare answers with a partner.

☐ I make a list of goals each day. It helps me plan my day.

☐ I have things I want to achieve over the next few years.

☐ I discuss my goals with my friends, parents, or teachers.

☐ I've had the same goals since I was six years old.

☐ I prefer not to set goals—I just take things as they come.

B Read about the students' goals. Are their goals realistic? Discuss them with a partner.

Here we are, the class of 2012! All of us just graduated from high school! Most of us will go to college. Our goal? To be successful at our jobs—and happy in our lives! Some of us, like David and Sue, want to be businesspeople. Their dream is to work in big, powerful offices. A few of us—like Jon and Lisa—want to work in jobs that help people. Solving problems is important to them. TJ's dream is to become a rock star—performing on stage is fun for her! We've also known Mike's dream forever. He's always loved the kitchen, so his dream of being a chef is no surprise! I love sports— but becoming a professional athlete probably isn't a reality for me. So my goal is to consider all the options.

C Look back at Parts A and B. Complete the tasks.

1. **Subject pronouns** (*I, you, she, he, it, we, they*) and **object pronouns** (*me, you, her, him, it, us, them*) take the place of nouns. Underline the examples in Parts A and B. What part of speech follows the subject pronouns? _____ What part of speech often comes before the object pronouns? _____

2. **Possessive adjectives** (*my, your, her, his, its, our, their*) show ownership. Circle the examples in Parts A and B. What part of speech do possessive adjectives modify? _____

3. As we saw in Chapter 11, **quantifiers** describe amounts. They answer the questions *How many?* and *How much?* Underline the quantifiers in Part B.

Reading

A WARM-UP What kinds of people set goals? What kinds of people don't care about goals? Discuss your ideas with a partner.

B SCANNING Scan the article for the following quotations. Match. Then go back and read the whole article.

Quotations	Speakers
_____ 1. "I have always wanted to be a rock star."	**a.** Professor Valerie Kenny
_____ 2. "My goal is to help students identify theirs."	**b.** Student Kevin McCann
_____ 3. "Life shapes me, not the other way around."	**c.** Psychologist Rafael Cardenas
_____ 4. "There's no 'one-size fits all' when it comes to goal-setting."	**d.** Sculptor Mee Chang

Goals for all and all for goals?

We know that establishing long- and short-term objectives is important. Whether you're a student, a small business owner, or a retiree, goal-setting is a good practice. But are we all goal setters?

Valerie Kenny, a Canadian sociology professor, uses the 2007 U.S. movie *Bucket List* to inspire students to do their own goal setting. The movie is about the adventures of two older men trying to fulfill their lifelong goals.

"All of my students are interested in setting at least some goals," Professor Kenny says. "Most claim they'd like to be successful. Some say they want to have families. All of them say that they want to enjoy life."

She says it's part of her responsibility to help her students set objectives for themselves "*My* goal," she says, "is to help students identify *theirs*."

Many researchers agree that, in fact, most of us are goal setters. We decide what we want to achieve in our lives and then work toward the attainment of those goals. What we do with our lists, however, varies from person to person.

"Mine are all in my head," says 18-year-old student Kevin McCann about his personal goals. "But everyone who knows me knows my dreams. I have always wanted to be a rock star. I'm confident that I'll achieve that goal and many more!"

Psychologist Rafael Cardenas says that being positive is the key. "The point of goal-setting," he says, "is to bridge the gap from where you are to where you want to be." Dr. Cardenas adds, "However, some of us may not feel the need to do this kind of exercise . . . and that's OK. There's no 'one-size-fits-all' when it comes to goal-setting."

For example, take the case of Mee Chang. This 54-year-old sculptor claims she's never had a list for herself. And mostly likely, she will never make one. As she puts it, "Life shapes me, not the other way around."

C UNDERSTANDING DETAILS Write *T* for the true statements and *F* for the false statements.

_____ 1. Establishing long-term objectives is only important for business owners.

_____ 2. Professor Valerie Kenny's goal is to tell students about her goals.

_____ 3. Student Kevin McCann writes his goals in a special notebook.

_____ 4. Dr. Rafael Cardenas says that being positive is very important.

_____ 5. Sculptor Mee Chang uses goals to shape her life.

Grammar Focus 1 Pronouns

Examples	Language notes
(1) **Jonathan** wants to be a nurse. [proper noun] **He** wants to be a nurse. [subject pronoun]	**Subject pronouns** *(I, you, he, she, it, we, they)* replace nouns and proper nouns as the subject of a sentence. They come before the verb.
(2) **Jonathan and I** want to help others. *Incorrect: ~~I and Jonathan~~* want to help others.	When you use subject pronouns to talk about yourself and others, **put others first**.
(3) Ryan helped **the girl**. [object] Ryan helped **her**. [object pronoun]	**Object pronouns** *(me, you, him, her, it, us, them)* replace the direct object of a verb. They come after the verb.
(4) <u>Give **me** the book</u> please! Teachers know what's best <u>for **us**</u> in school.	We also use **object pronouns** as **indirect objects** and as **objects of prepositions**.
(5) The **professor's class** is in that building. [possessive noun] **His class** is in that building. [possessive adjective] **My goal** is to graduate. **My goals** are to graduate and get a job.	We use **possessive adjectives** *(my, your, his, her, its, our, their)* to modify nouns. They show *who* owns or possesses something (noun). They come before the noun. *Note:* Possessive adjectives have only one form; they do not change with the subject.
(6) **My class** is filled with students! [possessive adjective + noun] **Mine** is filled with students! [possessive pronoun]	**Possessive pronouns** *(mine, yours, his, hers, its, ours, theirs)* also show ownership. They perform the same function as a possessive adjective + a noun.
(7) **Who** is going to the local college? **Who(m)** did you hire for that position?	To ask about people, use **who**. *Note: Whom* is an object pronoun and is considered very formal.
(8) **Q: Whose** bag is that? **A:** It's **my** bag. / It's **mine**. / **Mine**.	To ask about ownership, use **whose**. For **short answers**, use possessive adjectives with nouns, or possessive pronouns.
(9) **You're** a good student. [subject pronoun + *be*] What's **your** name? [possessive adjective] **It's** been hot. [subject pronoun + *has*] **It's** nice today. [subject pronoun + *is*] KU is a good school. I like **its** campus. [possessive adjective]	Be careful! It's easy to confuse **similar-sounding forms**: *you're = your; it's = its; they're = their = there; who's = whose.*

Subject pronoun	Object pronoun	Possessive adjective	Possessive pronoun
I	me	my	mine
you	you	your	yours
he	him	his	his
she	her	her	hers
it	it	its	its
we	us	our	ours
they	them	their	theirs

Grammar Practice

A Complete the sentences. Use subject and object pronouns.

1. Who's that guy over there? Why weren't we introduced to _____?

2. Where's Ms. James? I have to talk to _____ about my academic goals.

3. You can have my books from last semester. I don't need _____.

4. Maria's goal is to graduate this year, but _____ may need more time.

5. Frida can't find her keys. Where are _____?

6. They're going to visit the school. You can go with _____.

7. She just got the new computer she wanted! Have you seen _____?

8. We're going to talk to the director. Do you want to come with _____?

B Circle the correct words.

1. **A:** Is **their / theirs** class on the second floor?

   B: No, **their / theirs** is on the third floor. **Our / Ours** is on the second!

2. **A:** **Your / Yours** teacher seems really nice.

   B: She is. And **her / hers** classes are really interesting.

3. **A:** Is that **your / yours** book over there?

   B: No, it's **he's / his**. I've got **my / mine**.

4. **A:** What time is **their / there** school board meeting?

   B: **Its / It's** at 8:00. But we start **our / ours** at 9:00.

C Find and correct 10 mistakes in the email.

Hi Mom and Dad,

Greetings from New York! I feel like me life has changed completely since I left Belarus. School has been very interesting so far. My teachers are nice, though their accents are really different. Their are from all over the States. Our classes are fun, but sometimes we have too much homework! I try to read the newspaper every day, but the vocabulary is really difficult. Still, it gives we the chance to learn new words, grammar, and, of course, the latest news. The other students in the class are helpful. Their from all over the world, and they're situations are all different. I enjoy talking with they. Angelo, my new friend from Italy, has helped me a lot. In our free time, Angelo and me go to New York City together. The family I'm living with is also very nice. They always say, "Our house is you're house!" They make I feel at home. (But mom, you're cooking is still the best!)

Love, Alex

Grammar Focus 2 More quantifiers

Examples	Language notes
(1) I think it's great to have **several** <u>goals</u>! **All** <u>my classmates</u> plan to graduate next year.	As we saw in Unit 6, **quantifiers** describe the **amount** of something.
(2) **Each** <u>student</u> in my class sets personal goals. **Each** chooses his or her own goals.	*Each* emphasizes individuality. Use **each** before <u>singular count nouns</u>. We can also use *each* alone, as a pronoun.
(3) **Every** <u>student</u> in the school sets personal goals. <u>Almost</u> **every** student was prepared.	*Every* emphasizes completeness. We use **every** before <u>singular count nouns</u>. We also use **every** after <u>adverbs</u> (*almost, nearly, practically*, etc.).
(4) **Most** <u>teachers</u> assign homework. **All** <u>homework</u> must be completed! Here are **some** <u>pens</u>. **Q:** Do we have **any** <u>pens</u>? **A:** No. And we don't have **any** <u>paper</u>. There are**n't any** <u>chips</u>, and there's **no** <u>time</u> to buy some.	Use **all, most, a lot of, lots of, plenty of, some, (not) any**, and **no** before <u>plural count nouns</u> and <u>noncount nouns</u>. • Use **some** only in affirmative statements. • Use **any** only in questions and negative statements. • We can use **not any** or **no** with *There is / are*.
(5) **Several** <u>teachers</u> were at the meeting. **Both** <u>parents</u> say they like the school.	Use the quantifiers *(not) many, several, a couple of, both*, and *a few* before <u>plural count nouns</u> only.
(6) James and Luli are good students. **Both** <u>work</u> hard. **Each** <u>has</u> many challenges to overcome.	*Both* implies two and uses the <u>third person plural</u>. *Each* refers to one, but implies a total of two (or more), and uses the <u>third person singular</u>.
(7) He gives students **a great deal of** <u>homework</u>, but they get **a little** <u>class</u> time to work on it.	Use *a great deal of* and *a little* before <u>noncount nouns</u> only.
(8) They received **a little** <u>help</u> from her. She contributed **a few** <u>ideas</u>. They received **little** <u>help</u> from her. She contributed **few** <u>ideas</u>.	Use *a little* and *a few* in neutral or positive statements. Use *little* and *few* to mean "not enough."
(9) **Many** trees change colors in the fall. **Most** people live in cities. **All** books are expensive. **Few** schools have enough money.	We often use quantifiers to make **generalizations**.
(10) **Many** <u>of those trees</u> are evergreens. **Most** <u>of my friends</u> live in the city. **All** <u>of their books</u> are expensive.	Many **quantifiers** can be followed by <u>of</u> + <u>a determiner</u> to be more specific about a particular group.

Grammar Practice

A Circle the correct words.

1. **A:** Do you have a minute? I need **a little / a few** help with my homework.

   B: Sure, I have **some / any** time. Let me take a look.

2. **A:** Why does the teacher want **all / every** of us to raise our hands?

   B: She wants to be sure that **a great deal of / every** student has stopped writing.

3. **A:** **Several / Little** students seemed unprepared for the test.

   B: I know. I'm surprised because **both / every** student knew it was today.

4. **A:** I told my student to do the homework, but he said he didn't have **much / many** time.

   B: That's not good. If he gives **little / a little** time to his studies, he won't improve.

5. **A:** I always wanted to be a teacher because then you get **every / plenty of** summer off!

   B: I know. **Most / Both** teachers really value that time off!

B Complete the sentences. Use the words from the box.

a few	all	both	each	most	none

1. John got an A in Ms. Thomas's math class. Joe also got an A. So _____ students got As.

2. In Ms. Finer's drawing class, every student got a B. Can you believe that _____ students in that class got a B?

3. There are 30 students in Mr. Frank's music appreciation class. They all took the exam, but five didn't pass. So we can say that _____ students passed the test, but _____ didn't.

4. In Ms. Anderson's Spanish class, everyone passed the final exam. _____ of the students failed. After that, _____ student received a letter of congratulations from the principal!

C Think about your classes and classmates. Complete the sentences.

1. All of the students in my class _____.

2. Every assignment _____.

3. Most books _____.

4. Several projects _____.

5. A few teachers _____.

6. None of the classrooms _____.

Listening

A 🎧 UNDERSTANDING MAIN IDEAS Listen to the motivational speech. Check (✓) the best title.

☐ It's time to change!

☐ The vocabulary of success

☐ Your goals are my goals

☐ Most of us will always be students

B 🎧 UNDERSTANDING DETAILS Listen again. Complete the statements with the key words from the speech.

1. _____ gives you that feeling of "Wow! I did it!"

2. _____ is the *want* you feel for a certain goal.

3. _____ can come from another student or a professor.

4. _____ is the fire that helps you go forward.

5. _____ is the hunger for success.

6. _____ is the voice that encourages you when you're down.

C AFTER LISTENING What do you think about the speaker's advice? Which of the six words do you think is most important? What other words might you add to the list? Compare ideas with a partner.

Speaking

A Read the questions. Take notes.

Questions	Your answers
1. What do you like about school? Why? What don't you like about school? Why?	
2. In the past, what is a goal that you set for yourself? Did you reach it? How?	
3. What are your goals for the future? Where do you want to be five years from now?	
4. Generally, where does your motivation come from? Within? Or from outside (parents, friends, society, etc.)?	
5. What steps do you need to take to reach your goals?	

B Work with a partner. Talk about your answers. Are any of your answers similar?

C Now join another pair. Tell the other pair about your partner's goals. Share ideas for how to reach your goals. Look at the model.

> *Ruu's goal is to become a math teacher. In five years, he wants to have his own school in his country . . .*

Writing

MyEnglishLab

▶ Linking Grammar to Writing

A Interview a classmate about one of his or her goals. What steps do *you* think your partner needs to take to reach the goal? How much time is needed? Make notes about your ideas and suggestions.

Classmate _____

Goal: _____

_____

Steps / Timeline:

- _____

- _____

- _____

- _____

- _____

B Now write a paragraph using the information from Part A. Try to use the grammar from the chapter.

> Amina's short-term goal is to earn a degree in business. Her long-term goal is to open her own flower shop. The first step is to make a five-year plan for graduating. Amina is a mother of two. But all of her family is supportive, so she can attend school full time. . . .

C Share your paragraph with your class. Answer any questions.

MyEnglishLab

▶ Diagnostic Test

Grammar Summary

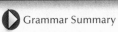

Count nouns are things we can count individually. They are singular or plural. **Noncount nouns** are masses, typically. They don't have a plural form. We use the **quantifiers** *many*, *much*, and *enough* with count and noncount nouns to talk about quantity. *Too + many / much* means more than wanted or necessary. *Not + enough* means an insufficient amount.

Count nouns	Noncount nouns
Where is your **classroom**? There are **too many problems** with that program. We have **enough students** to start the class.	Thanks for the **information**. Did I give them **too much homework**? There **isn't enough time** to study!

We use *wish* + a noun clause in the simple past or progressive form to express a desire about the present. We conjugate all forms of *be* as *were*. For wishes about future situations, use *wish* + simple past, past progressive, *be going to* + base verb, and *would* or *could* + base verb.

Present wish	Future wish
I **wish** we **had** a new computer! We **wish** we **were living** in Hawaii.	I **wish** your flight **left** later! They **wish** they **were going** fishing tomorrow. I **wish** we **were going to go** to the same school next year. We **wish** you **would come** to the party. She **wishes** her son **could participate**.

We use **pronouns** to take the place of nouns. They make sentences less repetitive. **Subject pronouns** (*I, you, she, he, it, we, they*) function as subjects. **Object pronouns** (*me, you, her, him, it, us, them*) receive the action of the verb or follow prepositions. Ask about people with *Who* (or *Whom*).

Subject pronouns		Object pronouns	
<u>Frank</u> is studying. <u>The boys</u> are in class.	**He** is studying. **They** are in class.	She gave <u>Sue</u> the notes. We enjoyed <u>the class</u>.	She gave **her** the notes. We enjoyed **it**.

Possessive adjectives (*my, your, her, his, its, our, their*) and **possessive pronouns** (*mine, yours, hers, his, ours, theirs*) mark possession and define who owns or possesses a particular noun. Ask about possession with *Whose*.

Possessive adjectives	Possessive pronouns
Please don't use **my** computer. **Their** class meets on Tuesdays.	Please don't use **mine**. **Theirs** meets on Tuesdays.

We use certain **quantifiers** depending on the nouns they're modifying. Some quantifiers are used with count nouns, some with noncount nouns, and some with both.

Rules	Quantifiers	Example
with <u>singular count nouns</u> only:	*each, every*	**Each** <u>student</u> receives a book.
with <u>plural count nouns</u> only:	*many, several, a couple of, both, a few, few*	**Both** <u>classes</u> meet on Fridays.
with <u>noncount nouns</u> only:	*a great deal of, a little, little*	They had **little** <u>time</u> to complete their assignments.
with <u>plural</u> and <u>noncount nouns</u>:	*all, most, a lot of, lots of, plenty of, some, any, no*	**Most** <u>students</u> don't like to have **any** <u>homework</u> on the weekend.

Self-Assessment

A (4 points) Circle all correct determiners.

1. a / this / the packages

2. an / your / six assignment

3. the / these / one truth

4. some / a / her attitude

B (4 points) Complete the sentences. Use the words from the box.

enough	not enough	too many	too much

1. The children can't focus. There are _____ distractions.

2. Every night the students worked for hours on assignments. Parents complained that teachers were giving _____ homework.

3. The teacher couldn't give the students _____ attention.

4. _____ students registered for the class, so the administration canceled it.

C (6 points) Complete the sentences. Use the correct form of the verbs. More than one correct answer may be possible.

1. The director wishes she _____ (have) more funding.

2. The students wish there _____ (be) more after-school programs.

3. The parents wish their son _____ (show) more interest in academics.

4. We wish we _____ (travel) around Europe next week.

5. Lin-Lin wishes the class _____ (watch) the movie, not reading the book.

6. Dia's good-bye party is today. We wish she _____ (not / leave) next month.

D (6 points) Replace the words in **bold** with pronouns or possessive adjectives.

1. You don't have notes? You can use **my notes**.

2. **Ana's** books are on the table.

3. Please give the computer to **Robert**.

4. **Mark and Gina** are great students!

5. Can you help **my friend and me**?

6. I have my books, but he left **his books**.

E (5 points) Which noun types can each word be used with? Check (✓) your answers.

	Singular count nouns Example: *student*	Plural count nouns Example: *books*	Noncount nouns Example: *work*
1. both	☐	☐	☐
2. not much	☐	☐	☐
3. a few	☐	☐	☐
4. each	☐	☐	☐
5. a lot of	☐	☐	☐

Unit Project: Civic proposal

A Work in a small group. Identify a problem in the community where you live now. Propose how to solve it. Follow the steps.

1. Choose one of the problems from the list, or think of one of your own.

- Too many homeless people and families
- Not enough parking places downtown
- Not enough public health services
- Not enough money for the arts

- Not enough police on the streets
- Too much graffiti
- Too many fast food restaurants

2. Research the problem and discuss possible solutions. Use the questions to help you. Take notes.

- What is the problem?
- Do any other cities have this issue? Which ones? What did those cities do to resolve it? How many people were involved?
- What solutions do you think might work for your community?
- What steps have already been taken?
- What steps can be taken?
- How much time is needed to solve this problem?
- How many people will need to work on it?

3. Use your notes from Step 2 to write your presentation. Use pictures, graphics (pie charts, etc.), and other visual aids to illustrate both the problem and the solutions.

B Present your research to the class. Invite questions at the end. Look at the model.

Problem:

Too many fast food restaurants

This is a picture of the corner of Broadway Boulevard and Main Street. As you can see, there is a fast food restaurant on every corner. We wish there were no fast food restaurants in our community. But that's not possible. So . . .

My**English**Lab

▶ Unit Test

My**English**Lab

▶ Search it!

Relationships

OUTCOMES

After completing this unit, I will be able to use these grammar points.

CHAPTER 13

Grammar Focus 1
Enough and *too*

Grammar Focus 2
Permission: Modals and expressions

Grammar Focus 3
Requests: Modals and expressions

CHAPTER 14

Grammar Focus 1
Reflexive and reciprocal pronouns

Grammar Focus 2
Unreal conditional

MyEnglishLab

 What do you know?

Getting Started

A Do you speak differently when you're talking to your friends, your boss, your family members, or your teacher? In what way? Discuss with a partner.

B Look at the pictures. Complete each conversation with the best response. Then compare answers with a partner.

_____ 1.
Would you please redo this report? It's not detailed enough.

May I borrow your phone? My battery is dead.
_____ 2.

Would you mind lending me that book sometime? I'd love to read it.
_____ 3.

_____ 4.
This exercise is too hard. Can I do it later?

a. No honey. Let me help you now.
b. Yes, sir. I'll do it right away.
c. Of course you can.
d. Not at all. I'd be happy to.

C Look back at the questions in Part B. Complete the tasks.

1. Permission asks someone to allow something. Circle the questions that ask permission.
2. Requests ask someone to do something. Underline the questions that make requests.
3. Which questions are more polite? Which are less polite? Write the questions.

More polite

_____

_____

_____

Less polite _____

Reading

A WARM-UP Rank the formality of these situations from *1* (most formal) to *5* (least formal). Then compare answers with a partner.

_____ **a.** Meeting your new boss for the first time

_____ **b.** Talking with a president or prime minister

_____ **c.** Chatting with your classmates at the beginning of the semester

_____ **d.** Catching up with your old friends from the neighborhood

_____ **e.** Speaking with a judge in a court of law

B SKIMMING Skim the article. Add the headings from the box. Then go back and read the article again.

WHAT DO YOU WANT?	WHERE ARE YOU?	WHO ARE YOU TALKING TO?

○ ○ ○

ARE YOU TALKING TO ME? "Would you mind if I sat here?" inquires an elderly woman as she steps onto a public bus. The next passenger to board, a teenager, says, "Is it OK if I sit here?"

Even when we're all speaking the same language, how we speak to one another depends on several factors. We often change our speaking—or our register—depending on who we're speaking with, where we are, and what kind of request we're making.

_____ Teenager Wes Peterson's grandmother always said there was no such thing as being too polite. But who we are addressing does impact word choices. He explains, "If I needed a chair and saw an older couple with an extra one, I would ask, 'Would you mind if I borrowed this chair?' But if there were kids my age, I would just say, 'Can I take this chair?'" Wes says if he spoke too formally to his peers, they would think he was being ridiculous!

_____ "The key to learning polite requests," says English teacher Lukas Murphy, "is to train your ear." He believes that students need to learn to recognize what's appropriate in which situation. Clearly there are enough instances of this in students' lives. For example, in an office or classroom, they might hear a lot of "Could you lend me your . . . ?" requests, but outside the class they might hear "Hey—can you give me that . . . ?"

_____ Register also depends on what the request is for. For example, imagine you are too busy to complete a project at work and need some help. A request to a colleague for help might begin with "I was wondering if you could possibly help me with . . . " However, this would be too formal for some situations. Requesting something simpler might only require a "Would you give me a hand with . . . ?" question.

In conclusion, learning about register is easy enough to do. Just observe language usage in a variety of situations. It's also helpful to be sensitive to the fact that it's not only what we are asking for, but clearly also who we are asking and where we are.

C UNDERSTANDING SUPPORTING DETAILS Where in the article could the following quotations be added? Write *1* for the first paragraph, *2* for the second paragraph, and so on.

_____ **a.** "When I want to ask my mom for the car, I'm always very careful to be polite."

_____ **b.** "The language we use depends on three different factors."

_____ **c.** "The language I use at work is different from the language I use at home."

_____ **d.** "Finally, if you listen to communication between different people—in different situations—you can learn a great deal."

_____ **e.** "Of course, if I were talking to a judge, I would address him or her as 'your honor.'"

Grammar Focus 1 *Enough* and *too*

Examples	Language notes
(1) She was **smart enough**, but she didn't try. Did he finish **quickly enough**? I **did**n't **study enough**. I failed the test.	As we saw in Chapter 11, the word **enough** means "sufficient" or "the right amount." It has a positive meaning. In addition to modifying nouns, *enough* can also modify **adjectives**, **adverbs**, and **verbs**. Use: **adjective / adverb / verb + enough**
(2) This report is **not detailed enough**. He did**n't** work **fast enough**. You are**n't** eating **enough**.	*Not enough* means that something is insufficient or less than the right amount. Use: **not + adjective + enough** **not + verb + adverb + enough** helping verb + **not** + verb + **enough**
(3) He didn't move fast **enough to get** a seat. Do you think she has **enough to do**?	We often add an **infinitive**: **enough + infinitive**
(4) Don't be **too friendly** with strangers. Does he speak **too formally** to his peers?	As we saw in Chapter 11, the word **too** means "more than is needed." The meaning is usually negative. In addition to modifying quantifiers, **too** can also modify **adjectives** and **adverbs**.
(5) My kids are**n't too interested** in history. Don't work **too hard**!	We use **not too** to say that something is **lacking**. Use: **not + too + adjective / adverb**
(6) You are **too busy to complete** a project. Did he arrive **too late to get** into the movie?	We often add an **infinitive**: **too + adjective / adverb + infinitive**
(7) There are **too many people** on the bus. There are **too few seats** on the bus. **Q:** Did the teacher present **too much information**? **A:** No, she presented **too little**. / She did**n't** present **enough**.	As we saw in Chapter 11, we can also use *(not)* **enough** and **too** with **count and noncount nouns**. • The opposite of **too many** is **too few** (for count nouns). • The opposite of **too much** is **too little** (for noncount nouns). We more commonly say "not enough."

Grammar Practice

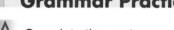

A Complete the sentences. Use *enough* or *too*.

1. I don't have _____ money to pay my taxi fare.

   Could you lend me some?

2. You are speaking _____ quickly. Would you mind slowing down?

3. Kevin hates to wait. He has _____ little patience.

4. I had no trouble finding your house. Your directions were easy _____.

5. Your instructions aren't clear _____. Can you say it in a different way?

6. Hal is _____ short to get the book off the shelf. He needs a ladder.

7. Nancy doesn't have a driver's license. She's not old _____.

MyEnglishLab

Grammar Plus 1
Activities 1 and 2

8. The movie is sold out. We arrived _____ late.

9. My grandma says I'm too thin. She always says, "You don't eat _____."

B Rewrite these sentences to say the opposite. Use *enough* or *too*. More than one correct answer may be possible.

1. She is walking too quickly. *She is not walking fast enough.*_____

2. He is old enough to enter the contest. _____

3. We were too slow to get seats on the subway. _____

4. There are too many people in our discussion group. _____

5. She was strong enough to lift the box. _____

6. There are too few grammar exercises in this book. _____

C Look at the picture. Write sentences with *enough* or *too*.

1. _____

2. _____

3. _____

4. _____

5. _____

6. _____

Grammar Focus 2 Permission: Modals and expressions

Examples	Language notes
(1) **Can** I do this exercise later? **Could** I do this exercise later? **May** I do this exercise later?	Permission asks someone to allow something. We **ask for permission** in a variety of ways. We commonly use the modal verbs *can*, *could*, and *may*.
(2) **Can I ask** a question? **Could they ask** a question? **May we ask** a question?	Like all modal verbs, *can*, *could*, and *may* have the **same form** for all subjects. Use: *Can / Could / May* + subject + **base verb**
(3) **May** I sit here, **please**? ⟶ More polite **May** I sit here? **Can / Could** I please <u>sit</u> here? **Can / Could** I sit here? ⟶ Less polite	The ways we ask permission can vary in **politeness**: • *May* is more polite than *could* or *can*. • We can add *please*—at the end of the question or before the <u>verb</u>—to make a question more polite.
(4) **I was wondering** <u>if I could sit</u> here. More polite **Would you mind** <u>if they sat</u> here? **Would it be OK** <u>if we sat</u> here? **Do you mind** <u>if he sits</u> here? **Is it OK** <u>if I sit</u> here? Less polite	There are several other **common expressions** of permission. Notice the verb form used with each: *I was wondering* + <u>*if*-clause with *could*</u> + **base verb** *Would you mind* + <u>*if*-clause</u> in **simple past** *Would it be OK* + <u>*if*-clause</u> in **simple past** *Do you mind* + <u>*if*-clause</u> in **simple present** *Is it OK* + <u>*if*-clause</u> in **simple present**
(5) You **can sit** here. He **may join** us. *Incorrect:* You ~~could~~ sit here.	To **grant permission** use: subject + *can / may* + **base verb** *Notes:* • *May* is considered formal in granting permission. • We can't use *could* in granting permission.
(6) You **cannot** sit here. / You **can't** sit here. You **may not** sit here. *Incorrect:* You ~~couldn't~~ sit here.	To **refuse permission**, add *not* after the modal. *Notes:* • Do not contract *may not*. • Do not use *could not* to refuse permission.
(7) **Q:** Could I borrow your phone? **A:** Sorry. I'm waiting for an important call.	We sometimes **apologize** and usually give a **reason** when we refuse permission. It's considered polite.

(8) **Q:** Could I do this later?
 	
    Affirmative   **Negative**
A: Yes, you can.   No, you can't.
    Yes, you may.   No, you may not.
    Sure. / Go ahead.   Sorry.
    Of course. / No problem.
	For **short answers** to requests for permission with *can*, *could*, or *may*, use *can* or *may*, or other short affirmative or negative expressions.

(9) **Q:** Do you **mind** if I borrow this chair? **A:** Yes, I do. *(I mind.)* [refusing] **Q:** Do you **mind** if I borrow this chair? **A:** No, I don't. *(I don't mind.)* [granting] **Q:** Do you **mind** if I borrow this chair? **A:** Sure. *(The seat is clearly free.)*	With *mind*, we use an affirmative reply to **refuse** permission and a negative reply to **grant** permission. *Note:* In **casual speech**, speakers often give a positive reply to grant permission. The context usually makes the situation clear.

Grammar Practice

A Circle the correct words.

1. A: Excuse me. Can I **sit** / sat here?

  B: Sure.

2. A: I was wondering if I can / **could** help.

  B: Of course.

3. A: Could we speak to your manager?

  B: Yes, you **can** / could. I'll get her.

4. A: Do you mind if I **call** / called you Mike?

  B: Well, actually, I prefer Michael.

5. A: Would it be OK if I will come / **came** late?

  B: No problem.

6. A: I'm sorry, but you **can't** / couldn't watch.

  B: Oh, really? I'm sorry.

7. A: Can I please stay out until midnight?

  B: No, you could / **may** not. Be home by 10:30.

8. A: Would you mind if we join / **joined** you?

  B: Not at all.

B Rewrite the questions. Make them more polite.

1. Can I borrow your newspaper? → Could *I borrow your newspaper, please* ?

2. Could we have a word with you? → May _____?

3. Do you mind if I open a window? → Would _____?

4. Would you mind if I looked at your notes? → I was _____?

C Read each scenario. Then write a conversation asking and granting or refusing permission.

1. You're cold because the classroom window is open. Ask the teacher.

  A: May _____?

  B: _____

2. You're at work and not feeling well. You want to go home early. Ask your boss.

  A: Would _____?

  B: _____

3. You and a friend are at a restaurant. You were seated near the noisy kitchen. Ask the waiter.

  A: Can _____?

  B: _____

4. You want to have a party at your house this weekend. Ask your roommate.

  A: I _____?

  B: _____

5. You'd like to finish a report for your colleague tomorrow instead of today. Ask your colleague.

  A: Do _____?

  B: _____

6. You want to reschedule your dentist appointment. Ask the receptionist.

  A: Could _____?

  B: _____

Grammar Focus 3 Requests: Modals and expressions

Examples	Language notes
(1) **Can** you **lend** me your laptop? **Would** you **lend** me your laptop? **Could** you **lend** me your laptop?	Requests ask someone to do something. We use the modal verbs **can**, **would**, and **could** to **make requests**. They do not change form. Use: **Can / Would / Could** + subject + **base verb**
(2) Could you **not play** music at your desk?	Request that someone **not do something** by placing *not* before the verb.
(3) Can you **please** give me a hand? Would you give me a hand, **please**? Could you **please** not pop your gum?	As with permission, requests are made more polite with **please**.
(4) **Q:** Could you lend me your phone? **A: Sorry. I'm not comfortable lending it out. /** **I'm afraid I can't. I'm using it right now.**	We sometimes apologize and usually give a **reason** when we don't grant a request. It's considered polite.
(5) Would you **mind helping** me? Do you **mind moving** over?	We can also use **mind** to make requests more polite. (*Mind* assumes that your request is annoying or imposing on the listener.) Use: **Would / Do you mind** + gerund
(6) **Q:** Would you **mind** changing seats with me? **A: I would, actually.** *(I would mind.)* [refusing] **Q:** Do you **mind** helping me? **A: Not at all.** I'd be happy to. *(I wouldn't mind.)* [granting] **Q:** Would you **mind** helping me? **A: Sure.** How can I help?	With *mind*, use an affirmative reply to **refuse a request** and a negative reply to **grant a request**. *Note:* In **casual speech** people may give a positive reply when granting a request. The context usually makes the situation clear.
(7) I **was wondering if <u>you</u> could** move over.	With *I was wondering . . .* change, *I* to *you*. **I was wondering if <u>you</u>** + **could / would** + base verb

Making a request	Granting / Refusing
Would **Could** } **you lend** me your laptop? More polite ↕ Less polite **Can**	Sure. No problem. / Sorry. I'm using it.
I was wondering if you'd mind changing seats? **Would you mind changing** seats?	Not at all. / Actually, I would. Sorry.

Grammar Practice

MyEnglishLab
▶ Grammar Plus 3
Activities 1 and 2

A Match all possible responses to the requests.

Requests

_____ 1. Could you finish the report by 5:00, please?

_____ 2. I was wondering if you'd mind helping me.

_____ 3. Would you mind closing that window?

_____ 4. Could you not leave dirty dishes in the sink?

_____ 5. Can you lend me your pen?

Responses

a. Sorry, but I can't complete it today.

b. Not at all. What do you need?

c. Actually, I'm using it.

d. No problem. I'm cold, too.

e. Of course. Sorry about that.

B Unscramble the words to make requests.

1. you / speak / could / please / more loudly / ?

_____

2. this letter / mind / mailing / would / you / for me / ?

_____

3. park / you / somewhere else / can / your car / ?

_____

4. not / you / would / in class / please / chew gum / ?

_____

5. you'd / was / I / if / our photo / wondering / mind / taking / .

_____

C Look at the pictures. Write a request for each one.

1. Could _____
_____ ?

2. Would _____
_____ ?

3. I was _____
_____ .

4. Do _____
_____ ?

D Role-play the situations in Part C. Agree or don't agree to each request.

Listening

A BEFORE LISTENING Have you ever helped a stranger? Have you ever asked a stranger for help? What happened?

B 🎧 UNDERSTANDING MAIN IDEAS Listen to the scenes from a drama. What happens in each scene? Circle the correct answers.

Scene 1
a. A man and woman bump into each other.
b. Two friends reconnect after a long time.
c. A woman talks about her love of vegetables.

Scene 2
a. There are many people buying movie tickets.
b. A couple goes to the movies.
c. Two people reconnect at a lecture.

Scene 3
a. The couple decides they will go to a movie sometime.
b. The man invites the woman to a café.
c. The couple says goodnight.

C 🎧 UNDERSTANDING DETAILS Listen again. Complete the sentences.

1. In scene one, after the "accident," Dan asks Lily: "_____ you a hand with these bags?"

2. Lily asks: "_____ them across the street to my apartment steps?"

3. In scene two, Dan asks: "Excuse me. _____ I sat here?"

4. Lily answers: "_____. This seat is taken."

5. Another woman asks: "_____ it down?"

6. In scene three, Dan asks: "_____ you a cup of coffee?"

Speaking

A Read the list of requests. Underline three requests you want to make. Think about what you will say.

A request . . .

☐ for a ride to the airport   ☐ for help moving to a new apartment

☐ for help with an essay   ☐ for help with homework

☐ for directions   ☐ to borrow a laptop

☐ to borrow a car   ☐ for a ride home

B Stand up and mingle with your classmates, making your requests. Mark the request with a checkmark when someone agrees. Grant every *other* request asked of you. Look at the model.

> *Excuse me. Could you tell me how to get to the Botanical Garden?*

> *No problem. First . . .*

MyEnglishLab

▶ Linking Grammar to Writing

Writing

A Think about requests you make of different people. Choose one from the list or think of your own.

- You want your teacher to speak more slowly in class.
- You want your teacher to explain some specific points more clearly.
- You want your siblings to not read your emails.
- You want your family to spend more time together.
- You want a friend of your parents to give you a job.
- You want your friend to teach you something (how to play a game, an instrument, etc.).

B Write an email making a request from Part A. Try to use the grammar from the chapter.

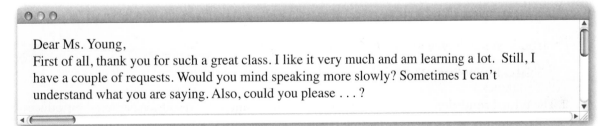

Dear Ms. Young,
First of all, thank you for such a great class. I like it very much and am learning a lot. Still, I have a couple of requests. Would you mind speaking more slowly? Sometimes I can't understand what you are saying. Also, could you please . . . ?

C Work with a partner. Imagine that you are the recipient of your partner's email. Role-play calling your partner to discuss the email.

MyEnglishLab

▶ Diagnostic Test

CHAPTER 14

Different Strokes for Different Folks

Getting Started

A What would you do in each situation? Circle your answers.

1. If you were having problems with a coworker, would you . . . ?
   a. keep the problem to yourself
   b. talk to your boss or another coworker
   c. quit your job

2. If you knew your sister's most important secret, would you . . . ?
   a. not say anything
   b. remind her to keep her secrets to herself
   c. tell everybody

3. If some of your classmates were getting credit for things they didn't do themselves, would you . . . ?
   a. let it go
   b. confront them
   c. tell the teacher

4. What would you do if you and a friend had a big argument?
   a. I would apologize.
   b. I would wait for the friend's apology.
   c. I would pretend that everything was just fine.

B Compare answers with a partner.

C Look back at the survey in Part A. Complete the tasks.

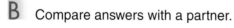

1. **Reflexive pronouns** restate subjects and objects for emphasis. They end in *-self* or *-selves*. Circle the examples.
2. The **unreal conditional** talks about untrue conditions and their results. What word introduces the unreal conditions in the survey questions? _____ What verb + verb form is used in the answers in item 4? _____ + _____

Reading

A WARM-UP What is your communication style? Discuss the questions with a partner.

When you have something to say, do you express yourself directly? Do you keep many feelings to yourself, or do you talk about them? Do you like when someone tells you his or her feelings directly?

B SCANNING Scan the article for answers to the question. Then go back and read the whole article.

What is the relationship between the people discussed in the three examples?

1. _____ 2. _____ and 3. Counselor, _____,

  partners _____ and _____

Communication Styles: Three Case Studies

When it comes to communication styles, we are not the same. In fact, we are very different from one another. Misunderstanding and misinterpretation are some of the most common frustrations we experience when we communicate with our coworkers, spouses, family, and friends. Even when people are from the same cultural background and speaking the same language, communication gaps are frequent.

Meet Jessica Franklin. She and her business partner are having some communication problems. Franklin feels frustrated. For help, she consulted a friend. Franklin told her friend, "Basically, my partner and I want to solve our issues ourselves. We're both 'I-can-do-it-myself' kinds of people: independent and headstrong." The friend asked, "How would your partner react if she knew your feelings about this?" Franklin thought about it and came to a realization. She said, "If I spoke to her directly, we might be able to reach an agreement, and move on."

Meet Alex Tyler. He and his girlfriend were not "on the same page" when it came to many things. Tyler always suggested going out with friends, but his girlfriend preferred they go out by themselves. The girlfriend expected Tyler to "read" her feelings—without having to say them. Tyler said, "Just tell me how you feel!" One day, Tyler said, "If you were more social, I would *want* to spend more time alone with you!" After that, his girlfriend started focusing on herself. She became more self-assured and started expressing herself better. Tyler learned to listen to her words—and body language.

Meet Donald Greene. An advisor at Smithtown High School, Greene counsels students *and* their parents. He says parents often declare, "If my kids spoke to me, I could help them!" Greene says students claim their parents only direct them. He always hears, "If my parents didn't tell me what to do all the time, I might be able to talk to them!" He works hard to get them all in the same room—and talking about the issues they face so they can better understand each other and eventually work it out by themselves.

C UNDERSTANDING INFERENCE Check (✓) the information that you can infer from the reading.

_____ **1.** Jessica Franklin's business was probably hurt by the communication problems.

_____ **2.** Alex Tyler and his girlfriend are probably going to get married.

_____ **3.** Donald Greene tries to be objective.

_____ **4.** All high school students and their parents go to counseling to work out problems.

Grammar Focus 1 Reflexive and reciprocal pronouns

Examples	Language notes
(1) **I** can't express **myself** easily. **He** asked **himself** a question.	We use **reflexive pronouns** when the subject and object of a sentence talk about the same noun (person, place, or thing).
(2) Did you see it **for yourself**? Rose started focusing **on herself**.	Reflexive pronouns are often the **object of a preposition**. Use: **preposition + reflexive pronoun**
(3) **I** can do this work **myself**. The **job itself** is fine. **Mike and I** want to solve our problems **ourselves**.	Use reflexive pronouns to **emphasize** a **noun**.
(4) I did it **by myself**. No one helped me. They worked it out **by themselves**.	To mean "alone," use: **by + reflexive pronoun**
(5) Help **yourself** to something to eat. *(said to one person)* Help **yourselves** to something to eat. *(said to two or more people)*	In **imperative sentences**, use *yourself* when the subject is singular. Use *yourselves* when the subject is plural.
(6) **Alex and Rose** looked at **each other**. *(Alex looked at Rose, and Rose looked at Alex.)* **The teacher and her students** learn from **one another**. *(The teacher learns from her students, and the students learn from their teacher.)*	*Each other* and *one another* are **reciprocal pronouns**. We use them in sentences that have compound subjects and objects that refer to the same people or things.
(7) **Alex and his girlfriend** didn't know how to communicate with **each other**. **My two business partners and I** communicate well with **one another**. The people in the audience looked at **each other**.	Use *each other* for two people. Use *one another* for three or more people. *Note:* In casual speech we often use *each other* with three or more people.
(8) The two tourists took **each other's** pictures. The school's large staff of teachers often borrowed **one another's** ideas.	Reciprocal pronouns can be **possessive**.

Subject pronoun	Reflexive pronoun	Examples
I	myself	Some mornings I have to force **myself** out of bed.
you	yourself	You need to admit the truth to **yourself**.
he	himself	He taught **himself** how to play the guitar.
she	herself	She prefers to solve problems by **herself**.
it	itself	The cat gave **itself** a bath.
we	ourselves	We are pushing **ourselves** to finish the job in time.
you	yourselves	You and Mika express **yourselves** in English well.
they	themselves	My parents treated **themselves** to a cruise.

See Appendix R on page A-8 for a list of other pronouns and possessive adjectives.

Grammar Practice

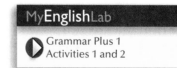

MyEnglishLab

Grammar Plus 1
Activities 1 and 2

A Complete the sentences. Use reflexive pronouns.

1. Mr. and Mrs. Lopez built their new house by _____.

2. My mother sometimes talks to _____.

3. I created this webpage by _____.

4. We introduced _____ to our new neighbors.

5. My brother is always looking at _____ in the mirror.

6. She put the presentation together by _____.

7. Tom and Lynne, if you want any food, please help _____.

8. Look at _____. You're covered in dirt!

B Look at the picture. Write sentences using words from the box. Use reflexive and reciprocal pronouns.

| buy | listen to | scratch | talk to |
| fan | ~~look at~~ | stand | wave |

1. Gary *is looking at himself in the mirror* _____.

2. David and Susie _____.

3. Lisa, Brad, and Brian _____.

4 Junko and Alicia _____.

5. Paul _____.

6. Teresa and Omar _____.

7. Penny _____.

8. Spike the cat _____.

Grammar Focus 2 Unreal conditional

Examples	Language notes
(1) If it **rains** tomorrow, I **will go** to the movies. *(There is a real possibility it will rain.)* [future real conditional]	As we saw in Chapter 8, we use the **future real conditional** to talk about possible or likely situations and their predicted outcomes.
If I **lived** in Brazil, I **would learn to dance** samba. *(It's unlikely I will live in Brazil, but I can imagine it.)* [unreal conditional]	In contrast, we use the **unreal conditional** to talk about unlikely or imagined present and future situations and their outcomes.
(2) **If** I **knew** her secret, I <u>**would tell** you</u>. *(But I don't know her secret.)* *Incorrect:* If I were having problems with a coworker I would talk to my boss.	The **if-clause** is the unlikely or imagined situation. The **main clause** is the imagined outcome. Use: **If-clause** = **If** + subject + **simple past /** **past progressive** + **main clause** = <u>subject</u> + **would** + **base verb** **Notes:** • The *if*-clause is in the simple past, but its meaning is not. • The *if*-clause is followed by a **comma** when it is at the beginning of the sentence.
(3) <u>I **would tell** you</u> if I knew her secret.	We can also **begin** unreal conditional sentences with the **main clause**.
(4) If I got into an argument, <u>I'**d** apologize</u>.	We often **contract** pronouns with *would* (I'*d*, you'*d*, she'*d*, etc.).
(5) If I spoke to her directly, <u>we **might be able to** reach an agreement</u>. If they needed money, <u>I **could help** them</u>.	When we are **less sure** about the result, we can use these modals in the <u>main clause</u>: *might* + **base verb** *could* + **base verb**
(6) If I **were** you, I **would tell** the truth. How **would** we **react** if we **were having** problems with a coworker?	With *be* in the *if*-clause, use **were** with all subjects. **Note:** In informal speech, you may also hear *was* used after *I*, *he*, *she*, and *it*.

If-clause: Simple past verb	Main clause: *Would / could / might* + verb
If I **got** into an argument,	I **would apologize**.
Main clause: *Would / could / might* + verb	**If-clause:** Past progressive verb
I **might** call you	if I **were having** problems.

See Appendix A on page A-1 for contractions with would.

Grammar Practice

A Complete the sentences. Use the unreal conditional with the simple past and *would*.

1. If I _____ (see) a classmate cheating, I _____ (tell) the teacher.

2. If my boss _____ (say) my name wrong, I _____ (not / correct) her.

3. I _____ (be) so happy if I _____ (get) promoted at work.

4. I _____ (live) in England if I _____ (can) live anywhere.

5. If my friends _____ (hear) I got married, they _____ (not / believe) it.

6. If someone _____ (not / tell) me the truth, I _____ (ask) why.

B Complete the sentences. Use your own ideas.

1. If I weren't getting along with someone in my class, I would _____.

2. If I improved my grades, I could _____.

3. If I could study anything, I would _____.

4. If I had more time in the day, I might _____.

5. If my friends suddenly stopped talking to me, I might _____.

6. If I could make a change in our school, I would _____.

C Complete the sentence. Make the result of one sentence the condition of the next sentence.

Example: If I had more time, *I would learn French* _____.

If I learned French, I could move to Paris. _____

If I moved to Paris, I might fall in love. _____

If I fell in love, . . . _____

1. If I had more time, I _____.

2. _____

3. _____

4. _____

5. _____

6. _____

D Discuss these questions in a group.

- Where would you go if you could go anywhere in the world?
- What would you do if your friends forgot your birthday?
- If you could meet one famous person, who would you meet?
- How would you feel if your parents stopped trusting you?
- What are some things you could do if you were older?
- If you could speak any language fluently, what language would you choose?
- If you could have one wish come true, what would you wish for?

Listening

A BEFORE LISTENING Do you like to do projects yourself, such as plumbing or house painting? Or do you prefer to hire someone else? Why?

B 🎧 UNDERSTANDING MAIN IDEAS Listen to an episode of the radio program *Tell Me Something I Don't Know.* Check (✓) the main idea.

☐ "Do-it-yourself" is a popular trend.

☐ If you do it yourself, you might save money.

☐ Musicians prefer record companies.

☐ "Do-it-yourself" is a fun new company.

C 🎧 UNDERSTANDING DETAILS Listen again. Then circle the correct answers.

1. Melanie Manchester, the show's host, says that the do-it-yourself trend started in . . .
  a. the 1940s.   **c.** the 1950s.
  b. the 1960s.   **d.** the 1970s.

2. The term *do-it-yourself* originally referred to . . .
  a. repairs and improvements.   **c.** music recording.
  b. a way to save money.   **d.** people's sense of pride.

3. One of the driving forces behind the do-it-yourself movement is . . .
  a. too many companies.   **c.** personal pride.
  b. a lot of free time.   **d.** early retirement.

4. A lot of do-it-yourself followers like Mark Roberts say if they had the money, they would . . .
  a. start their own companies.   **c.** buy better materials.
  b. hire help.   **d.** still fix things themselves.

5. Julie Jarmel has already . . .
  a. fixed a lot of things in her house.   **c.** released two CDs with her band.
  b. helped her parents build a bathroom. **d.** made a DVD with her friends.

6. Melanie Manchester suggests that the DIY movement is transferred from . . .
  a. country to country.   **c.** teacher to student.
  b. person to person.   **d.** business to business.

Speaking

A Read and think about the list of questions. Check (✓) the three that interest you the most.

☐ **1.** If you were president (prime minister, etc.) of your country, what would you do, and why?

☐ **2.** If you could spend an hour with any person, who would you spend it with? What questions would you ask him or her?

☐ **3.** If you had a coin that was worth $3 million, what would you do with it and why?

☐ **4.** If you could perform onstage as an actor or musician along with any other actors / musicians, who would it be? Why?

☐ **5.** If you could go on a free shopping spree with a family member to a favorite store, who would you take and to what store?

□ **6.** If someone were making a movie about you, who would star as you? As the other characters in your life?

□ **7.** If you had the chance to relive a particular moment with someone in your life, which one would it be?

□ **8.** If you were given the chance to give someone a special gift—anything—who would you choose? What would you give?

B Find students who are interested in some of the same questions from Part A and form a group. Take turns asking and answering the questions. Ask follow-up questions. Look at the model.

> So, if you were president of this country, what would you do?

> First, I would improve the healthcare system. . . .

Writing

MyEnglishLab
Linking Grammar to Writing

A Imagine that you are running for president of your country. What would you say to earn the people's support? Then imagine that you are giving a younger friend or sibling "life advice." How would your tone and language be different in these two situations?

B Write what you would say, first as a presidential candidate and then as an older sibling or friend. Try to use the grammar from the chapter.

> To my beloved countrymen and women,
>   I urge you to vote for me. If I were your president, I would
> change many things for the better. I would improve our educational
> system. I would make our health system better. I would also work hard to
> improve our opportunities as a country. You yourselves know what a great
> nation we have. . . .

CAMPAIGN 2016

> Hey Sis,
> I know it's sometimes tough for you to hear my advice, but I have to tell you something. First, you know I love you! But I'm very worried about your future. You're not working as hard as you could. I know you're smart! You really need to study hard so that you become successful —and happy. If you were a better student, you would have so many opportunities. If I were you, I'd make myself go to the library every night. There are too many distractions in the dorm. Also . . .

C Share your writing with a partner. Discuss the differences in register that you and your partner used.

MyEnglishLab
Diagnostic Test

Grammar Summary

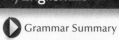

Enough means "sufficient" or "the right amount." Place it after adjectives, adverbs, and verbs. To say something is insufficient, use *not* + adjective / adverb / verb + *enough*. The meaning is usually negative. We can add an infinitive after *enough*.

Enough	Not enough
He's **tall enough to reach** the shelf.	He's **not tall enough to reach** the shelf.
She ran **fast enough to catch** the bus.	She didn't run **fast enough to catch** the bus.
I **studied enough**.	I **didn't study enough**.

The word *too* means "more than needed." Place it before adjectives and adverbs. The meaning is usually negative. We can add an infinitive after the phrase.

Too	
I'm **too tired**.	I'm **too tired to stay** awake.
He walks **too slowly**.	He walks **too slowly to keep** up with me.

We use *can*, *could*, and *may*, and other expressions to **ask permission**. We use *can*, *could*, and *would* and other expressions to **make requests**. By using expressions such as *Would you mind . . . ?* we imply that the action may be annoying or imposing. We can grant and refuse permission with *can* and *may (not)*: *Yes, you can. / No you may not.* We can grant and refuse requests with a variety of responses *(Sure. / Not at all. / Sorry.)*

Asking permission	Making requests
Can / Could / May I see your homework?	**Can you** open the door?
Is it OK if I sit here?	**Would you** say your name again?
Do you mind if I sit here?	**Could you not** make that noise, please?
Would it be OK if I sat here?	**Would you mind** turning down the TV?
Would you mind if I sat here?	**Do you mind** waiting?
I was wondering if I could sit here.	**I was wondering if** you'd mind helping.

Reflexive pronouns are used when the subject and object of a sentence refer to the same person or thing. We also use them for emphasis. *By* + a reflexive pronoun means "alone."

Singular	Plural
I forced **myself** out of bed.	We are pushing **ourselves** today.
Admit the truth to **yourself**!	You and Mika express **yourselves** well.
The cat gave **itself** a bath.	The children fixed breakfast **by themselves**.
He wanted to go hiking **by himself**.	

Use the **reciprocal pronouns** *each other* (for two people) and *one another* (for more than two people) when the subject and object refer to the same people or things.

Reciprocal pronouns
Bill and Carrie are looking at **each other**.
The group of students were helping **one another** finish the project.

We use the **unreal conditional** to talk about unreal or imaginary conditions. Use an *if*-clause (simple past or past continuous) + a main clause (*would / might / could* + base verb). Although the *if*-clause is in the simple past, it refers to the present or future.

If-clause	Main clause
If I **had** the time,	I **would travel** more.
If I **were** a pilot,	I **could see** the world.
If I **were earning** more money,	I **might travel** for six months.

Self-Assessment

A (5 points) Rewrite the sentences. Add *too* or *enough*.

1. Lara didn't eat. (enough) _____

2. I have little time to finish my report. (too) _____

3. Damien gave up the race easily. (too) _____

4. The presentation was not detailed. (enough) _____

5. They didn't read the map closely. (enough) _____

B (8 points) Circle the correct words.

1. **Can / May** you please speak more slowly?

2. Would you mind **close / closing** that window?

3. **May / Would** I please see your I.D. card?

4. I was wondering if you'd mind **help / helping** me.

5. Do you mind if I **borrow / borrowed** your notes?

6. Is it OK if I **move / moved** your bag over there?

7. **Do / Would** you mind if I sat here?

8. I was wondering if I **can / could** use your laptop.

C (6 points) Complete the sentences. Use reflexive or reciprocal pronouns.

1. Look at _____! You are wearing two different shoes!

2. After Pedro scored the winning goal, he and his coach looked at _____
   in disbelief.

3. My coworkers always try to solve their problems _____.

4. No one knows why Mr. Parker decided to give _____ a haircut.

5. For their birthdays, the three best friends bought _____ dinner.

6. Some people prefer to travel with a group, but I like traveling by _____.

D (6 points) Complete the sentences. Use the unreal conditional.

1. If my friends _____ (go) out without me, I _____ (be) upset.

2. If I _____ (not / live) so far away from campus, I _____ (walk)
   to school.

3. Tom _____ (not / be) in this advanced class if he _____ (not /
   study) so hard.

4. Kara _____ (quit) her job today if she _____ (have) any savings.

5. If I _____ (be) a veterinarian, I _____ (specialize) in cats.

6. If I _____ (see) a crime, I _____ (call) the police immediately.

Unit Project: Sphere of influence

A We all have people who influence us. These may be family members, friends, colleagues, bosses, teachers, or others. These people are part of our "sphere of influence." Work with a partner. Create your sphere of influence. Follow the steps.

1. Think of four people who have positively influenced you the most.
2. Tell your partner about them. Describe how they have enhanced your life.
3. Collect images, short written stories, or other things that represent these four people. Put them on a poster or create a webpage.

My mother taught me that anything was possible. I just have to believe in myself.

My grandfather taught me that humor and magic make the world a wonderful place.

My mom

Luisa (me)

My grandfather

My high school English teacher, Dr. Wolfe, taught me the beauty of literature.

My best friend Susan taught me the power of friendship.

Susan

Dr. Wolfe

B Present your sphere of influence to the class. Answer any questions.

MyEnglishLab
▶ Unit Test

MyEnglishLab
▶ Search it!

Investigations

CHAPTER 15 | Detective Work

Getting Started

A What aspects of detective work are interesting? What path might someone follow to become a detective?

B Read about the personal qualifications of a detective. Discuss the questions with a partner.

- Which qualifications do you think are most important? Why?
- Can you think of others?

All in a Day's Work

There are many physical requirements for a detective. But success in this field depends on personal qualifications as well.

- First and foremost, a good detective is mentally fit. This is important because the job presents a tremendous level of both external and internal stress.

- A good detective is responsible for his or her actions. In other words, a good detective has integrity. This is important because the people needing help are vulnerable.

- A good detective is also patient with others. Often a detective deals with folks who are very upset and can't communicate well. A well-trained detective reacts calmly to a variety of situations. This is important because so many situations are difficult and stressful.

- Additionally, a good detective is not afraid of challenging situations and can focus on work despite any and all distractions.

- Finally, a good detective is passionate about the community and the people in need of help.

If you are interested in a career as a detective, ask yourself if you have these qualifications and attributes. Then think about your interests. What types of detective work would interest you? You could even specialize in one specific type of work, such as cybercrime.

C Look back at the reading in Part B. Complete the tasks.

1. English has many **adjective + preposition** combinations *(responsible for)*. Circle the examples.
2. English also has many **verb + preposition** combinations *(depend on)*. Underline the examples.
3. Complete the chart with the examples.

Adjective + preposition	Verb + preposition

Reading

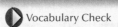
A WARM-UP These days people are very interested in crime investigations. What is some evidence of this fact?

B PREDICTING Read the headings in **bold** in the article. What kinds of information will the author probably give to support these headings? Discuss with a partner. Then go back and read the article. Were your guesses correct?

Detective Work from the Inside Out: Tips from an Insider

For 20 years, Tim O'Neil worked in law enforcement as a Chicago police officer. Now he's enthusiastic about his new career: detective. Being a detective, says O'Neil, is different from other jobs. According to him, you have to have a unique skill set beyond mere interest in the field. GetaClue.com asked Tim what it takes to be an effective investigator. Here he elaborates on what he says is most necessary.

Stay cool, calm, and collected. You are responsible for many different aspects of a crime scene. You need to be able to glance at a scene and take it all in. You can't be afraid of blood, frightened by situations that most people find disturbing, or feel sorry for the criminals. If you are, in fact, worried about your reactions, speak with someone in the field and get some advice. Everyone has limits, but you need to be strong. You may often be shocked by what you discover, but you always need to play it cool.

Do your homework. You need to have a lot of knowledge related to crime, criminals, and legal issues. The more you learn, the more prepared you'll be. Investigate. Read. Talk to experts. Research every detail related to the situations you are involved with. Protect yourself against possible danger and get your facts straight before you accuse someone of something. Learn the answers before you need to ask the questions.

Watch your back. Move cautiously and carefully, and always keep your eyes wide open. If you suspect someone of something, don't confront him or her immediately. Discuss your hunch with a colleague, but make sure it's a person you can confide in. Use your instincts and never apologize for being cautious.

O'Neil says that if you are good at reading people, passionate about helping society, and interested in making this world a safer and better place, then detective work may just be the field for you.

C UNDERSTANDING DETAILS Write *T* for the true statements and *F* for the false statements.

_____ 1. Detective O'Neil suggests becoming a police officer before becoming a detective.

_____ 2. Detectives are responsible for many aspects of a crime scene.

_____ 3. An effective detective can still be afraid of blood.

_____ 4. Detectives need to be familiar with legal issues.

_____ 5. If a detective suspects someone of a crime, it's best to accuse the person right away.

_____ 6. Detectives should never discuss cases with colleagues.

_____ 7. It's OK to use your instincts as a detective.

Grammar Focus 1 Adjective + preposition

Examples	Language notes
(1) Detectives need to be **passionate about** <u>what they do</u>.	English speakers often combine **adjectives** with **prepositions** in this pattern: **adjective + preposition +** <u>noun (phrase)</u>
(2) Tim is **enthusiastic about** his new career.	The following is a list of common **adjective + preposition** combinations. *angry / annoyed / crazy / excited / enthusiastic / furious / serious / worried / upset* **about** *something*
(3) She's **good at** science.	*excellent / bad / good / hopeless* **at** *something*
(4) She was **shocked at** the news. He was **surprised by** the discovery.	*amazed / annoyed / astonished / shocked / surprised* **at / by** *something*
(5) Don't feel **sorry for** the criminals. Be **responsible for** your actions.	*happy / (feel) sorry* **for** *someone* *famous / ready / responsible* **for** *something*
(6) A detective's job is **different from** other jobs.	*different* **from** *someone / something*
(7) I'm **interested in** unsolved crimes.	*interested* **in** *someone / something*
(8) You can't be **afraid of** blood as a detective.	*afraid / aware / fond / proud / scared / tired* **of** *someone / something*
(9) Good detective work is **dependent on** clues.	*dependent* **on** *someone / something*
(10) You need a lot of knowledge **related to** crime.	*opposed / related / similar* **to** *someone / something*
(11) Try to be **patient with** others.	*annoyed / bored / happy / patient / pleased / popular / satisfied* **with** *someone / something*
(12) If you are **good at** <u>reading</u> people, **passionate about** <u>helping</u> society, and **interested in** <u>making</u> this world a better place, then detective work may be for you. *Incorrect:* I'm passinate about ~~help~~ society.	<u>Gerunds</u> often follow **adjective + preposition** pairs.

Grammar Practice

MyEnglishLab
▶ Grammar Plus 1 Activities 1 and 2

A Circle the correct prepositions.

1. different **to** / **from**
2. interested **in** / **of**
3. serious **on** / **about**
4. aware **of** / **with**
5. bad **by** / **at**

6. astonished **to** / **by**
7. ready **for** / **by**
8. opposed **to** / **on**
9. dependent **to** / **on**
10. satisfied **with** / **in**

B Complete the conversation. Use adjectives from the box.

bored	famous	interested	similar	surprised	tired	upset

A: I'm really **1.** _____ with this detective story. Can you recommend something

else? I'm **2.** _____ of reading it.

B: You might be **3.** _____ in this one. I really enjoyed trying to solve the problem

while I read it.

A: What's it about?

B: It's about a woman who finds, and then loses, a mysterious necklace. She becomes really

4. _____ about losing it and goes to extreme measures to locate it.

A: It sounds **5.** _____ to another story I've read recently. That was called *The*

Case of the Missing Necklace. It's **6.** _____ for its ending. But you'll be

7. _____ by it.

B: That's it! That's the one I read!

C Complete the story about the famous detective Sherlock Holmes. Use the prepositions from the box.

about	at	for	in	on	with
about	by	from	of	with	

Scottish writer Sir Arthur Conan Doyle is famous

1. _____ creating perhaps English literature's most

popular detective—Sherlock Holmes. Doyle wrote 56 short

stories and four novels about the detective. Readers were crazy

2. _____ Sherlock Holmes from the time he first

appeared in 1887. Fans around the world are still interested

3. _____ him. Sherlock Holmes remains extremely

popular **4.** _____ new generations, as seen from the

2009 hit movie *Sherlock Holmes* and its 2011 sequel.

Sherlock Holmes is different **5.** _____ earlier

detectives in English literature. He is passionate **6.** _____

the cases he investigates as he uses his powers of observation. He

quickly becomes aware **7.** _____ key details that others would overlook and is excellent

8. _____ using logic to solve crimes. He is pleased **9.** _____ his superior

detective skills and responds well to compliments. Even with such skills, Holmes is dependent

10. _____ his friend and assistant, Dr. John Watson. Watson narrates all but four of the

stories about Holmes and is often surprised **11.** _____ Holmes's techniques. Famous

stories include *A Study in Scarlet* (1887) and *The Hound of the Baskervilles* (1902).

Grammar Focus 2 Verb + preposition

Examples	Language notes
(1) A good detective **depends on** <u>his or her instincts</u>.	English speakers often combine **verbs** with **prepositions** in this pattern: **verb + preposition +** <u>noun (phrase)</u>
(2) The detectives **argued about** the details of the investigation.	The following is a list of common **verb + preposition** combinations. *argue / be / boast / dream / worry* **about** something
(3) **Protect** yourself **against** possible danger.	*be / protect / protest* **against** something
(4) You'll need to **glance at** a scene and take it all in.	*glance / hint / marvel* **at** something
(5) The life of a detective does not **allow for** a traditional 9-to-5 day. The criminal **is** now **paying for** his crimes.	*allow / apply / account* **for** something *apologize / be / pay* **for** someone / something
(6) The police force **is suffering from** a lack of training. The TV cameras **distracted** the detective **from** his work.	*benefit / differ / resign / suffer* **from** something *distract* someone **from** something
(7) Make sure you **confide in** an honest person. You may **specialize in** one type of work.	*confide* **in** someone *result / specialize* **in** something
(8) She **accused** him **of** the crime.	*accuse / convict / remind / suspect* someone **of** something
(9) Tim **elaborated on** what is most necessary. Our success **depends on** you. I want to **congratulate** you **on** your new job. Don't **blame** Hank **for** the sloppy work.	*decide / elaborate / insist* **on** something *depend / impose* **on** someone *congratulate* someone **on** something *blame* something **on** someone
(10) Lacy **appealed to** the judge for leniency. Detectives need to **react to** a variety of situations with calmness. Can you **refer** me **to** your boss? I plan to **devote** myself **to** my community.	*apologize / appeal / attend* **to** someone *apply / confess / react / resort / see* **to** something *refer* someone **to** someone *apply / commit / devote* oneself **to** something
(11) Police officers often have to **deal with** a lot of paperwork. I want to **discuss** what I saw **with** a detective. The police officer **charged** the driver **with** reckless endangerment.	*coincide / collide / comply / deal / plead* **with** something *discuss* something **with** someone *charge / confront / provide / trust* someone **with** something
(12) Police officers **deal with** <u>having</u> a lot of paperwork.	<u>Gerunds</u> often follow **verb + preposition** pairs.

Grammar Practice

A Circle the correct prepositions.

1. coincide **with / of**
2. appeal **from / to**
3. insist **on / against**
4. protest **in / against**
5. confide **on / in**
6. hint **at / from**

7. dream **in / about**
8. benefit **from / at**
9. allow **for / with**
10. decide **for / on**
11. argue **about / from**
12. comply **in / with**

B Complete the tips for starting a career as a detective. Use the verbs from the box.

accuse	benefit	devote	is	specialize
apply	depends	elaborate	refer	suspect

1. **Get an education.** Many agencies require that private detectives obtain a four-year degree. However, you might _____ from an even higher degree.

2. **Learn what is public record.** As a good detective, you should _____ to all public records and case evidence as you build your case.

3. **Keep accurate notes.** Record the date, time, and location of an event or conversation. Then later _____ on these notes with more details.

4. **Ask questions.** Good detective work _____ on solid questioning techniques. To obtain more information, use open-ended questions.

5. **Read people.** If in your mind you _____ someone of a crime, first try to read the person's face and body language. Many people are terrible at hiding guilt.

6. **Have an eye for detail.** Cracking a case _____ about the details. Learn to focus not only on the bigger picture but also the smaller details that often go unnoticed.

7. **Take your time.** Don't jump to conclusions or _____ someone of something before you are sure.

8. **Get tech savvy.** _____ yourself to learning and using the latest technology in your work.

9. **Start a private detective business.** _____ for a business license and register all employees.

10. **Advertise.** If you _____ in a certain aspect of detective work—such as financial, legal, corporate, or computer—advertise it.

Speaking

A Could you be a sleuth (detective)? Ask your partner the questions and circle the answers. Total the results.

	Yes	No
1. Do you like to solve mysteries?	1	2
2. Are you good at research?	1	2
3. Are you interested in law?	1	2
4. Are you afraid of certain situations?	2	1
5. Do you confide in many people?	2	1
6. Are you afraid to confront people?	2	1
7. Do you sometimes read about crime cases?	1	2
8. Are you devoted to your community?	1	2
9. Are you good at working with others?	1	2
10. Do you enjoy work that's different from "usual" work?	1	2

Total points:

Key: 10–12 points: You would be a great sleuth.
13–15 points: You probably wouldn't be such a great sleuth.
16+ points: You might want to consider a different field of work.

B Work in a group. Discuss the results with your classmates. Look at the model.

> *My partner is perfect for a career as a sleuth. He is very good at everything related to detective work!*

> *My partner needs to choose a different field because she obviously isn't interested in this kind of work.*

Listening

A UNDERSTANDING MAIN IDEAS Listen to a private investigator's recorded notes. Circle the correct answers.

1. What is this case about?
   a. Missing documents.   **b.** Fake documents.   **c.** Stolen money.

2. What does the investigator think his current case is going to be like?
   a. Exciting.   **b.** Boring.   **c.** Scary.

3. How many different people does he consider suspects?
   a. One.   **b.** Two.   **c.** Three.

4. Does he solve the case?
   a. Yes.   **b.** No.   **c.** He doesn't say.

B 🎧 SUMMARIZING DETAILS Listen again. What happens on each day? Complete the sentences.

1. Day 1: The investigator meets Adam Minor. Minor claims someone stole a briefcase containing

_____ documents while he was out for a(n) _____.

2. Day 2: The investigator interviews Alice, Mr. Minor's _____. The investigator

feels that she wants to _____ something.

3. Day 3: The investigator talks to Alice's _____. The investigator has a(n)

_____ feeling about him.

4. Day 4: The investigator receives a(n) _____ from Alice. She says her boyfriend

owes people a lot of _____ and knew about Mr. Minor's walks.

5. Day 5: The investigator and some police officers drop by the boyfriend's house. They find

the briefcase _____ in a ceiling panel. Then the investigator mentions some

_____ news . . .

C AFTER LISTENING Talk with your partner. What do you think will happen next?

MyEnglishLab

▶ Linking Grammar to Writing

Writing

Occupational title	Employment, 2008	Projected employment, 2018	Change, 2008–2018	
			Number	% Change
Detectives and criminal investigators	112,200	130,900	18,700	17
Fish and game wardens	8,300	9,000	700	8
Police officers	665,700	723,300	57,600	9
Transit and railroad police	4,300	4,500	200	5

A Work with a partner. Look at the chart. According to data from the U.S. National Employment Matrix, where are the biggest areas of growth in police work?

B Choose one of the questions to write a paragraph about. Try to use the grammar from the chapter.

• Why are so many people interested in investigative work?
• What aspects of investigative work are you most interested in?
• What are the advantages and disadvantages of being a detective?
• Why do you think the need for investigators is increasing?

> *Detective work appeals to me for several reasons. First, I have always been*
> *interested in mystery novels, TV shows, and movies. I think I'm good at . . .*

C Share your writing with a partner who chose the same question. Do you have similar ideas?

MyEnglishLab

▶ Diagnostic Test

CHAPTER 16 New Tricks of the Trade

Getting Started

A What's the difference between a detective and a scientist? How are their jobs alike? Share your ideas with a partner.

B Read about *forensics*, the study of evidence discovered at a crime scene and used in a court of law. What three things are sometimes left behind?

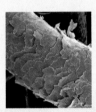

Hair today, gone tomorrow If you've watched crime movies or read mystery novels, then you know this: it's all about the clues! When detectives investigate, they count on getting good evidence. If they come across a single hair—whether it belongs to a victim or criminal—they can start to figure things out. After all, just one hair is enough to give researchers all the information they need to identify someone.

Fingerprints can finger the criminals Fingerprints are like snowflakes. No two are ever identical. We leave our mark almost everywhere we go. Although criminals may think that by wearing gloves they'll get away with a crime, often they aren't as cautious as necessary. Fingerprinting remains an amazingly accurate resource for detectives to determine exactly who the bad guys are.

Just a minute on the lips . . . A sip of soda—enough to leave a lipstick print at a crime scene—can be an extremely important piece of evidence. This is why detectives look over crime scenes carefully; they don't want to leave out even the smallest piece of evidence. Through methods ranging from microscopic analysis to chromatography (laboratory techniques used for the separation of mixtures), investigators can determine who wore the lipstick and what shade it is.

C Look back at the reading in Part B. Complete the tasks.

1. **Phrasal verbs** are multi-word verbs that are made up of a verb + one or two particles. The particles—usually prepositions or adverbs—change the meaning of the original verb. Find and circle the two-word phrasal verbs. (One has a noun between the verb and particle.)
2. Underline the three-word phrasal verb.
3. Complete the definitions with phrasal verbs.

   1. To *count on* _____ means to depend on.

   2. To _____ means to find accidentally.

   3. To _____ means to find a solution.

   4. To _____ means to do without being punished or caught.

   5. To _____ means to check or examine.

   6. To _____ means to omit.

Reading

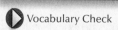

Vocabulary Check

A WARM-UP Work with a partner. *Forensics* is the analysis of evidence, and *anthropology* is the study of human beings. What do you think *forensic anthropology* is? How might it be used to solve crimes?

B SKIMMING Skim the article. Circle the best title. Then go back and read the article again.

    a. Technology can solve a crime   **b.** Crime doesn't pay   **c.** From crime scene to science lab

Forensic Anthropology: Getting down to the nitty-gritty

Today's crime solvers unite two key fields: science and investigation. Forensic anthropologists are able to bring up points that may have been ignored. They can also pick out and zero in on clues that greatly enhance investigations. Their research helps to bring closure to many mysteries. They work on crimes ranging from the identification of a missing person to the person's cause of death.

Here we briefly examine the field of forensic anthropology and discuss these scientists' roles in contemporary investigations.

First of all, what exactly is forensic anthropology? According to the American Board of Forensic Anthropology, it's the "... application of the science of physical or biological anthropology to the legal process." The field uses scientific techniques to identify human remains and to assist with the detection of a crime.

Secondly, what information can we get from the careful study of bones? Examination of skeletal remains can point out someone's gender, age, ethnicity, and height, as well as verify the amount of time since death. In some cases, it can even determine cause of death and contribute additional information about a person's lifestyle. These findings not only help identify victims but also allow investigators to back up their hunches with concrete data and rule certain things out. In short, bones provide a tremendous amount of insight.

Finally, how do forensic anthropologists and other colleagues collaborate? While some investigators may come up with theories related to a case, they all need clear-cut evidence to fall back on, especially when it comes time to take a case to court. Therefore, forensic anthropologists and investigators need to get along well, discuss assumptions and findings, and put "the pieces of the puzzle" together.

In conclusion, scientific discoveries have brought about many changes in our world, and crime solving is no exception. Today's investigators are able to break down cases into parts that were previously untouchable. In doing so, they clear up assumptions, get down to the "nitty-gritty" of crime solving, and ultimately, wrap up the case.

C UNDERSTANDING INFERENCE Check (✓) the information that you can infer from the reading.

☐ **1.** These days a background in science is helpful in investigating crimes.

☐ **2.** A forensic anthropologist can see things that regular people would often miss.

☐ **3.** The only way a forensic anthropologist can identify a victim is through dental remains.

☐ **4.** It's very difficult to prove a case in court without evidence.

☐ **5.** Because of forensic anthropology, more cases are solved today than in the past.

☐ **6.** Most of the forensic science seen on TV shows is not accurate.

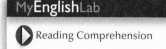

Reading Comprehension

Grammar Focus 1 Phrasal verbs: Inseparable

Examples	Language notes
(1) Detectives **count on** the collection of evidence.	**Phrasal verbs** are a type of multi-word verb. Two-word phrasal verbs have a **verb + a particle**. The particle is usually a preposition or adverb.
(2) Witnesses said the suspect **got in** a white van. Investigators **break down** cases into parts.	The most common **prepositions** in phrasal verbs are *in, on, about,* and *for.* The most common **adverbs** in phrasal verbs are *up, down, off,* and *on.*
(3) The police **brought up** the knife from the basement. *(carried up the stairs)* The suspect **brought up** the topic. *(mentioned)*	Unlike verb + adjective forms, **phrasal verbs change in meaning** when the particle is added.
(4) Let's **discuss** our findings. [more formal] Let's **talk over** our findings. [less formal]	Phrasal verbs are common in **speech**. They are usually less formal than their single-word synonyms.
(5) We didn't **come across** a single hair. ***Incorrect:*** We didn't ~~come a single hair across~~.	Phrasal verbs can be separable or inseparable. **Inseparable** phrasal verbs must keep the verb and particle together.
(6) The investigator **ran into** her colleague at the crime scene. [object = noun] The investigator **ran into** him at the crime scene. [object = pronoun] Forensic anthropologists and other colleagues need to **get along**. [no object]	Inseparable phrasal verbs can be **transitive** or **intransitive**. *Transitive* means the action of the verb impacts something (the object). The object can be a noun or a pronoun. *Intransitive* means the verb does not take an object.
(7) Some criminals wear gloves in an effort to **get away with** crimes.	Some inseparable phrasal verbs have **three words**—a verb + two particles.

Common inseparable phrasal verbs and their definitions		
account for = explain	fall apart = collapse	look into = investigate
blow away = move due to wind	find out = see	run into = meet unexpectedly
break into = enter forcibly	get away = escape	stick to = follow
call for = require	go through = experience / search	take after = resemble
come across = find	look after = guard	take place = happen
drag on = continue	look for = seek	watch over = supervise

See Appendix S for page A-8 for more inseparable phrasal verbs.

Grammar Practice

 A Complete the steps using words from the box.

> come across   find out   look into   stick to   take place

Assessing the scene When police **1.** _____ a crime and study a crime scene, they must
2. _____ certain procedures. Their first action is to **3.** _____ the scene—
for example, notice the size—and isolate the area. They must preserve the scene as they found it and
record anyone who enters or leaves. They then aim to **4.** _____ if the site is a primary or
secondary crime scene. In other words, did the crime **5.** _____ there or somewhere else?

> broke into   got away   look for

Locating the evidence Detectives then try to determine exactly what happened and where. In some cases the criminal **6.** _____ the area, so the detectives look at how he or she possibly entered and **7.** _____. They document the crime scene with written descriptions, photos, videos, and sketches. Regardless of the size of the crime scene, it's important that the police **8.** _____ clues within the secure area.

> account for   blow away   calls for   drag on   fall apart

Collecting the evidence Clear-cut evidence is essential to prove guilt or innocence in a court of law. In any case, this will **9.** _____ a big part of any case as "proof beyond all reasonable doubt." Without this, a case can quickly **10.** _____, or the case may **11.** _____ for a long period of time without resolution. Therefore, detectives gather the most vulnerable evidence first, such as hairs or fibers that may **12.** _____. All evidence is collected in packets using gloves and tweezers. Collecting evidence without cross-contaminating **13.** _____ patience and skills.

B Look back at Part A. Circle the transitive phrasal verbs. Draw a rectangle around the intransitive phrasal verbs.

C Unscramble the three-word phrasal verbs to complete the sentences.

1. Too many people _____ (with / get / away) crimes. We need more police.
2. Why did she _____ (along / go / with) it? She knew it was wrong.
3. The jury tried to _____ (keep / with / up) the lawyer's argument.
4. Can you _____ (up / come / with) a better explanation?
5. It's almost dark. The detective might _____ (out / of / run) daylight.
6. Solving a crime _____ (to / comes / down) the evidence.
7. I _____ (to / up / look) police officers. It's not an easy job.
8. We _____ (look / to / forward) our day in court.

D Look back at the phrasal verbs in Part C. Circle the correct meanings.

1. **a.** escape punishment from   **b.** pay attention to
2. **a.** argue against   **b.** take the same view as
3. **a.** ask questions about   **b.** not fall behind
4. **a.** produce   **b.** tell the truth about
5. **a.** take a short break   **b.** have no more
6. **a.** means or signifies   **b.** arrives from
7. **a.** call when needed   **b.** admire or respect
8. **a.** anticipate   **b.** fear

Grammar Focus 2 Phrasal verbs: Separable

Examples	Language notes
(1) The detectives **looked** <u>the crime scene</u> **over**. [object = noun] The detectives **looked** <u>it</u> **over**. [object = pronoun]	All separable phrasal verbs are **transitive**—meaning they have an <u>object</u>. The object can be a noun or pronoun.
(2) Investigators **break down** <u>cases</u> into parts. Investigators **break** <u>cases</u> **down** into parts.	In **separable** phrasal verbs, the <u>object</u> can go after or between the verb and particle: **verb + particle + <u>object</u>** **verb + <u>object</u> + particle**
(3) The investigator was able to **figure** <u>it</u> **out**. [pronoun] *Incorrect:* The investigator was able to ~~figure out it~~.	When the object is a pronoun, the <u>pronoun</u> must follow the verb: **verb + <u>pronoun</u> + particle**
(4) Forensic anthropologists are able to **bring up points that may have been previously ignored**. *Incorrect:* Forensic anthropologists are able to **bring** ~~points that may have been previously ignored~~ **up**.	A <u>long object</u> is best placed after the **phrasal verb**.

Common separable phrasal verbs and their definitions	
burn down = destroy by burning	pay back = repay
call off = cancel	pick up = lift with hands or fingers
carry out = fulfill or accomplish	rule out = eliminate
clean off = clear the surface of	seal off = prevent people from entering
clear up = clarify	send off = send in the mail
figure out = understand	throw away = discard
fill in = complete a form	try out = attempt or test
give back = return	work out = solve
leave out = omit	write down = record in writing
look over = study	write up = prepare a document
mix up = confuse one for another	

See Appendix S on page A-8 for more separable phrasal verbs.

Grammar Practice

 A Circle the correct particles.

1. Would you please fill **in / down** this form? Include as much detail as possible.

2. Have you been able to work **away / out** who the killer was?

3. If you aren't sure that you want to buy it, why don't you try it **out / up** first?

4. She left **out / on** some important details from her final report.

5. Can you clear something **up / out**? How exactly did the burglar enter the locked house?

6. Never throw **up / away** evidence until 10 years after a case has closed.

7. I'm happy to lend you some money. Just pay me **out / back** by the end of the month.

8. Please give **back / down** Ms. Turner's belongings. She is free to go.

B Rewrite each sentence twice: (a) Put the object between the verb and the particle. (b) Replace the object with a pronoun.

1. The criminal burned down three houses.

   a. *The criminal burned three houses down.*

   b. *The criminal burned them down.*

2. Do not pick up that glove.

   a. _____

   b. _____

3. The police ruled out Mike Conners as a suspect.

   a. _____

   b. _____

4. Do not clean off this surface yet.

   a. _____

   b. _____

5. Why did the detective call off the investigation?

   a. _____

   b. _____

6. Please write up your lab results as soon as possible.

   a. _____

   b. _____

C Complete the paragraph. Use the phrasal verbs from the box.

carry out	figure out	mix up	pick up	seal off	send off	write down

Fiber evidence at a crime scene can be used to link a suspect to a crime. How fibers are collected at crime scenes depends on their size. When fibers are large, investigators
1. _____ them _____ with their fingers and place them inside a small envelope. They then seal it and 2. _____ the details of the evidence. When smaller fibers are found at a crime scene, investigators will
3. _____ the area where they were found, and 4. _____ them _____ to forensic scientists for analysis. These objects must be handled with care so investigators do not 5. _____ the fibers. When forensic scientists 6. _____ their analysis of fiber evidence, they can usually
7. _____ if the fibers are of a certain type of clothing. They can't always determine if fibers came from one specific piece of clothing. However, this evidence is still significant.

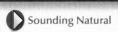

Speaking

A Work in groups of three. A crime has occurred in Grandma Rose's living room. Imagine that you and your partners are the investigative team on the case. (Each partner chooses one role: police officer, detective, or forensic scientist.) Look at the pictures and work as a team to come up with answers to the questions.

What crime was committed? (Was it a theft? A kidnapping? A murder? etc.) What evidence was collected? (Be specific!) What five questions will you ask each of the suspects? Who "dunnit"?

Grandma Rose

Archie, grandson

Betsy, neighbor

Frank, gardener

Crime scene

B As a group, present your case to the class. Look at the model.

> *First of all, we believe the crime was a theft. How do we back up that claim? The evidence . . .*

Listening

A UNDERSTANDING MAIN IDEAS Listen to the podcast interview. Check (✓) the main idea.

☐ Many people these days are inspired to work in forensics by TV shows, especially *CSI*.

☐ Lucy Moreno plans to be a detective and work in forensics.

☐ A 15-year-old student already knows she wants to become a medical examiner.

B 🎧 UNDERSTANDING DETAILS Listen again. Then circle the correct words.

1. Lucy wants to pursue a(n) **internship / career** as a medical examiner.

2. A medical examiner is in charge of the **forensic / criminal** investigation of a death.

3. Lucy has always been **interested in / bored by** science.

4. Lucy has never **seen / been grossed out by** blood.

5. A medical examiner is **involved in / in charge of** both the legal and the medical sides of the investigation.

6. Lucy's eighth grade teacher **brought in / brought up** a healthy lung and a smoker's lung.

C AFTER LISTENING Think back to when you were younger. What did you want to be when you grew up? What were the reasons? What are you now interested in?

Writing

My**English**Lab

▶ Linking Grammar to Writing

A One of the most popular genres (styles) of writing is the mystery story. Detective stories are a kind of sub-genre. You are going to write a detective story. Read the story titles, starters, and endings.

Titles
- The Mystery of the Missing Key
- The Case of the Barking Dog
- Lipstick on the Napkin

Starters
- It was a dark and stormy night. Nobody was on the street. Muddy footprints led up from the doorway to the stairway of the apartment building.
- She thought she had put her key in the pocket of her fuzzy sweater. Now it wasn't there. She heard a noise behind her and began to panic.
- Suddenly there was a loud bang and then the noisy city went quiet—except for a dog barking in the distance.

Endings
- He grinned, but the look of pain was still visible on his face.
- "I'm always careful, honey," the detective whispered into the phone.
- Despite everything, she never returned to that city again.

B Now write a detective story. Use a title, starter, or ending from Part A. Try to use the grammar from the chapter.

> It was a dark and stormy night. Nobody was on the street. Muddy footprints led up from the doorway to the stairway of the apartment building. Emily hesitated at the bottom of the stairs. The situation called for courage, but Emily felt unsure. . . .

C Work in a small group. Exchange your stories. Read and make comments. Then choose one to share with the class.

My**English**Lab

▶ Diagnostic Test

Grammar Summary

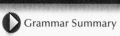

English has many **adjective + preposition** and **verb + preposition** combinations.

Adjectives	Verbs	Prepositions
angry / annoyed / crazy / excited / enthusiastic / furious / serious / worried / upset	argue / be / boast / dream / worry	about
—	be / protect / protest	against
amazed / annoyed / astonished / excellent / bad / good / hopeless / shocked / surprised	glance / hint / marvel	at
happy / (feel) sorry / famous / ready / responsible	account / allow / apologize / apply / be / pay	for
different	benefit / differ / resign / suffer / distract	from
interested	confide / result / specialize	in
afraid / aware / fond / proud / scared / tired	accuse / convict / remind / suspect	of
dependent	decide / elaborate / insist / depend / impose	on
opposed / related / similar	apologize / appeal / attend / apply / confess / react / resort / see	to
annoyed / bored / happy / pleased / popular / satisfied	charge / coincide / collide / comply / confront / deal / discuss/ plead / trust	with

A **phrasal verb** is a verb paired with one or more particles (usually an adverb or preposition). The particle changes the meaning of the verb. Phrasal verbs can be inseparable or separable and transitive or intransitive.

Inseparable		Separable	
get along	take place	back up	figure out
run into	wait on	carry out	throw away

	Transitive (with object)	Intransitive (without object)
Inseparable	The investigator **ran into** <u>her colleague</u> at the crime scene.	Forensic anthropologists and other colleagues need to **get along**.
Separable	The investigator **wrapped** <u>the case</u> **up**.	—

With **transitive separable phrasal verbs**, the <u>object</u> can be placed after the particle or between the verb and the particle. When the object is a pronoun, it can only be placed between the verb and particle.

Transitive separable phrasal verbs
Detectives need to **look over** <u>the crime scene</u> carefully.   Detectives need to **look** <u>the crime scene</u> **over** carefully.   Detectives need to **look** <u>it</u> **over** carefully.

Three-word phrasal verbs are usually inseparable.

Three-word phrasal verbs
Why do some people think they can **get away with** crimes? They usually get caught.   After 10 years, the criminal is going to **get out of** jail. DNA analysis has just proved his innocence.

Self-Assessment

A (5 points) Cross out the adjective that cannot go with the preposition.

1. **a.** excited   **b.** serious   **c.** responsible   + **about**

2. **a.** ready   **b.** different   **c.** famous   + **for**

3. **a.** interested   **b.** fond   **c.** proud   + **of**

4. **a.** opposed   **b.** related   **c.** excellent   + **to**

5. **a.** annoyed   **b.** astonished   **c.** satisfied   + **with**

B (7 points) Complete the sentences. Use prepositions.

1. My cousin is going to apply _____ a position on the police force.

2. Lydia accused her neighbor _____ theft.

3. No one ever confessed _____ the murder.

4. The criminal pleaded _____ the judge for leniency.

5. Allison is specializing _____ forensic anthropology in graduate school.

6. The detective devoted himself _____ solving the case.

7. Do you think criminals can benefit _____ watching TV shows about crime?

C (5 points) Rewrite the sentences. Replace each underlined word with a phrasal verb from the box. For separable phrasal verbs, place the object between the verb and particle.

call off   fall apart   leave out   look for   pay back

1. Be sure to <u>repay</u> the money. _____

2. Always <u>seek</u> clues in unexpected places. _____

3. The case will <u>collapse</u> without a witness. _____

4. Chief Lee will <u>cancel</u> the press conference. _____

5. Why did you <u>omit</u> the quotation? _____

D (8 points) Complete the story about a dumb criminal. Circle the correct phrasal verbs.

A woman had an unusual way of robbing people. First, she would knock on people's doors and tell them that her car **1. fell apart / broke down**. Next, she would ask to use the phone to **2. call for / look over** help. But she never got an answer. Finally, she would ask to use the restroom, but what she really did was **3. watch over / go through** the victims' drawers and cupboards. After the woman thanked the people and left, they would **4. find out / back up** that they were missing cash, jewelry, and credit cards. Her tricks worked well until one day one of her victims offered to fix her car. Of course, it started right away. She panicked, ran, and **5. got away / paid back**. Then the police **6. accounted for / figured out** that the number she was calling was her own number. The police simply **7. stuck to / looked for** the woman and **8. came across / dragged on** her at her home, where she was arrested.

Unit Project: Science profile

A Some real-life forensic scientists are famous for their research as well as for solving difficult cases. Work with a partner. Research and give a presentation about someone in the field of forensics. Follow the steps.

1. Here are some famous forensics experts. Choose one from the list or think of another one.

Sir Alec Jeffreys

Clea Koff

Henry C. Lee

- Dr. Michael Baden
- William Bass
- Dr. Joseph Bell
- Sir Alec Jeffreys
- Clea Koff

- Henry C. Lee
- Herbert Leon MacDonell
- Dr. Laura Pettler
- Dr. Khunying Porntip Rojanasunan
- Dr. Cyril Wecht

2. Research your expert with your partner. Use the questions to help you.
- Where is he / she from?
- What degree(s) does he / she hold?
- What started him / her in the career of forensics?
- What is he / she most famous for?
- What are some cases he / she has worked on?
- What books has he / she written?
- What is he / she currently doing?
- If you had the opportunity to meet him / her, what three questions would you ask?

B With your partner, present your findings to the class. Answer any questions. Look at the model.

> *Clea Koff is a forensic anthropologist, author, and humanitarian. She grew up living in different countries around the world. . . .*

MyEnglishLab

▶ Unit Test

MyEnglishLab

▶ Search it!

From Garden to Table

OUTCOMES

After completing this unit, I will be able to use these grammar points.

CHAPTER 17

Grammar Focus 1
Present passive

Grammar Focus 2
Time signals

CHAPTER 18

Grammar Focus 1
Advice: Modals and expressions

Grammar Focus 2
Necessity: Expressions

CHAPTER 17 | Behind the Scenes

Getting Started

A Discuss the questions with a partner.

- Do you drink coffee? If so, how many cups do you drink a day? How do you like it prepared?
- Why do you think coffee is so popular with so many people?

B Complete the questionnaire. Circle your answers.

What do you know about coffee?

1. Coffee is grown in about (**a.** 25 **b.** 50 **c.** 125) countries worldwide.
2. Coffee is traded more than any other commodity except (**a.** oil **b.** rice **c.** chocolate).
3. Coffee beans are the seeds of a fruit similar to a (**a.** banana **b.** pineapple **c.** cherry).
4. Most coffee in the world is cultivated in (**a.** Brazil **b.** Colombia **c.** Ethiopia).
5. About (**a.** 2 **b.** 7 **c.** 12) million tons of green coffee beans are produced each year.
6. Most coffee beans are picked (**a.** by machine **b.** by hand) as soon as they're ripe.
7. Arabica coffee beans are cultivated at an altitude above (**a.** 492 feet/150 m **b.** 1,640 feet/500 m **c.** 1,946 feet/600 m).
8. It takes (**a.** 3 to 5 **b.** 13 to 15 **c.** 30 to 50) years for a coffee tree to reach maturity.
9. For 1 pound (about .5 kg) of roasted coffee, (**a.** 1,000 **b.** 2,000 **c.** 4,000) beans are needed.
10. Flavored coffees are created (**a.** before **b.** after) the roasting process.

1.b 2.a 3.c 4.a 5.b 6.b 7.c 8.b 9.c 10.b

C Look back at the questionnaire in Part B. Complete the tasks.

1. **Time signals** help explain the order of events. Circle the examples that show order.
2. We use the **passive voice** when the action is the focus. It is formed with *be* + the past participle of the verb. Underline the past participles. Then complete the chart.

Subject	Be + past participle

Reading

A WARM-UP What do you know about caring for plants? What about how coffee is grown?

B SKIMMING Skim the article. Put the steps in order (1–4). Then go back and read the article again.

_____ **a.** Roast the beans.   _____ **c.** Hull, polish, grade, and sort the beans.

_____ **b.** Transplant the seedlings.   _____ **d.** Dry the cherries.

Today's Harvested Cherries: Your Future Roasted Beans

Origins Have you ever considered where your steaming, aromatic cup of fresh-ground coffee comes from? Coffee cultivation started in the eighth or ninth century, experts believe. According to legend, a shepherd in Ethiopia spotted his goats eating flaming red cherries, then frolicking about energetically. When the shepherd tried a few himself, he felt a surge of energy! This was the start of coffee consumption.

Starting with a seed Coffee seeds are found inside those brightly-colored cherries. They are first planted in large beds. As soon as seedlings sprout, they are transplanted into special pots and watered frequently. As they grow, the seedlings are shaded from harsh sunlight. When they are bigger and strong enough, they are replanted outside. This generally occurs during the wet season so that the roots of the young plants stay moist and can easily expand in the soil. Coffee trees are ideally grown in high altitudes, where the soil is rich.

From tree to cherries Depending on the variety, it takes three or four years for coffee plants to produce the bright-red coffee cherries. In most cases, the moment the cherries ripen, they are harvested, either by hand or machine, and processed.

Processing the cherries With the more traditional dry method of processing, the cherries are then spread out on extensive surfaces. After that, they are dried in the sun. For thorough drying, the cherries are raked and turned several times a day. For protection from moisture, the cherries are covered at night. This entire process may take several weeks.

Drying and roasting After the cherries are dried, the outer layers are removed and the beans are exposed. Before the beans are exported, they are hulled, polished, graded, and sorted. Next, the defective beans are discarded. The rest are stored to await roasting—the step in which the green coffee beans are transformed into the rich brown aromatic beans that we find in our markets.

C UNDERSTANDING SUPPORTING DETAILS Where in the article do the following sentences belong? Write *1* for the first paragraph, *2* for the second paragraph, and so on.

_____ **1.** Roasting is generally performed by the importing company.

_____ **2.** In addition to healthy soil, the seedlings need water frequently.

_____ **3.** The surge is caused by caffeine.

_____ **4.** A good picker can harvest about 110 to 220 pounds (50 to 100 kg) of coffee cherries a day.

_____ **5.** In the wet method of processing coffee cherries, the pulp is removed after harvesting, and the bean is dried with just the parchment skin left on.

Grammar Focus 1 Present passive

Examples	Language notes
(1) The seeds **are dried** in the sun. *(It's not important who put the seeds out.)* Coffee seeds **are found** inside brightly colored berries. *(Anyone who looks inside the berries finds seeds.)*	We use the **passive voice** when we want to focus on the action, not the doer (the person or thing doing the action). We may also use it if the doer is unknown or universal.
(2) Coffee **is grown** in many countries around the world. The seedlings **are transplanted** into special pots.	To form the passive in the simple present, use: **be + past participle**
(3) Farmers **plant** <u>coffee seeds</u> in large beds. [active] Coffee seeds **are planted** in large beds. [passive]	In **active** sentences, the doer is the subject of the sentence; the receiver of the **action** is the <u>object</u>. In **passive** sentences, the receiver is the subject of the sentence. Therefore, only **transitive verbs** (verbs that take an object) can be used in the passive voice. Use: **receiver + be + past participle of transitive verb** **Note:** The passive voice is more commonly used in formal writing. In speech, most sentences are active.
(4) Coffee seeds are planted in large beds **by farmers**.	If we want to include the doer, we can include that information near the end of the sentence, using *by*. Use: **receiver + be + past participle + by + doer**

See Appendix J on page A-5 for a list of irregular past participles.

Grammar Practice

MyEnglishLab

▶ Grammar Plus 1
Activities 1 and 2

A Read the sentences. Write *A* (active) or *P* (passive).

_____ 1. A lot of coffee is grown in the relatively small country of Guatemala.

_____ 2. Coffee is cultivated in the highlands of Antigua.

_____ 3. The highlands rise 5,573 feet (1,700 m) above sea level.

_____ 4. Many coffee lovers visit Antigua every year.

_____ 5. Antiguan coffee has an exceptional taste.

_____ 6. Antiguan coffee is known for a rich and lively aroma.

B Complete the sentences. Use the verbs from the box. Use the present passive.

~~grow~~ harvest need plant purchase roast see transplant

The process

1. Some coffee plants *are grown* _____ by people inside the home in large pots, though ideally it's best to do it outside.

2. To grow a coffee tree, fresh coffee cherries _____ for planting. However, because cherries are not always available, it's also possible to use coffee seeds.

3. Seeds _____ from special stores or through the mail.

4. Next, the seeds _____ an inch or two (2.5 to 5 cm) deep in a pot. At four months, the first leaves _____, though they don't really look like adult coffee plant leaves.

5. At nine months, the plant _____ into the ground if the climate is right.

6. Coffee cherries _____ after several years.

7. After processing and drying, the coffee beans _____.

C Rewrite the sentences. Use the present passive.

1. More than 50 percent of Americans over the age of 18 consume coffee every day.

_____

2. People enjoy 65 percent of all coffee during breakfast hours.

_____

3. Some people dispute the health effects of coffee.

_____

4. Thirty-five percent of coffee drinkers request black coffee.

_____

5. A typical espresso drive-through business sells an average of 250 cups of coffee a day.

_____

6. People in the United States import more than $4 billion of coffee a year.

_____

D Complete the sentences. Use the simple present. Use the active or passive form of the verbs.

We **1.** _____ (depend on) agriculture. No matter where we are in the world, different kinds of crops **2.** _____ (find). Many crops **3.** _____ (raise) for food. The three most popular are sugar cane, corn, and wheat.

Sugar cane **4.** _____ (produced) in around 107 countries worldwide. Brazil and China **5.** _____ (be) responsible for more than 50 percent of the world's production.

Corn **6.** _____ (cultivate) throughout the world. It **7.** _____ (call) *maize* in many countries in the world.

More of the earth's surface **8.** _____ (cover) by wheat than by any other food crop. Mostly, it **9.** _____ (grow) in China, Russia, the United States, India, and Canada. The world's farmers **10.** _____ (grow) enough wheat every year to fill a freight train long enough to stretch around the world two and a half times!

Grammar Focus 2 Time signals

Examples	Language notes
(1) **As soon as** they sprout, the seedlings will be transplanted. Should the cherries be harvested **after** they're bright red?	**Time signals** can help explain the order of events in a story or steps in a process. We also use them to give instructions. We use them with a variety of verb forms.
(2) We went to visit the coffee plantation. **Afterwards**, we enjoyed delicious coffee. **After that**, we decided which coffee was our favorite. We will visit the coffee plantation again next year, and **then** we'll buy a lot more coffee.	The adverbs ***afterwards***, ***after that***, and ***then*** mean *subsequently, at a later time,* or *following.* They explain the time relationship between the first piece of information and the second.
(3) **First**, the seeds are planted. **Next**, they are harvested. **Finally**, they are sold in stores.	The adverbs ***now***, ***first*** (*second,* etc.), ***next***, and ***finally*** indicate chronological order—as in a recipe, story, or sequence of events.
(4) <u>**Before** exportation</u>, the beans were processed. <u>**The moment** they ripen</u>, they will be harvested. *Incorrect:* ~~The moment,~~ they will be harvested.	Other time signals cannot stand alone. They are part of a time phrase / clause. Use: **time signal** + noun (+ verb) Examples of these words include *after, as soon as, before, the moment,* and *when.*
(5) **After** the farmers picked the cherries, they spread them out to dry.	***After*** . . . means *later in time.*
(6) **As soon as** the cherries are ripe, we'll let you know. Did the people buy the coffee **once** it was available?	***As soon as*** . . . means *immediately after.* Similar signals include ***Once*** . . . , ***The moment*** (*that*) . . . , and ***Now that*** . . . .
(7) **Before** she saw the coffee trees in Costa Rica, she thought they were much taller.	***Before*** . . . means *at an earlier time.*
(8) I was reading an article **when** he arrived.	***When*** . . . means *at that time.*
(9) **Afterwards**, we had coffee and cake. **First**, the plants are transplanted. **After the sun rose**, the workers arrived. **Once you get here**, call me.	We usually place a **comma** after time signals that come at the beginning of a sentence.

Grammar Practice

MyEnglishLab
▶ Grammar Plus 2
Activities 1 and 2

 A Read about how the best coffee is made. Circle the correct words.

1. For the best flavor, coffee is ground immediately **before** / **when** it's used.

2. **After** / **First** the pot is filled with water, the coffee is brewed.

3. **Next,** / **As soon as,** water is poured into the coffee maker.

4. **Now that** / **After that**, one heaping teaspoon of ground coffee per cup is put into the filter.

5. **Then,** / **When** the coffee is ready, pour yourself a cup.

6. **After** / **Now** your breakfast is finished, you may want another cup.

7. **Finally,** / **Now that** you know how to make an excellent cup of coffee, share it with your friends.

B Look at the pictures and read the steps. Then put them in order (1–6).

_____ **a.** Next the mixture is pasteurized, homogenized, and left for four hours to let cool and form into crystals.

_____ **b.** When ingredients are added, the ice cream is packaged and frozen.

_1_ **c.** First, the basic ice cream ingredients are weighed and combined.

_____ **d.** Before the mix is packaged, nuts and other elements are added.

_____ **e.** Finally, the ice cream is enjoyed.

_____ **f.** After the mix has rested for four hours, fresh fruits, flavors, or colors are added.

C Work with a partner. Describe a process that you follow to prepare something. Choose a process from the list or think of your own. Use time markers.

• How to boil an egg
• How to make popcorn
• How to make rice
• How to make a cup of tea

Listening

A BEFORE LISTENING Are you a connoisseur of (an expert on) a particular food or drink? What do you like about it? What do you know about where it comes from?

B 🎧 UNDERSTANDING INFERENCE Listen to an interview with a coffee connoisseur. What can you infer about coffee, based on the interview? Check (✓) the statement(s).

☐ **1.** Coffee is good for you.

☐ **2.** Tea is more popular than coffee.

☐ **3.** Coffee is popular with people around the world.

C 🎧 UNDERSTANDING DETAILS Listen again. Write *T* for the true statements and *F* for the false statements.

_____ **1.** Java is one of many places where coffee is cultivated.

_____ **2.** More than 400 billion cups of coffee are consumed each year.

_____ **3.** Nearly 55 million farmers worldwide depend on coffee for their livelihood.

_____ **4.** Coffee is best stored at room temperature.

_____ **5.** Coffee is best when it is consumed not too long after purchase.

_____ **6.** Adding cinnamon, nutmeg, or chocolate to coffee is suggested.

Speaking

A *Eating habits* are what and how people eat. What are your eating habits? Discuss the questions in a small group.

1. When did you learn food etiquette (the rules that define how and what you eat)?
2. When seasons change, many people change their food choices. In your culture, how are food choices affected by the seasons?
3. What typical foods are eaten in your culture? What foods are not permitted or not usually eaten?
4. What are some cultural "guidelines" for food combinations? Are there certain foods that are never combined?

5. In your culture, how many and what types of meals are eaten during the day?

6. What advice is given to visitors to your home country about food and eating—for example, practices before, during, and after meals? Look at the model.

> In my country, we are told by our parents what time we eat—and what we eat!

> In my family, we always share a Sunday dinner together.

> In wintertime, we usually eat a lot of soups. In the summer, we often eat spicy foods.

B As a class, talk about your answers from Part A.

Writing

MyEnglishLab

▶ Linking Grammar to Writing

A How is breakfast traditionally prepared in your home or home country? Consider the questions in the list.

• How is the table set?
• What else is placed on the table or serving area?
• What main dish is prepared? What foods are placed on the table?
• What side dishes or condiments are served?
• What drinks are served?

B Write a paragraph about the process of breakfast preparation in your home or home country. Assume your audience is unfamiliar with the process. Try to use the grammar from the chapter.

Breakfast in Canada

Breakfast in Ethiopia

Breakfast in Lebanon

> Breakfast on Sunday is a very important meal in my house. First, the table is set with small plates, forks, and spoons, and cloth napkins. My mother usually places fresh flowers on the table, too. Next, my father's favorite red tea is prepared in a large pot. We use tea glasses from Turkey, my father's home country. Fresh yogurt and flatbread are also placed on the table. Once we sit down to eat, tea is served. After that . . .

C Share your writing with a partner and compare the similarities and differences. Then tell the class what you learned.

MyEnglishLab

 ▶ Diagnostic Test

CHAPTER 18

Redefining Gardens:
Urban Farming

Getting Started

A If you want to enjoy fresh vegetables and you live in a city, what are your options? Should you buy your vegetables from a store? Should you grow them?

B Read the tips for urban farmers. What's something farmers must do when starting their "garden"? What's something they shouldn't do?

○ ○ ○

Growing our own—in the city

Let's face it, big city living isn't the healthiest lifestyle. How can we still enjoy fresh produce when we live in the center of a concrete jungle? Of course, eating fresh vegetables is something we **have got to** do in order to be healthy. Buying from local farmers is something we **should** do, but **it's also a good idea to** grow our own! Here are some tips:

Do your homework.

🌱 As soon as you decide to start a garden, you **must** invest in soil testing to check contaminants; you **must not** use soil that will "poison" your plants!

🌱 Before you choose the plants you want to grow, you **have to** look into the conditions they require.

Join forces.

🌱 You **might want to** collaborate with a neighbor on your garden project.

🌱 You **had better** seek advice from people who have urban garden expertise. If you don't, your garden may fail.

Recycle and reuse.

🌱 Once you decide to start your garden, you **ought to** start composting! Learn how to use scraps to enrich your dirt.

🌱 Look around for containers you are no longer using. But be careful! You **shouldn't** use materials that you're unsure about.

C Look back at the tips in Part B. Complete the tasks.

1. Notice the words in **bold**. What do they have in common in terms of form?
2. What's the tone of the words? Which express **advice**? **Necessity**?

Reading

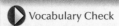
A WARM-UP How do you think urban gardens might be different from country gardens?

B SCANNING Scan the article. What three things does Will Allen believe about farming? Then go back and read the whole article.

IT TAKES A FARMER

Can smarter farming save a community? What about our planet? Expert urban gardener Will Allen thinks so. Allen, a former pro basketball player, is now the CEO of Growing Power, a non-profit sustainable farming project based in Milwaukee, Wisconsin. As the unofficial leader of the so-called "local food" movement, Allen and his organization are dedicated to spreading the word about farming where you live, be it urban or rural.

According to Allen:

- All people should have access to fresh, safe, affordable, and nutritious foods regardless of their economic circumstances.
- We have to educate ourselves about gardening in order to live healthier lives. For example: We must not use synthetic chemicals, including fertilizers, pesticides, and herbicides. We need to learn about the hazards of these products. And then we need to stay away from them.
- We ought to deal with pests the old-fashioned way—for example, with ladybugs and foliar compost tea, to assist in controlling pest and bacteria problems. If necessary, we should use only certified organic pesticides, such as Neem oil and pyrethrum (a pesticide made from chrysanthemum leaves).

These beliefs are alive and well at Altgeld Gardens, one of Allen's urban farm sites. The farm sits on 2.5 acres (1 hectare) in Chicago's South Side neighborhood. The farm not only produces healthy food but also creates job opportunities in an impoverished and isolated community. The message is that we have got to educate ourselves and our community if we want to live healthy lives.

As for the planet? The message has a global application, as well. We had better work together to make this planet a delicious and healthful place for all, or our health, and our earth, will suffer.

C UNDERSTANDING MAIN IDEAS AND DETAILS Answer the questions.

1. Who is Will Allen? _____

2. What does Allen promote? _____

3. What does "local food" mean? _____

4. How does Allen feel about synthetic chemicals? _____

5. How can sustainable farming help a community? The world? _____
_____

Grammar Focus 1 Advice: Modals and expressions

Examples	Language notes
(1) You **should** use ladybugs, not pesticides. They **ought to** grow tomatoes in their garden. He**'d better not** use too much water.	We can **express advice** with a variety of modals and expressions, and with a range of politeness.
(2) You **should** eat more vegetables.	Use **should** to give advice or to talk about what is right.
(3) We **ought to** do what we enjoy.	We use **ought to** in the same way we use *should*, but it's not used as frequently.
(4) We **had better** get started. We**'d better** learn more about how to safely protect our crops.	*Had better* is stronger than *should* and *ought to*. We use it to imply that there may be consequences if the person doesn't follow the advice. We often contract *had* (*'d*) with subject pronouns in speech and informal writing.
(5) Everyone **should have** access to fresh, safe, affordable, and nutritious foods. We **ought to grow** our own vegetables. We **had better work** together to make this planet a healthful place.	With *should*, *ought to*, and *had better*, use: subject + **modal** + **base verb**
(6) We **shouldn't have** to search far for healthy foods. He **had better not use** pesticides on his farm.	Use **should not** and **had better not** to advise against something.
(7) **Maybe** you ought to visit your local farmer's market. I **think** (that) we'd better use this soil. I **don't think** (that) you should eat meat.	To make a suggestion with *should*, *ought to*, or *had better* more polite, use: **Maybe** + advice subject + (**do** + **not**) **think** (that) + advice **Note:** The "that" at the start of the noun clause is often dropped.
(8) **It's a good idea to use** organic pesticides. **If I were you, I would find** a way to grow herbs. **You might want to work** with a neighbor.	Other ways to politely make suggestions include: • **It's a good idea to** + base verb • **If I were you, I would (not)** + base verb • **You might want to** + base verb
(9) Q: **Should** we **start** a garden? A: **Yes, you should. / No, you shouldn't.** Q: **What should** I **wear**? A: **Something casual.**	Use *should* to **ask** for advice. For **short answers** to *yes / no* questions, use *should*.

Grammar Practice

MyEnglishLab

▶ Grammar Plus 1
Activities 1 and 2

 Circle the correct answers.

1. I love chocolate, but I _____ eat too much or I'll get sick!
   a. ought to   **b.** had better   **c.** shouldn't

2. That farm uses a lot of dangerous pesticides. You _____ eat those vegetables.
   a. had better not   **b.** should   **c.** ought to

3. _____ find out more information about eating locally.
   a. Shouldn't   **b.** Had better not   **c.** It's a good idea to

4. At that farm, you can pick your own berries. So you _____ bring a big basket!

    a. ought to   **b.** shouldn't   **c.** had better not

5. Before I plant my garden, _____ I check the soil?

    a. had better not   **b.** ought to   **c.** should

6. The chef says that we _____ first visit the farmer's market and *then* decide what to prepare for dinner.

    a. ought to   **b.** shouldn't   **c.** had better not

7. He has diabetes, so he _____ be careful about eating sugary foods.

    a. shouldn't   **b.** had better   **c.** had better not

B   Match the advice to the situations.

Situation	Advice
_____ **1.** I don't know much about starting a garden.	**a.** It's a good idea to eat something before working in the garden.
_____ **2.** The birds are eating all the blueberries.	**b.** She should apply some aloe vera cream.
_____ **3.** His back hurts after weeding all day.	**c.** You had better water it.
_____ **4.** She got sunburned after working in the sun.	**d.** You might want to put a net over the bushes.
_____ **5.** The shoes were too small; now she has blisters.	**e.** He shouldn't bend over so much.
_____ **6.** The garden is too dry.	**f.** You ought to first read about gardens.
_____ **7.** I'm so hungry that my head hurts.	**g.** She should start her garden inside.
_____ **8.** She can't have a garden outside.	**h.** She had better not wear those shoes again.

C   Read the lists of garden tools. They are categorized by importance. Give advice using words from the list.

Recommended items for starting a vegetable garden

Very important	Important	Don't get!
high-quality shovel and hoe	5-gallon (19 li) bucket	~~poorly made gardening boots~~
organic seeds	lightweight gloves	expensive pruners
organic soil	long garden hose	small watering can

1. *You had better not buy poorly made gardening boots.* _____

2. _____

3. _____

4. _____

5. _____

6. _____

7. _____

8. _____

9. _____

Grammar Focus 2 Necessity: Expressions

Examples	Language notes
(1) We **have to** educate ourselves and our community. They **have got to** learn about sustainability. We **need to** get some ladybugs. We **must** learn about gardening.	Use **have to**, **have got to**, **need to**, and **must** to express the idea that something is necessary.
(2) I **have to** plant my garden this weekend. We **need to** use organic pesticides.	We use **have to**, **have got to**, and **need to** in everyday speech.
(3) You **must** learn about healthy planting so that you can protect the soil, your food, and your family.	*Must*, on the other hand, is very strong. Use it to give orders or make strong suggestions.
(4) They **must follow** the steps in order to have a successful garden.	With **have to**, **have got to**, **need to**, and **must**, use: subject + **modal** + **base verb**
(5) You **don't have to have** a yard in order to start a garden. She **doesn't need to water** the garden today. You **needn't worry** about watering because it's rained so much this week. We **must not use** synthetic chemicals. *(Something very bad will happen if we do, so do not do that.)*	To express **lack of necessity**, use: subject + **do** + **not** + **have to** + **base verb** subject + **do** + **not** + **need to** + **base verb** We can also use **needn't** (*need not*) + **be** to express lack of necessity, but it's not common. **Note:** The negative form of *must* (**must not / mustn't**) expresses prohibition.
(6) She **had to get** a city permit before she started the garden on her building's rooftop. They **will need to stop** at the garden store for compost.	To express **necessity in the past / future**, use: subject + **had to / will have to** + **base verb** subject + **needed to / will need to** + **base verb**
(7) It's **necessary to learn** a few things before we start a garden. They **are not required to wear** gloves. We **are supposed to use** certified organic pesticides.	Other expressions of necessity include: subject + **be (not) necessary to** + **base verb** subject + **be (not) required to** + **base verb** subject + **be (not) supposed to** + **base verb** *Be required to* and *be supposed to* are similar in meaning.
(8) **Q:** **Do** we **have to** go? **A:** Yes, you **do**. / No, you **don't**. *Incorrect:* Yes, you ~~have~~. / No, you ~~haven't~~. **Q:** When **do** you **need to** know? **A:** By tomorrow.	Use *have to* and *need to* to **ask** about necessity. For **short answers** to *yes / no* questions, use *do*.

Grammar Practice

A Complete the sentences. Use the correct form of words from the box.

| had to   have to   must   mustn't   not have to |

1. Yesterday I _____ finish my plant research.

2. He will _____ investigate the area before he starts his garden there.

3. We _____ forget to water the new plants!

4. Before you start your roof-top garden, you _____ get permission from the building's owner.

5. You _____ help me in the garden. But I would be grateful if you did.

B Rewrite the rules. Use the expressions of necessity.

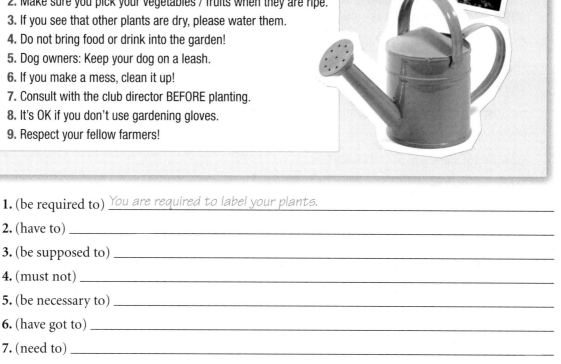

Let's Grow Together: College Garden Club

1. Please label your plants.
2. Make sure you pick your vegetables / fruits when they are ripe.
3. If you see that other plants are dry, please water them.
4. Do not bring food or drink into the garden!
5. Dog owners: Keep your dog on a leash.
6. If you make a mess, clean it up!
7. Consult with the club director BEFORE planting.
8. It's OK if you don't use gardening gloves.
9. Respect your fellow farmers!

1. (be required to) *You are required to label your plants.* _____

2. (have to) _____

3. (be supposed to) _____

4. (must not) _____

5. (be necessary to) _____

6. (have got to) _____

7. (need to) _____

8. (not / need to) _____

9. (must) _____

Redefining Gardens: Urban Farming   **185**

Speaking

 A The idea of "gardening" means different things to different people. Work with a partner. Read the quotations. Together choose the one that interests you most.

"When one of my plants dies, I die a little inside, too." ~*Linda Solegato*

"Adopt the pace of nature: her secret is patience." ~*Ralph Waldo Emerson*

"Gardening is cheaper than therapy and you get tomatoes." ~*Author unknown*

"In search of my mother's garden, I found my own." ~*Alice Walker*

"Always do your best. What you plant now, you will harvest later." ~*Og Mandino*

"I want death to find me planting my cabbages." ~*Michel de Montaigne*

"Sometimes the tiniest flowers smell the sweetest." ~*Emilie Barnes*

"There are no gardening mistakes, only experiments." ~*Kilburn Phillips*

 B Tell your classmates the following: 1) What the author meant, 2) How you might rephrase the quote (say it in a different way), and 3) What it means to you—why you and your partner chose it. Look at the model.

> We chose the Ralph Waldo Emerson quotation.

> We think he means we should . . .

Listening

A BEFORE LISTENING Would you be interested in having your own garden? If so, where would it be? What would you grow? If not, why not? Discuss with a partner.

B 🎧 UNDERSTANDING MAIN IDEAS Listen to classroom guest speaker Frank Velez. Circle the topics he discusses.

The kinds of vegetables that urban gardeners in Russia grow

His inspirations for becoming an urban gardener

His favorite recipes

How he got started as an urban gardener

What compost is

All the uses of coffee grounds

 C 🎧 UNDERSTANDING DETAILS Listen again. Answer the questions.

1. What's one thing that inspired Frank Velez to become an urban farmer?

_____

2. What are some vegetables that don't require deep plant beds?

_____

3. What is compost?

_____

4. What are some things you can put in compost?

_____

5. What mustn't you put in compost?

_____

 Writing

MyEnglishLab

▶ Linking Grammar to Writing

A Read the website forum about starting a garden. What is the writer proposing? Now think of a food- or environment-related project you would encourage others to try. Work with a partner to brainstorm project ideas.

○ ○ ○

Food for Thought

Do you want to help yourself, your family, and your society? All of us should start learning about the value of natural food so that we can help ourselves. After all, there is nothing more gratifying than watching your food grow, and then eating it. You don't have to have a yard, but you must have desire! This is not as complicated as you might think. If you have access to a terrace, a roof, or a patch of ground the size of a flowerbed, you can learn to feed yourself and others. All you need is time and patience. Today is the day to begin a garden!

B Write a blog entry about your project idea. Use the questions to help you. Try to use the grammar from the chapter.

- What steps must someone take to get a project started?
- What items are necessary? Why?
- What steps and items are good ideas? Why are they important?
- What _doesn't_ someone have to do? Why not?

○ ○ ○

Hello friends!
I've been thinking a lot about food lately, and about gardening. I know many of you enjoy seeing things grow—and thrive. For that reason, I'm making a suggestion—you ought to start your own garden. Do you have a shelf in your kitchen? You should transform that into a little plant-growing center. (My blog will provide you with recipes!) You should start small, maybe with basil, mint, and small tomatoes. You don't need too much . . .

C Share your blog entry with your classmates. Are their blog entries convincing? Discuss why or why not.

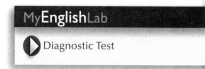

MyEnglishLab

▶ Diagnostic Test

Grammar Summary

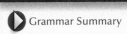

Use the **present passive** (*be* + past participle) when the action, not the doer, is the focus. Only transitive verbs—those that take an object—can be used in the passive voice. The passive form is used a lot in formal writing. Add *by* + person / thing to include the doer.

Active form	Passive form
She **waters** the garden every day.	The garden **is watered** every day.
The farmer **transplants** the seedlings.	Seedlings **are transplanted by the farmer**.

Use **time signals** to talk about the sequence of events. Some function independently (*afterwards, after that, then, now, first, next, finally*) while others begin clauses and phrases (*after . . . , as soon as . . . , once . . . , the moment . . . , now that . . . , before . . . , when . . .*). We usually place a comma after a time signal that begins a sentence.

Time signals
First, you need to prepare the plant beds.
Second, you should plant your seeds.
Once the seedlings are strong enough, they are transplanted.
Afterwards, they must be fed and watered.
After that, you will see them grow.
Finally, you will be able to harvest your vegetables!

Use *should (not)* and *ought to* + base verb to give **advice**. For stronger advice, usually implying that there are consequences, we use *had better (not)*. We often contract *had* with subject pronouns (*She'd better . . .*). We can add *maybe* or *I (do + not) think* to make advice more polite. Other expressions of advice include *It's a good idea to . . . , If I were you, I would (not) . . .* , and *You might want to*. We also use *should* to **ask for advice**.

Should, ought to, had better + base verb	Other expressions + base verb
You **should take** this opportunity.	**It's a good idea to visit** Polyface Farm.
We **ought to visit** Polyface Farm.	**If I were you, I wouldn't** go on Saturday.
You**'d better take** this opportunity.	**You might want to call** first.
Should I go today, or tomorrow?	

Use *have to, have got to,* and *need to* to show **necessity**. *Must* is stronger and can be used to show that something is urgent or, in the negative form, prohibited. *Not + have to / need to* indicates that something is not necessary. The past form of *have to* is *had to*; the past form of *need to* is *needed to*. Other expressions of necessity include *It's (not) necessary to, be (not) required to*, and *be (not) supposed to*.

Have to, have got to, need to, must + base verb	+ Not
We **have to stop** eating meat.	We **don't have to stop** eating eggs.
I **had to stop** drinking milk.	
He **has got to change** his diet.	
You **need to buy** a sturdy hoe.	You **don't need to use** special tools.
She **needed to get** a hat.	
They **must use** organic pesticides on that farm.	

Other expressions + base verb
It's not necessary to come early.
We**'re required to wear** uniforms.
They**'re not supposed to be** here.

Self-Assessment

A (5 points) Use the words to write passive sentences. Use the simple present.

1. (many vegetables / harvest / in August) _____

2. (the garden / water / every day) _____

3. (some berries / eat / by the birds) _____

4. (fruit trees / not planted / in the summer) _____

5. (the weeds / pull / every week) _____

B (7 points) Circle the correct words.

How should you make a great cup of coffee? **1.** As soon as / First, purchase excellent quality coffee beans. **2.** Next, / Before make sure the beans are stored in a cool, dry place. **3.** Second / Before you put the beans in the coffee maker, grind the beans. **4.** Now / Once the beans are ground, put them into your coffee machine. **5.** After that / As soon as the water starts to run through the beans, you will smell the aroma of the coffee. **6.** Then / After just a few minutes, you can pour your coffee. **7.** Finally, / After you can relax and enjoy your cup of freshly brewed coffee.

C (7 points) Circle the correct answers.

1. We _____ water the garden today, or we will lose all of our fruits and vegetables!
   a. had better   **b.** shouldn't   **c.** ought to

2. If you are worried about getting fat, you _____ eat fast food every day.
   a. ought to   **b.** had better   **c.** shouldn't

3. You _____ eat healthy, low-fat foods, such as fruits and vegetables.
   a. had better not   **b.** ought to   **c.** shouldn't

4. Mrs. Powers, it's really raining outside right now. _____ borrow my umbrella, or you'll get wet.
   a. I wouldn't   **b.** You shouldn't   **c.** I think you'd better

5. Where _____ we have lunch today—at home or in a restaurant?
   a. had better   **b.** should   **c.** ought to

6. It's a good idea to _____ in the morning when you have a lot of energy.
   a. exercise   **b.** exercises   **c.** exercising

7. If I were you, _____ sign up for the gardening class today. It fills up fast!
   a. I had better   **b.** you should   **c.** I would

D (6 points) Circle the correct words.

1. You **must / must not** submit an incomplete job application. If the form is not accurate, you will **have to / must** reapply in the future.

2. Tomorrow is a holiday, so I **must not / don't have to** go to work. However, we have an important conference next week, and my boss has said that I have no choice; I **have / must** attend.

3. When in the mountains, you must / need look out for bears. They're dangerous. You **don't have to / must not** go near them.

Unit Project: Advertising campaign

A Work in a small group. Create an advertising campaign that promotes a food and explains the process for producing the food. Follow the steps.

1. Imagine that your group is an advertising agency. A representative from the food industry comes to you and asks you to create a campaign. It should explain to the public a) the food's benefits and b) how the food is made. Choose one of the foods to research, or choose your own.

Food

beef / chicken / turkey / duck / goose
bread
cheese
frozen yogurt

pie or other fruit-based pastries
tea
wheat to pasta
yogurt

2. Now choose from the list <u>two</u> forms of media to use in your campaign.

Forms of media

airplane banner
billboard ads
bus / subway banners
Internet ads

interviews with the media
magazine ads
newspaper ads

press releases
radio ads
TV ads

3. Create a slogan (a memorable expression). Your slogan must appear in both media pieces.
4. You must explain the process of how your food is made / grown.

B With your group, present your campaign to the class. Show your two media pieces and explain the process. If possible, provide samples of your food item. Answer any questions. Look at the model.

We chose pasta because we love it, and it's a global food. Our slogan is "Gotta have pasta!" By that we mean "I have got to have pasta!" . . .

Here are the steps involved in producing pasta. Most pasta is made from wheat. So first, the wheat is harvested . . .

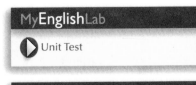

MyEnglishLab

▶ Unit Test

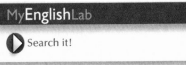

MyEnglishLab

▶ Search it!

Earth—and Beyond

MyEnglishLab

 What do you know?

CHAPTER 19

Earth's Neighbors

Getting Started

A Discuss the questions in a small group.

- When was the last time you looked up at the sky at night? What did you notice?
- When you look at the sky and think about the universe, how do you feel?

B Work with a partner. Take the quiz about the planet Venus. Circle your answers.

1. T F Venus is named after the Roman god of war.
2. T F Venus is always brighter than any star (except the Sun).
3. T F Venus is about as big as Earth.
4. T F Mercury is closer to Earth than Venus is.
5. T F Venus was discovered in the early 20th century.
6. T F Venus and Earth rotate in opposite directions.
7. T F Venus has one moon.
8. T F The volcanoes on Venus are more massive than those on Earth.
9. T F Venus is both hotter and colder than Earth.
10. T F One day on Venus is 243 Earth days long, making a Venus day longer than an Earth year.

1. False. Venus is named after the Roman god of love and beauty. 2. True 3. True 4. False. Venus is closer to Earth. 5. False. Venus has been known since pre-historic times. 6. True 7. False. Venus has no moons. 8. True. 9. False. It is hotter but not colder. It's always about 860 degrees Fahrenheit (460°C) on Venus. 10. False. An Earth year is 365 days long.

C Look back at the quiz in Part B. Complete the tasks.

1. Circle the **comparative adjectives** that end in *-er*.
2. Underline the **comparative adjective** that has *more* before it.
3. Double underline the adjective between the words *as . . . as*.
4. Complete the chart.

Adjective + -er (with *than*)	More + adjective (with *than*)	As + adjective + as

Reading

MyEnglishLab
Vocabulary Check

A WARM-UP What do you know about the planet Mars? How is it different from Earth? In what ways might it be similar to Earth? Discuss with a partner.

B SCANNING Scan the article for the information. Then go back and read the whole article.

1. Diameter of Earth: _____

2. Height of Olympic Mons: _____

3. Length of day on Mars: _____

4. Average temperature on Earth: _____

Sibling Rivalry

The study of Mars can tell us a lot about our own planet, Earth. In many ways, comparing the two provides scientists with a control set as they look at geology, climate, and the potential for life in other worlds.

Mars is similar to Earth in some ways but is very different from it in other ways. Science fiction has tried to show us that Mars is a twin planet of Earth—colder and farther from the Sun but about the same size as Earth. In fact, Mars is much smaller than Earth, although the land area of the two is

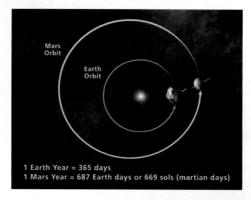

1 Earth Year = 365 days
1 Mars Year = 687 Earth days or 669 sols (martian days)

roughly the same. Mars's diameter is 4,225 miles (6,800 km), while Earth's is 7,953 miles (12,800 km). And Mars has only 10 percent of the mass of Earth. Because of the smaller diameter and lower mass, Mars has only 38 percent of Earth's gravity. This means that things are much heavier on Earth. For example, if you weighed 220 pounds (100 kg) on Earth, you would weigh just 84 pounds (38 kg) on Mars.

The geologic histories of Earth and Mars are quite different. Mars has no oceans, and its crust is not as stable as Earth's. There are no long chains of mountains. But Mars does have several large volcanoes that resemble those in Hawaii, though the ones on Mars are much larger. Volcanoes on Earth aren't as big because the movement of the Earth's plates separates volcanoes from their lava source, their source of growth. Martian volcanoes don't move and, consequently, continue to grow bigger and bigger. One mountain —Olympic Mons—rises 14 miles (23 km) above the surrounding plains.

A day on Earth is about as long as a day on Mars (24 hours, 40 minutes). In addition, while the planetary tilt of Mars is 25 degrees, on Earth it's 23.5 degrees. This means both have similar seasons. But since Mars takes twice as long to go around the Sun as Earth does, its year, at 687 days, is much longer than ours. Therefore, the seasons on Mars are more extreme. Mars is much colder than Earth. The average temperature on Mars is –82 degrees Fahrenheit (–63°C). On Earth it's 59 degrees Fahrenheit (15°C). That makes for a cold Martian summer, but an even colder winter.

C MAKING COMPARISONS Compare Earth and Mars. Write *S* for the *similar* features and *D* for the *different* features.

_____ 1. Size

_____ 2. Land area

_____ 3. Mass

_____ 4. Presence of mountains chains

_____ 5. Presence of volcanoes

_____ 6. Length of days

_____ 7. Length of seasons

_____ 8. Average temperature

MyEnglishLab
Reading Comprehension

Earth's Neighbors **193**

Grammar Focus 1 Adjectives: Comparatives

Examples	Language notes
(1) Seasons on Mars are **longer than** seasons on Earth.	To compare two things, use: **comparative form of adjective + *than***
(2) Winters on Mars are **colder** *(than winters on Earth)*.	It is common to **drop** the ***than* . . .** part of the comparison if the meaning is clear.
(3) She's more interested in space **than him**. She's more interested in space **than he is**.	In speech and informal writing, people commonly use ***than* + object pronoun** instead of ***than* + subject pronoun + verb**.
(4) Mars is **much smaller** than Earth.	We can make a comparative **stronger** with: ***much* + comparative form of adjective**
(5) Mars is **smaller** than Earth.	For most **one-syllable adjectives, add -*er***: *small* → *smaller* *long* → *longer* Exceptions: *more fun, more tired*
(6) Earth is **larger** than Mars.	For adjectives already **ending in -*e*, add -*r***: *large* → *larger* *nice* → *nicer*
(7) You will be **heavier** on Earth than on Mars.	For adjectives **ending in a consonant + *y*, change *y* to *i* + -*er***: *heavy* → *heavier* *pretty* → *prettier*
(8) Mars's volcanoes are **bigger** than Earth's.	For one-syllable adjectives ending in a **single vowel + single consonant, double the consonant**: *big* → *bigger* *thin* → *thinner*
(9) Seasons on Mars are **more extreme** than on Earth.	For **most two-** and **three-syllable adjectives, use *more* + adjective**: *extreme* → *more extreme* Exceptions: *simpler, quieter*
(10) The nights are **quieter** than the days. *Incorrect:* The nights are ~~more quieter~~ than the days.	Never add *more* to a comparative adjective that ends in -*er*.
(11) Earth's geologic history is **more well known** than Mars's geologic history. Mars's geologic history is **less well known** than Earth's geologic history.	The opposite of *more* is *less*. Never add *less* to a comparative adjective that ends in -*er*.
(12) Mars is **farther** from the Sun than Earth is.	Some adjectives have **irregular** comparative forms: *good* → *better* *bad* → *worse* *far* → *farther / further*

Grammar Practice

MyEnglishLab

▶ Grammar Plus 1
  Activities 1 and 2

A Complete the conversation. Use the comparative form of the adjectives.

   A: I see you bought a telescope. Is this the one you told me about?

   B: No, this one is actually **1.** _____ (small) and **2.** _____ (light) than that one. But it was **3.** _____ (expensive), unfortunately.

A: Well, I'm sure it's **4.** _____ (good). So what do you look at through it?

B: Mostly the Moon. Here, take a look.

A: Wow! It's huge! It's much **5.** _____ (big) than I expected. And it's so much **6.** _____ (clear).

B: It almost doesn't look real, does it? Here, let me see if I can find Mars. It's **7.** _____ (difficult) to spot, but if I keep looking . . . there it is. Let me just focus it.

A: Look at that! Amazing. It's **8.** _____ (red) than I imagined.

B Find and correct the mistake in each sentence.

1. Venus is visibler when it's low in the sky.

2. Stars are usually bright in the country than in the city.

3. The first Moon landing was more exciting the last moon landing.

4. It is more hard to send people to Venus than Mars.

5. The International Space Station is more bigger than a soccer field.

6. Astronaut Neil Armstrong is more famouser than Michael Collins.

7. It's more easy to see when the Moon is full.

8. Space tourism is less cheaper than it was in the past, but it's still extremely expensive.

C Complete the sentences. Use the comparative form of the adjectives. Add *than* when necessary.

When you look at the Moon, it's hard to get a sense of how big it really is. The diameter of the Earth is 7,918 miles (12,742 km). That's **1.** _____ (much / big) the Moon's diameter of 2,159 miles (3,474 km). As for surface area, at 317 million square miles (510 million sq km), the Moon is **2.** _____ (small) Asia.

As seen from space, the Earth is **3.** _____ (bright) the Moon. Why? The Earth has reflective clouds; the Moon has only rock and dirt. And the Earth is **4.** _____ (old) the Moon. Many scientists believe the Moon was formed after a Mars-sized body hit the Earth, sending material into its orbit. Some of this material later became the Moon.

The Moon orbits the Earth at an average speed of 2,289 miles (3,683 km) per hour. The Moon's orbital speed is **5.** _____ (slow) when it is **6.** _____ (far) from the Earth and **7.** _____ (fast) when it is **8.** _____ (near) the Earth.

Both the Sun and the Moon affect ocean tides on the Earth. The Sun is **9.** _____ (large), but because the Moon is **10.** _____ (close) to the Earth, its effect is **11.** _____ (great). When a full moon is directly overhead, you will experience **12.** _____ (high) tides. A second full moon within a month is called a blue moon, giving us the idiom "once in a blue moon."

Grammar Focus 2 Adjectives: *As . . . as*

Examples	Language notes
(1) A day on Earth is **as long as** a day on Mars.	To show how two things are **alike**, use: *as* + **adjective** + *as*
(2) Mars's crust is **not as stable as** Earth's crust.	To show how two things are **different**, use: *not* + *as* + **adjective** + *as*
(3) He's not as interested in space **as her.** He's not as interested in space **as she is.**	In speech and informal writing, people often use *. . . as* + **object pronoun** instead of *. . . as* + **subject pronoun** + **verb**.
(4) A day on Earth is **just as long as** a day on Mars.	Add *just* to emphasize that two things are alike. ***Note: Just about*** means *almost.*
(5) Winters on Earth **aren't as cold** (*as winters on Mars*).	It's common to **drop** the **second part** of the comparison if the meaning is clear.
(6) The land area of Mars is about **the same as** the land area of Earth. Mars has about **the same** land area **as** Earth. The land area on Mars and Earth is about **the same.**	We can also say two things are alike with ***the same*** (*as*).
(7) When you look up at the night sky, Jupiter **looks like** a star.	Use *look* (*be, seem,* etc.) *like* to express similarity.
(8) Mars is **similar to** Earth in some interesting ways.	Use *similar to* to say two things are similar but not exactly the same.
(9) The length of the seasons on Mars is **different from** those on Earth.	Use *different from* to say that two things are not alike.

Grammar Practice

MyEnglishLab
 ► Grammar Plus 2
 Activities 1 and 2

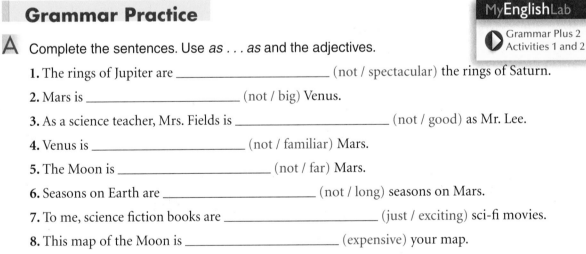

A Complete the sentences. Use *as . . . as* and the adjectives.

1. The rings of Jupiter are _____ (not / spectacular) the rings of Saturn.

2. Mars is _____ (not / big) Venus.

3. As a science teacher, Mrs. Fields is _____ (not / good) as Mr. Lee.

4. Venus is _____ (not / familiar) Mars.

5. The Moon is _____ (not / far) Mars.

6. Seasons on Earth are _____ (not / long) seasons on Mars.

7. To me, science fiction books are _____ (just / exciting) sci-fi movies.

8. This map of the Moon is _____ (expensive) your map.

9. Venus is _____ (just / about / large) the Earth.

B Rewrite sentences 1 to 5 from Part A. Use comparative adjectives with *than*.

A model of the planet Saturn

1. *The rings of Saturn are more spectacular than the rings of Jupiter.* _____

2. _____

3. _____

4. _____

5. _____

C Look at the chart comparing Venus and Mars. Write true sentences. Use *not as . . . as* and the adjectives.

	Venus	Mars
1. Distance from Sun	67,238,000 mi (108,209,000 km)	141,6333,000 mi (227,937,000 km)
2. Duration of rotation (Earth days)	243 days	1.03 days
3. Orbit around Sun (Earth years)	224 years	1.88 years
4. Minimum surface temperature	864° F (462° C)	−125° F (−87° C)
5. Maximum surface temperature	864° F (462° C)	23° F (−5° C)
6. Surface area	285,976,346 sq mi (460,234,317 sq km)	89,708,223 sq mi (144,371,391 sq km)

1. (close) _____

2. (short) _____

3. (long) _____

4. (hot) _____

5. (cold) _____

6. (large) _____

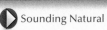

Speaking

A Work with a partner. Look at the images and think about how Martians and other aliens have been depicted over the years—in movies and books, in video games, in the news, and as children's toys. Choose two and take notes comparing them.

A poster from the 1958 movie *The Blob*

E.T. from the 1982 movie *E.T.: The Extra-Terrestrial*

An action figure from the Transformer toy series

Keanu Reeves as Klaatu in the 2008 remake of the movie *The Day the Earth Stood Still*

B Join another pair. Compare your aliens. How are they different? Look at the model.

> *We chose the alien E.T. from the movie E.T. and Klaatu from the movie* The Day the Earth Stood Still.

> *E.T. looks like an alien. Klaatu, on the other hand, looks like a human. E.T. is a more interesting character in some ways because . . .*

C What do you think an alien looks like? Draw a picture of an alien. Then compare with a partner. How are your aliens similar? How are they different?

Listening

A 🎧 UNDERSTANDING MAIN IDEAS Listen to the film studies lecture. Check (✓) the movies and books the professor mentions.

☐ *Red Planet Mars*   ☐ *2001: A Space Odyssey*   ☐ *Red Planet*

☐ *War of the Worlds*   ☐ *Star Wars*   ☐ *Voyage to Mars*

☐ *Mars in Space*   ☐ *Mars Invasion*   ☐ *Mission to Mars*

☐ *Invaders from Mars*   ☐ *Total Recall*   ☐ *Moving Mars*

B 🎧 UNDERSTANDING DETAILS Listen again. Answer the questions.

1. How many films have been made about Mars and Martians? _____

2. What is the professor's favorite movie? _____

3. What 1990 movie about Mars was a big hit? _____

4. What year did the fad in movies about Mars start? _____

5. What probably caused the fad to end? _____

C AFTER LISTENING Do you like science fiction movies? What movies about Mars have you seen? What sci-fi movie is popular now? Have you seen it?

Writing

A What do you know about the International Space Station? Read about some aspects of daily life.

Daily routine Astronauts have the same hygiene needs as people on Earth. But keeping clean can be a challenge in space. They wash their hair with a special rinseless shampoo.

Exercise Astronauts need to exercise two hours a day to prevent muscle and bone loss. Lifting weights in space is easy because there is no gravity, so astronauts need special machines that offer resistance.

Food Eating in space is a lot like camping. Astronauts can eat some food as is, but a lot of food requires water. Salt and pepper are in liquid form. Drinking is done through straws.

Work Astronauts work hard in space. They are busy cleaning, fixing things, updating computers, and checking support systems.

Play All work and no play is no fun for anyone. Astronauts also need time to relax. They play games, read, play music, or just look out the window. And like most people, they get weekends off.

Sleep With no gravity, astronauts can sleep in any position they like, even upside down, but they must be attached so they don't bump into anything. They sleep eight hours a day.

B Imagine that you are an astronaut on the International Space Station. Write an email home describing how life in space is similar to and different from life on Earth. Try to use the grammar from the chapter.

○○○

Dear Lida,
Life in space is more difficult than life on Earth, but it's not as bad as I imagined it. Keeping clean is more challenging because we can't take an ordinary shower. We use a rinseless shampoo. I'm looking forward to a long, hot bath! Also, I'm much more active here. I exercise two hours a day. I also . . .

C Imagine you are on a video chat with a friend on Earth. Read your email to your partner. Answer any questions.

CHAPTER 20   Extreme Space

Getting Started

A   Imagine that you could mail a box of items into space for aliens to find. What kinds of things would you put in the box to show or tell about life on Earth?

B   Read about two remarkably successful space probes. Which one has traveled the longest? Which has traveled the farthest?

Voyager 1 is a 1,592-pound (722-kg) space probe. It was launched in 1977 by NASA (the U.S. National Aeronautics and Space Administration). Its primary mission ended in 1980 after encountering Jupiter in 1979 and Saturn in 1980, but it is still operational. It was the first probe to provide detailed images of the two largest planets and their moons. For the past few decades, it has sent incredible images back to Earth, along with data that has rewritten astronomy books.

Voyager 2, an identical spacecraft, was launched almost a month earlier than *Voyager 1*. *Voyager 2* has explored space longer than any other probe but doesn't travel as fast as *Voyager 1*. So *Voyager 1* has traveled the farthest. It is now the most distant human-made object from Earth. It has visited Neptune and Uranus and is now far beyond Pluto.

There are other probes now in our solar system, but *Voyager 1* is still the fastest and one of the most remarkable. It travels at over 11 miles (17 km) a second and continues to transmit data to Earth. It is expected to continue to send data back for at least another decade. On board each probe is a gold disc containing images of Earth and its life forms as well as recordings of classical music, whales, waves crashing, babies crying, and greetings in various languages.

C   Look back at the reading in Part A. Complete the tasks.

1. Circle the **superlative adjectives** that end in *-est* and those that have *the most* before them.
2. Underline the **comparative adverbs** that end in *-er + than*.
3. Double underline the **superlative adverb** that ends in *-est*.
4. Draw a rectangle around the adverb between the words *as . . . as*.
5. Complete the chart.

Adjective + *-est* and *the most* + adjective	Adverb + *-er* + *than*	Adverb + *-est*	As + adverb + as

Reading

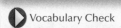
A WARM-UP Work with a partner. Cover the picture in Part B. Try to name the planets in our solar system in order from the Sun. Look at the picture to check your answers.

B SCANNING Scan the article. Which three planets' moons are mentioned? Then go back and read the whole article.

Strange Worlds

Our solar system (and beyond) is full of extremes.
Let's explore!

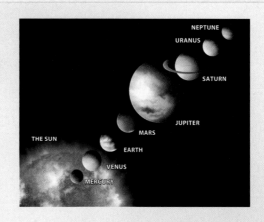

As the planet nearest to the Sun, Mercury hosts temperatures that can reach 842 degrees Fahrenheit (450°C). With no atmosphere to trap heat, temperatures can drop to −274 degrees Fahrenheit (−170°C). This temperature swing is the greatest in the solar system. And Mercury orbits the Sun faster than any other planet. It travels at an average speed of 106,876 miles (172,000 km) per hour. It also has the shortest orbit. One year on Mercury equals 88 Earth days.

After the Moon, Venus is the brightest object in the night sky, and often shines just as brightly as a star. Its atmosphere, which consists mostly of carbon dioxide, is the densest of all the planets. A younger Venus was believed to have possessed Earth-like oceans, but these all evaporated as temperatures rose.

Craters on the Moon's south pole are some of the coldest places in the universe. The floors on the crater are permanently in shadow. The temperatures never rise above −396 degrees Fahrenheit (−238°C). Ice has been discovered in these craters.

Jupiter is equal to more than 1,300 Earths in size. The most extraordinary feature on Jupiter is the Great Red Spot, a giant storm. At its widest point, the spot is roughly three times as wide as Earth. Jupiter's moon Io has the most active volcano in the solar system.

Saturn, the second largest planet after Jupiter, is most famous for its spectacular rings. Titan, the largest of Saturn's 62 moons, is bigger than the planet Mercury. Saturn is less dense than water. In fact, it could float in a bathtub, if there were a bathtub big enough.

Uranus was the first planet discovered with a telescope. No planet tilts as heavily as Uranus. Its north-south poles lie where most planets have their equators. This makes for some extreme weather.

Considered the least understood planet, Neptune is the farthest planet from the Sun. (The farthest planet used to be Pluto, but Pluto was recently downgraded to a dwarf planet). At 1,600 miles (2,575 km) per hour, the winds of Neptune blow the fastest of any measured in the solar system.

VY Canis Majoris is the largest star we have ever discovered. It's 2,000 times wider than the Sun. If you replaced our Sun with VY Canis Majoris, its radius would extend past Saturn.

C UNDERSTANDING DETAILS Complete the information.

1. Brightest object at night: _____

2. Second largest planet: _____

3. Moon bigger than Mercury: _____

4. Largest star ever discovered: _____

5. Fastest planet: _____

6. Windiest planet: _____

7. Most active volcano: _____

8. Farthest planet from Sun: _____

MyEnglishLab

▶ Reading Comprehension

Grammar Focus 1 Adjectives: Superlatives

Examples	Language notes
(1) Venus is **the brightest** object in the night sky.	To **compare three or more things** from a group, use the superlative form of an adjective.
(2) Saturn is the second largest *(planet after Jupiter)*.	It's common to **drop** the **second part** of the comparison if the meaning is clear.
(3) The Moon's south pole is **one of the coldest places** in the universe.	A common structure is: **one** *(some, most, many) of* + superlative + **plural noun**
(4) Saturn's rings are **the most spectacular in the solar system**.	We often use **the superlative** with <u>prepositional phrases</u> to provide context.
(5) That's **the most incredible** thing (that) <u>I've ever heard</u>!	A clause with *that* + the <u>present perfect</u> sometimes follows **the superlative**. We often drop *that*.
(6) Mercury is **the nearest** planet to the Sun.	For most **one-syllable adjectives, use:** *the* + **adjective** + *-est* *near → the nearest bright → the brightest* Exceptions: *the most fun, the most tired*
(7) Titan is **the largest** of Saturn's moons.	For adjectives already **ending in -e**, use: *the* + **adjective** + *-st* *large → the largest dense → the densest*
(8) Neptune is **the windiest** planet.	For adjectives **ending in a consonant + y**, use: *the* + **adjective, change y to i + est** *windy → the windiest heavy → the heaviest*
(9) **The biggest** planet is Jupiter.	For one-syllable adjectives **ending in a single vowel + single consonant**, use: *the* + **adjective, double the consonant** *big → the biggest thin → the thinnest*
(10) **The most famous** feature on Jupiter is the Great Red Spot.	For **most two-** and **three- syllable adjectives**, use: *the most* + **adjective**: *famous → the most famous* *beautiful → the most beautiful* Exceptions: *the simplest, the quietest*
(11) Venus has **the densest** atmosphere. **Incorrect:** Venus has ~~the most densest~~ atmosphere.	Never add **the most** to a superlative adjective that ends in -*est*.
(12) I think Jupiter is **the most interesting** planet. What is **the least interesting** planet?	The opposite form of **the most** is **the least**.
(13) Neptune is **the farthest** planet from the Sun.	Some adjectives have **irregular** superlative forms: *good → the best bad → the worst* *far → the farthest / furthest*

MyEnglishLab
▶ Grammar Plus 1
Activities 1 and 2

Grammar Practice

A Write the superlative form of the adjectives.

1. close _____   6. dim _____

2. heavy _____   7. fun _____

3. boring _____   8. good _____

4. beautiful _____   9. bad _____

5. far _____   10. tired _____

B Complete the information. Use the superlative form of the adjectives.

The Sun is **1.** _____ (close) star to Earth.
2. _____ (near) star after our Sun is over 4.2
light years away. The Sun is by far **3.** _____
(large) thing in our solar system. In fact, a million Earths
could fit inside the Sun.

One of **4.** _____ (fascinating)
things about the Sun is its solar flares.

5. _____ (big) ones have extended hundreds of thousands of miles into
space. In fact, **6.** _____ (intense) flares have impacted life here on Earth,
including communications devices that rely on the transmission of radio waves. One of
7. _____ (common) ways we are affected is through cell phone interference.

June 2011 marked one of **8.** _____ (massive) solar flares people have
ever observed and recorded. This stunning explosion from the Sun created some of
9. _____ (beautiful) Aurora Borealis, or Northern Lights, seen in a long
time. **10.** _____ (good) places to see these dancing lights are in the northern
and southern hemispheres.

You can't get very close to study the Sun. Too much exposure would be dangerous.
One of **11.** _____ (safe) places to study the Sun is here on Earth.

C Find and correct the mistake in each sentence.

1. Mercury has the thinest atmosphere of all the planets.

2. Some of the most beautiful meteor shower in the northern hemisphere are in August.

3. I think dumbest thing you can do is look directly at the Sun.

4. Which planet is the closer to Earth—Mercury, Venus, or Mars?

5. The less understood planet of all is Neptune.

6. The most best time to view Venus is in the early morning.

7. The baddest place to see the Northern Lights is at the equator.

8. That's the brightest shooting star I've ever saw.

Grammar Focus 2 Adverbs: Comparatives and superlatives

Examples	Language notes
(1) Mercury **revolves** around the Sun **faster than** Earth *(revolves around the Sun)*.	To compare the **action** of **two** things, use: **verb + comparative form of adverb + *than***
(2) These probes performed **better than** those. Those probes performed **worse than** these. *Voyager 1* has traveled **farther than** *Voyager 2*.	Some adverbs have **irregular** comparative forms: *well* → *better than* *badly* → *worse than* *far* → *farther / further than*
(3) Venus often shines **as brightly as** a star.	To show how two actions are **alike**, use: ***as* + adverb + *as***
(4) Venus often shines **just as brightly as** a star.	To emphasize that two actions are alike, use: ***just* + *as* + adverb + *as***
(5) The earlier interplanetary probes did**n't fly as fast as** the later ones.	To show how two actions are **different**, use: ***not* + verb + *as* + adverb + *as***
(6) The winds of Neptune **blow the fastest** of any measured in the solar system.	To compare the **action** of one thing with the actions of **two or more** other things from a group, use: **verb + superlative form of adverb**
(7) *Voyager 1* travels **the fastest**.	For most **one-syllable adverbs**, use: ***the* + adverb + *-est***
(8) Jupiter spins **the most quickly** of any planet.	For **most two-** and **three- syllable adverbs**, use: ***the most* + adverb**
(9) Jupiter spins **the fastest**. *Incorrect:* Jupiter spins ~~the most fastest~~.	Never add *more* or *the most* to an adverb that ends in *-est*.
(10) Venus spins **the least quickly** of any planet.	The opposite form of *the most* is *the least*.
(11) The later Mars rovers performed **the best**. The earlier Mars rovers performed **the worst**. *Voyager 1* has traveled **the farthest**.	Some adverbs have **irregular** superlative forms: *well* → *the best* *badly* → *the worst* *far* → *the farthest / furthest*
(12) The earlier interplanetary probes didn't fly **as fast** *(as the later interplanetary probes)*.	It's common to **drop** the **second part** of the comparison if the meaning is clear.

Grammar Practice

MyEnglishLab

▶ Grammar Plus 2
Activities 1 and 2

A Complete the sentences. Use the adverb form of the adjectives.

1. Mars doesn't shine as _____ (bright) as Venus.

2. The Viking missions lasted _____ (long) than anyone imagined.

3. I performed _____ (good) on today's astronomy quiz than on last week's.

4. Jupiter spins the _____ (fast) of all the planets.

5. Through a telescope, you can't see Jupiter's rings as _____ (easy) as Saturn's.

6. The *Vanguard 1* satellite was launched in 1958. Although contact was lost in 1964, it continues to

   orbit as _____ (regular) as any other satellite.

B Read the information about the *Sojourner* and the *Spirit,* two robotic rovers that explored the surface of Mars. Write two sentences comparing each fact. More than two correct answers may be possible.

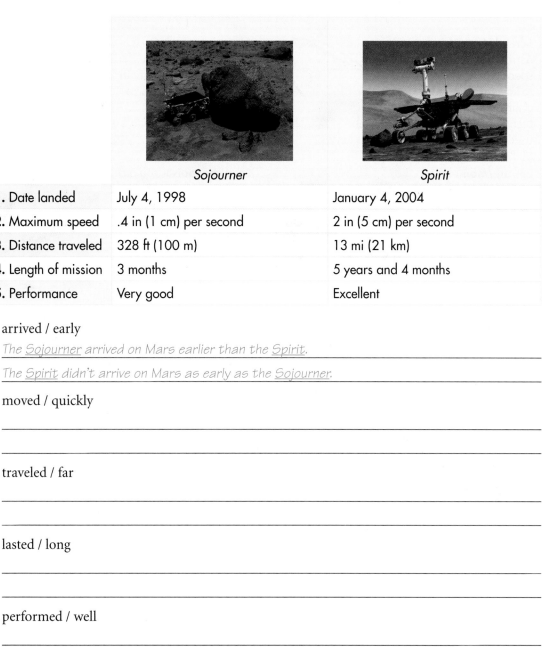

	Sojourner	Spirit
1. Date landed	July 4, 1998	January 4, 2004
2. Maximum speed	.4 in (1 cm) per second	2 in (5 cm) per second
3. Distance traveled	328 ft (100 m)	13 mi (21 km)
4. Length of mission	3 months	5 years and 4 months
5. Performance	Very good	Excellent

1. arrived / early

   The Sojourner arrived on Mars earlier than the Spirit.

   The Spirit didn't arrive on Mars as early as the Sojourner.

2. moved / quickly

   _____

   _____

3. traveled / far

   _____

   _____

4. lasted / long

   _____

   _____

5. performed / well

   _____

   _____

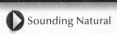

Speaking

A Space exploration has led to inventions that have everyday use. Read about six of these inventions.

Scratch-free lenses Astronauts needed a special plastic coating to keep instruments clean and safe. This technology is now used in scratch-resistant eyeglass lenses.

Smoke alarms A fire is dangerous anywhere, but it can be a disaster in space. The smoke alarm was invented in the 1970s to alert astronauts of possible fires.

Ear thermometers It's not always easy to take someone's temperature, but it got easier with the ear thermometer. It uses infrared technology to measure heat to take an accurate temperature measure.

Cordless tools If you pick up dirt around the house with a cordless vacuum, you can thank the space program for assisting in the research that made these and other lightweight tools possible.

Water filters Astronauts needed to clean the water they brought with them, and keep it clean for long periods of time. Water filters with charcoal were used.

Shoe insoles When Neil Armstrong first stepped onto the Moon, he said it was "one giant leap for mankind." He wasn't kidding! Shoe companies have borrowed the technology found in moon boots to put more "spring" into athletic shoes.

B Discuss the questions in a group. Look at the model.

> *I use a water filter when I go camping—it's safer than drinking directly from a stream.*

- Which of the inventions have you used?
- Which inventions do you think are the most useful?
- Which are the least useful?
- Which is the most surprising to you?

Listening

A BEFORE LISTENING What's the most you'd be willing to pay for a trip into space? What would be the best part of going? What would be the worst part? Discuss with a partner.

B UNDERSTANDING MAIN IDEAS Listen to the student presentation. Circle the topics the student discusses.

Alternatives to space tourism	The dangers of space tourism	The costs of space tourism
Past space tourists	Training needed for space flights	What companies are planning

C 🎧 UNDERSTANDING DETAILS Listen again. Answer the questions.

1. How much could space tourism as an industry be worth in the future? _____

2. Who was Dennis Tito? _____

3. Where will space tourists stay in space? _____

4. Can you make a reservation for a trip to space right now? _____

5. What are two reasons people want to travel to space? _____

6. According to reports, how low might the cost of a trip to space drop? _____

7. Are people able to experience weightlessness without going to space? _____

8. How much does the airplane experience cost? _____

Writing

MyEnglishLab

▶ Linking Grammar to Writing

A   Read the news blurb. What do you think? Do you agree or disagree with this decision? Discuss your opinion with a partner.

Space Funding Increases

The government has announced a 50 percent increase in funding for space exploration. The government is investing in new technologies that could see a human-occupied spacecraft land on the Moon in the next decade. There are plans to increase the current sales tax by 1 percent to pay for this significant investment. The announcement has started a debate on whether the government should invest more money in space exploration or should cut funding to pay for . . .

B   Write a letter to a government leader expressing your opinion. Use the questions to help you. Try to use the grammar from the chapter.

• What might be some of the benefits of this investment? What might be some drawbacks?
• Is this the best investment of public money? Is there something else that might make a better investment? What are some of the biggest impacts (pros or cons) of such a plan, in your opinion?

Dear Sir or Madam:

I am writing to express my gratitude that you are increasing funding for space exploration. There may be some drawbacks, such as not having enough money for other important projects. But I believe that the benefits will outweigh these. For example, the technology we gain can transfer to other industries, such as aircraft and robotics. One of the most important things will be . . .

C   Work in a small group. Share you letters with people who have a different opinion from yours. After hearing others' letters, has your opinion changed?

MyEnglishLab

▶ Diagnostic Test

Grammar Summary

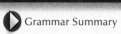

One way to make **comparisons** is to use the **comparative form of an adjective** + *than*. For most one-syllable adjectives, form the comparative form by adding *-er* (*small = smaller*) or more (*fun = more fun*). Use the **superlative form of an adjective** to compare three or more things. To make the superlative form, use *the* + adjective + *-est* or *the* + *most* + adjective. The opposite of *more* is *less* and the opposite of *most* is *least*. There are **irregular** comparative and superlative adjectives.

Adjectives	Comparative	Superlative
long	longer than	the longest
large	larger than	the largest
heavy	heavier than	the heaviest
big	bigger than	the biggest
distant	more / less distant than	the most / least distant
beautiful	more / less beautiful than	the most / least beautiful
Irregulars		
good	better than	the best
bad	worse than	the worst
far	farther / further than	the farthest / furthest

Use the **comparative form of an adverb** + *than* to compare two actions. To compare the action of one with the actions of three or more other things from a group, use the **superlative form**. Some adverbs have **irregular** comparative and superlative forms.

Adverbs	Comparative	Superlative
fast	faster than	the fastest
slowly	more / less slowly than	the most / least slowly
Irregulars		
well	better than	the best
badly	worse than	the worst
far	farther / further than	the farthest / furthest

We can **drop the second part of a comparison** when the meaning is clear.

Main clause
The landscape there is **less hospitable** *(than the landscape here)*.
The earlier interplanetary probes didn't fly **as fast** *(as the later ones)*.
Jupiter is the **biggest** *(of all the planets in the solar system)*.

Use *as* + adjective / adverb + *as* to make comparisons when two things are alike. Emphasize that they are alike by adding *just*. To express that they are **not alike**, add *not*. (We can use comparatives with *than* to express the same thing.)

Adjectives	Adverbs
I am (just) **as old as** you. *(We are the same age.)*	I can run (just) **as quickly as** you. *(We can both run quickly, at the same speed.)*
I am **not as old as** you. *(You are older than me.)*	I can**not** run **as quickly as** you. *(You can run faster than I can.)*

Self-Assessment

A (5 points) Write sentences comparing Jupiter and Saturn. Use the adjectives and *than*.

	Jupiter	Saturn
1. Distance from Sun	483,683,000 mi (778,412,000 km)	886,526,000 mi (1,426,725,000 km)
2. Orbit period (Earth years)	11.8 years	29.4 years
3. Cloud thickness	31 mi (50 km)	155 mi (250 km)
4. Diameter	88,846 mi (142,984 km)	74,898 mi (120,536 km)
5. Brightness from Earth	Bright	Not very bright

1. (far) _____

2. (much / long) _____

3. (thick) _____

4. (massive) _____

5. (bright) _____

B (7 points) Rewrite the sentences. Use *as . . . as* or *not as . . . as*.

1. Earth is denser than Saturn. _____

2. The Moon is brighter than Venus. _____

3. Venus and Earth are about the same size. _____

4. VY Canis Majoris is bigger than our Sun. _____

5. Geology is more interesting than astronomy. _____

6. Venus is equally hot in the summer and winter. _____

7. Mercury is closer to the Sun than Mars is. _____

C (7 points) Complete the sentences. Use the superlative form of the adjectives.

The Hubble telescope was not the first in space, but it was **1.** _____ (versatile).
The telescope is 43.3 feet (13.2 m) long and at its **2.** _____ (wide) measures
only 13.8 feet (4.2 m). It has made many of **3.** _____ (dramatic) discoveries in
astronomy and has taken some of **4.** _____ (detailed) images of
5. _____ (distant) objects in our universe. One of **6.** _____
(famous) images is that of a dying star and **7.** _____ (frequent) image is of Earth.

D (6 points) Find and correct the mistake in each sentence.

1. Mars was discovered much early than Neptune and Uranus.

2. Which space probe has traveled more far: *Voyager 1* or *Voyager 2*?

3. Stephen Spielberg has directed some of the best science fiction film of all time.

4. Your telescope doesn't work as good as my telescope.

5. Which planet in the solar system spins the more quickly?

6. I scored worst on today's exam than on last week's exam.

Unit Project: Class debate

 In your view, what has been the greatest accomplishment in space exploration and invention? Work in a small group. Prepare an argument and then debate your classmates. Follow the steps.

1. Assign each group member an accomplishment from the list to research, or choose your own.

   Greatest accomplishments

   - Launch of the Hubble telescope
   - Living on the International Space Station
   - Rovers exploring surface of Mars
   - Space probes exploring outer solar system

   - The first Moon landing
   - The first person in space
   - The first satellite in space
   - The reusable space shuttle

2. As a group, discuss the research. Which accomplishment was the most significant? Why? This is the accomplishment that your group will present.

3. Divide sections of your argument among group members. Prepare notecards and visual aids.

I. Introduction

II. Arguments (A, B, C)

III. Acknowledgement of other accomplishments

IV. Summary

B With your group, present your argument. Listen to your opponent's argument and rebut the claims. The class votes for the best argument. Look at the model.

> We feel that the greatest all-time accomplishment is the launch of the Hubble telescope, shown in this photo. . . .

> One reason why we say this is . . .

> There are other incredible accomplishments, of course, but nothing is as incredible as . . .

> To summarize, we feel that the Hubble telescope is the best . . .

MyEnglishLab

▶ Unit Test

MyEnglishLab

▶ Search it!

Appendices

A Contractions

Affirmative		Negative
be		
I am → I'm you are → you're he is → he's she is → she's	it is → it's we are → we're they are → they're	is not → 's not / isn't are not → 're not / aren't was not → wasn't were not → weren't
do		
—		does not → doesn't do not → don't
will		
I will → I'll you will → you'll he will → he'll she will → she'll	it will → it'll we will → we'll they will → they'll	will not → won't
have		
I have → I've you have → you've he has → he's she has → she's	it has → it's we have → we've they have → they've	has not → hasn't have not → haven't
would		
I would → I'd you would → you'd he would → he'd she would → she'd	it would → it'd we would → we'd they would → they'd	would not → wouldn't

B Simple present: *Be*

Affirmative statements			Negative statements			
I	**am**		I	**am**		
He / She / It	**is**	in the classroom.	He / She / It	**is**	**not**	in the library.
You / We / They	**are**		You / We / They	**are**		

Yes / No questions			Short answers			
Am	I		Yes,	you	**are.**	
				I	**am.**	
Are	you	in Room A?		he / she / it	**is.**	
				we / they	**are.**	
Is	he / she / it		No,	you	**'re not / aren't.**	
				I	**'m not.**	
Are	we / they			he / she / it	**'s not / isn't.**	
				we / they	**'re not / aren't.**	

Wh- questions with *be*			Short answers	Long answers
Where	**am**	I?	In Room B.	You're in Room B.
Who What When	**is**	he? it? the test?	A friend. A ring. Tomorrow.	He's a friend It's a ring The test is tomorrow.
Why How	**are**	you here? they?	Because I live here. Fine.	I'm here because I live here. They're fine.

C Present progressive

Affirmative statements				Negative statements			
I	am			I	am		
You / We / They	are	studying.		You / We / They	are	not	exercising.
He / She	is			He / She	is		
It	is	raining.		It	is		snowing.

Yes / No questions				Short answers			
Am	I			Yes,	you	are.	
					I	am.	
Are	you				he / she / it	is.	
		working?			we / they	are.	
Is	he / she / it			No,	you	're not / aren't.	
					I	'm not.	
Are	we / they				he / she / it	's not / isn't.	
					we / they	're not / aren't.	

Wh- questions				Short answers	Long answers
Who	am	I	calling?	An old friend.	You're calling an old friend.
What	is	he	doing?	Sleeping.	He's sleeping.
Where		she	going?	To the store.	She's going to the store.
Why		you	crying?	Because I'm sad.	I'm crying because I'm sad.
How	are	we	paying?	With cash.	We're paying with cash.
How much		they	taking?	About $300.	They're taking about $300.
When	is	it	starting?	At 7:00.	It's starting at 7:00.

D Spelling rules for -ing endings

Rules	Examples of present progressive verbs / gerunds	
For verbs that end in a **consonant + -e**, drop the -e and add -ing.	advertise → **advertising** come → **coming** give → **giving** have → **having**	make → **making** take → **taking** use → **using** write → **writing**
For verbs that end in a **consonant + vowel + consonant**, double the final consonant and add -ing. *Exceptions: w, x, y endings.*	begin → **beginning** blog → **blogging** cut → **cutting** get → **getting**	jog → **jogging** plan → **planning** run → **running** sit → **sitting**
For **most other verbs**, add -ing with no change to the verb.	do → **doing** download → **downloading** eat → **eating** happen → **happening**	looking → **looking** rain → **raining** send → **sending** text → **texting**

E Simple present

Affirmative statements			Negative statements				
I / You / We / They	eat like have	cereal for breakfast.	I / You / We / They	do	not	eat like have	yogurt.
He / She	eats likes has		He / She	does			

Yes / No questions				Short answers		
Do	I / you / we / they	**own** a tablet? **go** to State College? **do** homework at night?	Yes,	you / I / we / they	**do.**
Does	he / she			he / she	**does.**
			No,	you / I / we / they	**don't.**
				he / she	**doesn't.**

Wh- questions				Short answers
Who What When Where	**do**	I you we they	**study** with? **have** for homework? **catch** the bus? **live?**	Friends. Nothing. At 2:00. In Iceland.
Why How much	**does**	he she	**want** to know? **owe?**	Because he's curious. Not much.

Note: It *takes the same forms as* He / She

F Spelling rules for -s endings

Rules	Examples of simple present verbs	
For verbs that end in a **vowel + y**, add -s.	buy → **buys**	pay → **pays**
For verbs that end in a **consonant + y**, change the y to i, and add -es.	cry → **cries**	dry → **dries**
For verbs that end in -*ch*, -**s**, -**sh**, -**x**, or -**z**, add -es.	catch → **catches** discuss → **discusses** brush → **brushes**	mix → **mixes** buzz → **buzzes**
For **most other verbs**, add -s.	call → **calls** like → **likes**	put → **puts** talk → **talks**

G Simple past: Regular verbs

Affirmative statements			Negative statements			
I / You / He / She /We / They	**talked** about it. **looked** upset. **planned** a trip. **raked** the yard. **hurried** home.		I / You / He / She / We / They	**did**	**not**	**talk** about it. **look** upset. **plan** a trip. **rake** the yard. **hurry** home.
Yes / No questions			Short answers			
Did	I / you / he / she / we / they	**talk** about it? **hurry** home?	Yes, No,		you / I / he / she / we / they	**did.** **didn't.**

Note: It *takes the same forms as* He / She

H Spelling rules for -ed endings

Rules	Examples of simple past verbs	
For verbs that **end in -e**, add d.	achieve → **achieved** create → **created**	decide → **decided** notice → **noticed**
For verbs that end with **consonant + -y**, change -y to -i and add -ed.	hurry → **hurried** marry → **married**	study → **studied** try → **tried**
For verbs that end in **consonant + vowel + consonant**, double the consonant and add -ed. *Exception: If the stress is on the first syllable, do not double the consonant.*	occur → **occurred** plan → **planned** travel → **traveled**	stir → **stirred** stop → **stopped** wonder → **wondered**
For **most other verbs**, add -ed.	enroll → **enrolled** explain → **explained**	open → **opened** treat → **treated**

Simple past: Irregular verbs

Affirmative statements		Negative statements			
I / You / He / She /We / They	**caught** a cold. **read** the book. **made** plans. **did** the chores. **ate** lunch.	I / You / He / She / We / They	**did**	**not**	**catch** a cold. **read** the book. **make** plans. **do** the chores. **eat** lunch.
Yes / No questions			Short answers		
Did	I / you / he / she / we / they	**catch** a cold? **eat** lunch?	Yes, No,	you / I / he / she / we / they	**did**. **didn't**.

Note: It *takes the same forms as* He / She

Irregular simple past verbs / Irregular past participles

Simple present	Simple past	Irregular past participles
be	was / were	been
do	did	done
drink	drank	drunk
eat	ate	eaten
feel	felt	felt
have	had	had
hear	heard	heard
get	got	gotten
go	went	gone
say	said	said
see	saw	seen
tell	told	told

Simple past: *Wh-* questions

Wh- questions				Short answers	Long answers
Who What When Where Why How How long	**did**	I you he she we they it	**see**? **think**? **start**? **live**? **stay** here? **feel**? **last**?	Friends. It was nice. Yesterday. On Main Street. Because it was free. Upset. Two days.	You **saw** friends. I **thought** it was nice. He **started** yesterday. She **lived** on Main Street. We **stayed** here because it was free. They **felt** upset. It **lasted** two days.

L · Simple past: *Be*

Past affirmative statements			Past negative statements			
I / He / She / It	**was**	on time.	I / He / She / It	**was**	**not**	late.
You / We / They	**were**		You / We / They	**were**		

Yes / No questions			Short answers			
Was	I		Yes,	you		**were.**
				I		**was.**
Were	you			he / she / it		**was.**
		at home?		we / they		**were.**
Was	he / she / it		No,	you		**weren't.**
				I		**wasn't.**
Were	we / they			he / she / it		**wasn't.**
				we / they		**weren't.**

Wh- questions with *be*			Short answers
Who What When Where	**was**	there? she? he here? it?	Lots of people. An artist. Last year. In Bercher Auditorium.
Why How How much	**were**	you late? we? they?	The bus broke down. Very good. Only $10.

M · Past progressive

Affirmative statements			Negative statements			
I / He / She	**was**	**thinking** about something else.	I / He / She	**was**	**not**	**listening.**
You / We / They	**were**		You / We / They	**were**		

Yes / No questions			Short answers			
Was	I		Yes,	you		**were.**
				I		**was.**
Were	you			he / she / it		**was.**
		trying?		we / they		**were.**
Was	he / she / it		No,	you		**weren't.**
				I		**wasn't.**
Were	we / they			he / she / it		**wasn't.**
				we / they		**weren't.**

Wh- questions				Short answers	Long answers
Who What Where	**was**	I he she	**helping?** **baking?** **living?**	A neighbor. A pie. In Laos.	You were helping a neighbor. He was baking a pie. She was living in Laos.
Why How How much	**were**	you we they	**hiding?** **doing?** **charging?**	Because I was scared. Great. About $50.	I was hiding because I was scared. We were doing great. They were charging about $50.

Note: **It** *takes the same forms as* **He / She**

N Future: *Will*

Affirmative statements				Negative statements			
I / You / He / She / We / They	**will**		**call** you.	I / You / He / She / We / They	**will**	**not**	**text.**

Yes / No questions			Short answers			
Will	I / you / he / she / we / they	**carry** that box?	Yes,	you / I / he / she / we / they	**will.**	
			No,		**will not / won't.**	

Wh- questions				Short answers
Who		I	**invite?**	Friends.
What		you	**do?**	Relax.
When	**will**	he	**know?**	By next week.
Where		she	**go** on vacation this year?	To Canada.
How		we	**travel** there?	By bus.
How long		they	**be** in town?	For a couple of weeks.

Note: It *takes the same forms as* He / She

O Future: *Be going to*

Affirmative statements				Negative statements				
I	**am**			I	**am**			
You / We / They	**are**	**going to**	**drive.**	You / We / They	**are**	**not**	**going to**	**fly.**
He / She	**is**			He / She	**is**			

Yes / No questions				Short answers		
Am	I			Yes,	you	**are.**
					I	**am.**
Are	you				he / she / it	**is.**
		going to	**be** late?		we / they	**are.**
Is	he / she / it			No,	you	**'re not / aren't.**
					I	**'m not.**
Are	we / they				he / she / it	**'s not / isn't.**
					we / they	**'re not / aren't.**

Wh- questions				Short answers
Who	**am**	I	**know** at the party?	Maybe no one.
What		he	**wear?**	Jeans.
When	**is**	she	**get** a haircut?	Soon.
Where		it	**be?**	At the stadium.
Why		you	**do** that?	Because I want to.
How	**are**	we	**fix** it?	Very carefully.
How many		they	**buy?**	Two.

Note: It *takes the same forms as* He / She

P Present perfect

Affirmative statements				Negative statements				
I / You / We / They	**have**	arrived. tried. left.		I / You / We / They	**have**	**not**	arrived. tried. left.	
He / She	**has**			He / She	**has**			

Yes / No questions				Short answers		
Have	I / you / we / they	arrived? tried? left?		Yes,	you / I / we / they	**have.**
					he / she	**has.**
Has	he / she			No,	you / I / we / they	**haven't.**
					he / she	**hasn't.**

Wh- questions				Short answers
Who What When Where	**have**	I you we they	**met?** **made** in sewing class? **seen** him? **traveled?**	Several nice people. A shirt. At lunch. Around the world.
Why How	**has**	he she	**quit?** **been?**	Because of pay. Great.

Note: It *takes the same forms as* He / She

Q Count and noncount nouns

Irregular count nouns	Noncount nouns
child – children, man – men, mouse – mice, person – people, wife – wives, woman – women	baseball, bread, economics, furniture, gold, milk, rain, sand, space, stress, technology

R Pronouns and possessive adjectives

Subject pronouns	Object pronouns	Possessive adjectives	Possessive pronouns	Reflexive pronouns
I you he she it we they	me you him her it us them	my your his her its our their	mine yours his hers its ours theirs	myself yourself / yourselves himself herself itself ourselves themselves

S Phrasal verbs

Inseparable		
come up with = think of die down = become quiet go over = review hold on = grasp keep up with = stay on pace	look back = reflect pick on = bully put up with = endure settle up = pay a debt stand for = believe in	take over = become the leader tell on = report wait on = serve wait up = stay awake watch out for = care for

Separable		
bring about = cause to happen cheer up = make happy clear up = clarify cut off = interrupt dress up = wear nice clothes	fill out = complete give up = quit trying hang up = suspend keep up = continue let out = release	rule out = eliminate shut off = turn to "off" position throw away = put in trash turn down = say "no" to wear out = use until finished

Index

Credits